5/2007

THE CAIRO DOCUMENTS

MOHAMED HASSANEIN HEIKAL

INTRODUCTION BY EDWARD R. F. SHEEHAN

THE CAIRO DOCUMENTS

THE INSIDE STORY OF NASSER AND HIS
RELATIONSHIP WITH WORLD LEADERS,
REBELS, AND STATESMEN

Doubleday & Company, Inc., Garden City, New York, 1973

Unless otherwise noted, the photographs used in this book are the property of the author and *Al Ahram.*

962.05
H

ISBN: 0-385-06447-0
Library of Congress Catalog Card Number 76–182696
Copyright © 1971, 1972, 1973 by Mohamed Heikal and The Sunday Telegraph
Introduction Copyright © 1973 by Edward R. F. Sheehan; Copyright © 1971 by
The New York Times Company
All Rights Reserved
Printed in the United States of America
First Edition in the United States of America

CONTENTS

Rebels and Statesmen

This book evolved from the intense pressure put upon me by my friends and by publishers all round the world to write a biography of Gamal Abdel Nasser, from my own desire to write about my great friend and leader—and from my own inability to do so.

It is still too early to write his story, for it is not yet finished. The struggle for which he lived and died continues. There are matters of great importance to his biography that cannot yet be told for reasons of national security. And I am still too emotionally involved with his memory to be able to write about him in the detached fashion necessary. For these reasons I must wait before embarking on Nasser's biography until I can try to give it the historical value and validity the subject demands.

How, then, can I write about him at all?

There really was only one possible answer. That is to write about

Nasser as a man and to tell the story of his years of power from a personal point of view.

The result is not a biography. It is not the story of any one battle that he fought. It is not the complete story of Suez. It is not the complete story of 1967. It is largely the story of his personal relations with twelve men, giants of the international scene, rebels and statesmen, whom he met in conflict or friendship—and occasionally both. And in telling this story it touches upon the events, principles, and issues that have made the world what it is today.

Gamal Abdel Nasser played a vital role in the affairs of the world from the time he came to power as an unknown colonel on July 23, 1952, until his premature death eighteen years later. But for anyone to understand what he actually did for Egypt it must be realized that he started the basic social transformation of his country. His was not a simple coup d'état, the exchange of one government for another: he changed everything.

Before Nasser, Egypt's foreign and internal trade was virtually controlled by foreigners. Those Egyptians who were rich were very rich indeed. One half a per cent of the population owned 50 per cent of the nation's wealth. He took away the power of the ruling classes. He nationalized their wealth. He made foreigners subject to Egyptian law. He gave Egypt back to the Egyptians.

And—this is very important—it was done without bloodshed. The revolution was carried out during the ice ages of the Cold War; it was interrupted three times by fighting—Suez in 1956, Yemen in 1962, and in the war of 1967—and yet it was accomplished without terror. It must be unique for a nation to carry through such a fundamental social and economic revolution and still maintain its unity without violence. To accomplish this it was necessary for Nasser to restrain normal party politics, but the results more than justified the restraint.

This example transformed itself into a highly charged current that flashed through the Arab world. Nasserite parties were created in every Arab country, often against his wishes. In the end it was the passion that he aroused among Arabs which led to his most important achievement: the linking of Egypt to the rest of the Arab world and the linking of the Arabs as an entity to the ideas and values prevailing in the world today.

I hope that in this book I have been able to give some idea of what Gamal Abdel Nasser stood for, how he fought for his principles, and what he achieved.

In writing it I have been fortunate in the help I have been gladly given by many people. It is a pleasure to record my gratitude to them. First of all, there are the people who encouraged me to write the book, particularly Dennis Hamilton of the London *Times* and C. L. Sulzberger of the New York *Times*. I must thank Cy Sulzberger doubly because his book *The Last of the Giants* provided a model for my own work. My thanks are also due to my staff at *Al Ahram* who kept my papers in order—a monumental, painstaking task that they carried out patiently and impeccably. The research department of *Al Ahram*'s library helped me with great skill and persistence. They provided all the names, dates, and figures that I needed—no mean accomplishment. To everybody who helped me I give my thanks.

I would also like to record my gratitude to the English author and journalist Christopher Dobson, who collaborated with me in writing this book in English. It was a happy and fruitful partnership.

Cairo, 1972

Mohamed Hassanein Heikal

The Most Powerful Journalist in the World, His Newspaper, and His Book
by Edward R. F. Sheehan

He is a rather short, solidly built man whose dark face and cool brown eyes exude a self-assurance that can sometimes hint of arrogance. He sits silently in his sumptuous office, perfectly tailored in an American-style business suit, behind an immense, immaculate desk, puffing on a Cuban cigar, encouraging you to do all of the talking as he measures you in his mind and calculates how he wishes to respond. When finally he begins to talk, his replies are torrential. "All that I am, I owe to the history of Egypt. . . ."

He was the late Gamal Abdel Nasser's *alter ego,* and he is a close and influential friend of President Anwar el Sadat. His writings are devoured by Arabs from the casbahs of Morocco to the oil derricks of the Persian Gulf, by diplomats from Foggy Bottom to Peking, for auguries of events to come in the convulsive

Middle East. He is Mohamed Hassanein Heikal, editor of *Al Ahram* and perhaps the most powerful journalist in the world.

When Heikal visited London soon after Nasser's death in 1970, he was received like a chief of state. He lunched at the Foreign Office, then motored to Number 10 Downing Street for a chat with Prime Minister Edward Heath on Middle Eastern problems. While in London, Heikal was approached by several publishers who urged him to write a book on Nasser, and the competition for such a book was intense. In the end he sold the world rights to *The Sunday Telegraph* for a prodigious sum. The *Telegraph* is the most conservative of Britain's quality newspapers, and Nasser had been its bête noire for more than fifteen years, but the decision was typical of Heikal's political acumen (no sense preaching to the converted), his business ability, his love of challenge, and his sense of humor.

At home, Heikal is Egypt's most eminent propagandist and the anointed prophet of Nasserism. His long, weekly editorial "Frankly Speaking," though sometimes turgid and repetitious, is read by millions for its continuing exegesis of Nasser's thought, just as the news columns of *Al Ahram* are the most informative source of what is happening in Egypt and the clearest index of Cairo's policies at any given moment. *Le Monde,* the BBC, the New York *Times,* the entire Arab press, all quote Heikal regularly and at length, since they know that he not only enunciates Egyptian policy, he sometimes inspires it. Heikal has often counseled President Sadat on the formulation of crucial decisions in domestic and foreign affairs, and he played a key role in advising Sadat how to foil the conspiracy mounted against him in May of 1971 by seven of his own ministers. Heikal ingenuously denies such influence ("I simply talk to the President without inhibitions," he says), but in fact he unquestionably continues to be one of the half dozen most important men in Egypt.

Though he served as Minister of Information for six months in 1970 (at Nasser's insistence), Heikal has always resisted the burdens of office; he prefers influence without formal responsibility. Otherwise he relishes all of the rewards of wielding power. He is vain, emotional, amusing, quick-witted, cunning, vulnerable to flattery, and a perceptive judge of men. Prominent journalists from the West besiege his door, seeking audiences with him and President Sadat; cheerfully he instructs his secretaries to send most of them away, though he knows better than they do that without his blessing the President probably will not see them; it was the same while Nasser lived.

Curiously, Heikal agrees to see me. His inner sanctum is a huge, dark-paneled place where he sits among modern paintings, the latest books from London, and push buttons at his fingertips. He talks on; I scribble away; his telephone buzzes sweetly. "Would you mind stepping outside for a few minutes?" he says smilingly, in perfect English. "The President is on the line." As I close the door, I can hear Heikal greeting Sadat with a burst of uproarious pleasantries.

Heikal's significance is not confined to his counsel behind the throne; he remains as well the catalyst of a continuing debate that concerns the whole future of Egyptian society. Many of Egypt's thinkers used to plead that their society could not be radically improved before the confrontation with Israel was resolved. Heikal has dumped that argument upside down, insisting in his columns that Egypt can never face up to the Israeli challenge unless it discards its own backwardness—and that to accomplish that, it must create an open society, animated by the rule of law, endowed with democratic institutions, and freed of most of the police-state restraints that have burdened the country for the last twenty years. With a truly democratic system, Heikal's argument runs, Egypt would not have been defeated by Israel in 1967. Moreover, until

the whole society is changed, through efficiency and moderniza-
tion born in freedom, Egypt is doomed to new defeats.

"Egyptian society," Heikal asserts, "will always be unhealthy if
a main current of contemporary political thought—any current,
Marxist or otherwise—is dealt with through the police. Unless we
allow all ideas to be expressed freely—unless we allow this ferment,
conflict, dialogue—we will remain a society in a test tube. I am,
of course, talking about peaceful dissent, not the dissent of terrorists
and conspirators."

In a cautious way, Heikal has long since applied his personal
philosophy of freedom and efficiency to *Al Ahram* itself, with
some degree of success, particularly on the level of technical expertise. The new *Ahram* building, finished a year and a half
after the defeat of 1967, is one of the half dozen most advanced
newspaper complexes in the world. When A. M. Rosenthal, man-
aging editor of the New York *Times,* visited the building in 1970,
he was astonished. "There isn't anything in America to compare
with it," he stated.

Faintly futuristic in style, designed by an Egyptian architect,
the building rises fourteen stories and houses the most sophisticated
printing equipment that Western technology can offer. Immense
marble reception halls, adorned with gouache paintings and
ceramic sculpture, lead to antiseptic rooms where technicians in
immaculate smocks tend electronic perforators, American computers, and British typesetting machines in making up the newspaper. The electronic data processing center on the eleventh floor
is especially impressive. There, programmers trained in England
and America feed facts on finances, circulation, and advertising
into IBM System 360 Model 30 computers—not only for *Al Ahram*
but for a score of other large companies as well. Heikal is fascinated by the American mystique, and the bright young editors
who roam his gleaming corridors, all of them dressed as impec-

cably as he, seem to evince a sort of Islamic New Frontier. They are, in terms not only of appearance but of talent, a refreshing contrast to the mediocrity and shabbiness of the larger part of Egyptian journalism.

Though it is limited by a shortage of newsprint, *Al Ahram* is a handsomely composed paper that endeavors to strike a balance between local, Arab world, and international events. The preponderance of news is local, since like most people the Egyptians want mainly to read about themselves. But *Ahram* subscribes to all of the leading Western wire services and prints an abundance of news from Israel. In 1968 *Ahram* gave extensive coverage to the Soviet invasion of Czechoslovakia and criticized it editorially, much to the displeasure of the Soviet Embassy in Cairo. *Ahram's* editorials are usually not distinguished; they are full of slogans and predictable repetitions of the government line on the zeal of the Egyptian Army, the errors of the United States, the perfidy of Israel—except when Heikal writes them. He is always interesting, often funny, and sometimes maddening. He writes as he talks: his favorite subject is himself, and he is so fond of elaborate digressions that he can consume thousands of words before he comes to his point. He is a master of the overwrought purple-patch: "The sultans of the dark have fallen," he wrote of the abortive conspiracy in 1971 against President Sadat, "and the phantoms of fear have vanished. Twice Providence intervened to undo the disaster that would have plunged Egypt into the pit of night, causing her to lose her sweetest and most precious possession. . . ."

It reads better in Arabic. Heikal's column appears on Fridays, the Moslem sabbath, when *Ahram's* circulation climbs to nearly a million copies; it is 650,000 on weekdays, which makes it the most widely read publication in the Arab world. The company claimed about $5,000,000 in net profits for 1970, half of which were redistributed to the newspaper's employees. The advertising department prospers not only from its advertisements for Swiss watches, Gulf Oil, Marlboro cigarettes, but above all from its obituary columns—one of the main sources of the newspaper's revenue. After all, "Al Ahram" means "the Pyramids," and that association with the entombed Pharaohs of antiquity reminds modern Egyptians that they must continue to honor their dead. Egypt may be a socialist state, but Heikal prefers advertising from the private sector. Heavy reliance on nationalized industries, he feels, might paralyze his freedom to criticize the government.

Every nook and cranny of the *Ahram* building breathes Heikal's presence, particularly his obsession with cleanliness. The elevator boys ooze the spit and polish of West Point cadets and in polite English remind you that you must not smoke inside their lifts; the cafeteria on the twelfth floor is the best and cleanest in Cairo, and the same seems so of the free workers' clinic. In a country where scruffy coffee boys bearing sloppy trays of refreshments seem almost a cultural compulsion, *Ahram*'s coffee boys look like orderlies in a Swedish hospital. The night cleaning crew have permanent instructions to throw away any papers they find on top of desks and to confiscate the contents of unlocked drawers. Any worker who is dirty or who soils a wall with his hands or feet is docked a day's pay. "We have won our fight," says Dr. Fuad Ibrahim, general manager of *Ahram*, "against *la nonchalance orientale*. And if we can do it here, why not in the whole country? Mr. Heikal feels that all of Egypt can be run like *Al Ahram*."

All of Egypt, however, is not run like *Al Ahram*. Ironically, the *Ahram* building is situated in the Bulak quarter, not far from the Nile, one of the poorest sections of Cairo. Within thirty seconds of exiting the newspaper's back door, one is lost in a labyrinth of almost medieval alleys, where one confronts multitudes of impoverished Egyptians, many of them still clad in flowing galabias and striped pajamas. The alleys are too squeezed for motorcars, but donkeys, goats, and cackling hens abound, as do horseflies and djinns of dust kicked up by ragged, undernourished children playing games in the dirt. The smell is from another century—an almost sensuous amalgam of roasting coffee, perfumed women, fried fish, butchers' mutton rotting in the sun. A policeman urinates against a wall beneath a fading photograph of Anthony Quinn, and an old hunchback will utter imprecations against *Al Ahram*, should you dare to raise the subject. In fact, when the *Ahram* building was going up, the people of Bulak threw garbage and animal droppings at it, so fearful were they that this futuristic invasion would spread throughout the district (as it has begun to do) and banish them from their homes.

Mohamed Hassanein Heikal has spent a lifetime waging war with the Bulak mentality. He has had an extraordinary career. Born in Cairo in 1923 of rather humble middle-class origins, his rise in Egyptian journalism was meteoric, and he was already well known in Egypt by the time he was twenty-four. Though extremely anti-British, he began his career at nineteen as a reporter on the English-language *Egyptian Gazette* under the tutelage of a British journalist, Scott Watson. After covering the battle of El Alamein and the equally tempestuous Egyptian parliament in 1942 and 1943, he moved to the magazine *Akher Saa'* and embarked upon investigative reporting. He won his first of three King Farouk Prizes in journalism before he was twenty-five, for his coverage of a cholera epidemic in which 17,000 people died.

Akher Saa' was sold to the weekly *Akhbar al Yom*, and in 1946, at Heikal's insistence, his new employers sent him to Syria and Palestine to report on the brewing war between the Arabs and the Jews. Over the next three years Heikal returned to Palestine frequently, and his articles made him famous in the Arab world. He met David Ben Gurion and became an intimate of King Abdullah of Jordan; he stressed the strength of the Haganah and warned the

Arabs against waging an unprepared war—a theme of realism that enraged many Arabs but which was to recur as a leitmotif in Heikal's writings later on.

It was in 1948, during the first Arab-Israeli war, that Heikal met Gamal Abdel Nasser. Legend claims that they forged their friendship then, but in truth—so Heikal told me—they exchanged only a few perfunctory words. Nasser was a major commanding a battalion at Iraq al-Manshiya, in the Negev desert, and when he was introduced to Heikal he said simply, "I've read your articles. I expected to meet an older man." They did not meet again until the beginning of 1951, when Nasser came to Heikal's office in Cairo to borrow a book he had written about Iran and to talk to him about coups d'état in Syria, a subject on which Heikal had become an expert. Their conversation that day was the catalyst of their ensuing friendship, and the dialogue they started continued to the day of Nasser's death, with no small consequences for Egypt.

In the meanwhile, Heikal had been hastening to the four corners of the world, making a name in Cairo as a foreign correspondent and acquiring a *Weltanschauung* that was unprecedented in Egyptian journalism. He covered the Communist guerrilla war in Greece in 1947 and 1949, roamed all over Ethiopia, Uganda, and the southern Sudan, wrote his book about Mohammed Mossadegh and the Persian oil crisis, visited India and Indochina, and covered the Korean War—not to mention the American presidential elections of 1952. His acceptance of a State Department Leader Grant for that trip gave rise to rumors that he was an "American agent," an untrue demagogic charge he has never completely been able to live down.

But from 1952 Heikal spent most of his time at home, for the simple reason that Egypt itself was coming apart. The country was convulsed with riots and assassinations, inspired largely by the British occupation of the Suez Canal Zone, and Farouk's corrupt monarchy was tottering. Sensing something momentous in the wind, Heikal cultivated several members of Nasser's clandestine Free Officers movement, and soon he was being shadowed by Farouk's secret police.

"The whole Egyptian underground was in contact with me," Heikal recalls in conversation. "Everybody was fascinated by me, fascinated by my foreign experience and by my knowledge of coups d'état. But I did not definitely know there was a conspiracy afoot until four days before the revolution took place. On July 18, 1952, Nasser took me into his confidence. I was visiting General Mohammed Naguib at his home when Nasser walked in, wearing a white shirt and gray flannels. I said, 'The Army failed in 1948 defending its honor. Now it does not even have its honor.' Nasser replied, 'What do you suggest we do? Do you want the Army to make a coup d'état?' I knew from that moment of his intentions—and on July 22 he carried them out."

From the day of the revolution, Heikal grew ever closer to Nasser. Soon enough he was as powerful as most cabinet ministers, and many ministers themselves were calling on him as a means of catching Nasser's ear. It is believed that in 1953 he wrote much of Nasser's famous pamphlet *The Philosophy of the Revolution*, in which Nasser outlined the ambitious foreign policy that was eventually to reap for Egypt—and the whole Arab world—such mixed, and sometimes catastrophic, consequences. "In this region," Nasser wrote, "there is a role wandering aimlessly about in search of an actor to play it. . . ." The role was the leadership of the Arab, Islamic, and African worlds, and *The Philosophy of the Revolution* suggested that the most suitable actor to play the part was Egypt itself.

By this time Heikal had moved from the editorship of *Akher Saa'* to the more important post of editor of the huge daily *Al*

Akhbar. He had already introduced a novel and vivacious style into Arab journalism which he used to support Nasser in his successful effort to consolidate his power after the deposition of President Mohammed Naguib and which he consecrated to Nasser's ends for sixteen years thereafter. *Al Akhbar* specialized in bedroom scandals and sensational gossip that offended Nasser's puritan sensibility, and Heikal grew uneasy under the hand of the newspaper's owner. In 1957 Heikal left *Al Akhbar* to become editor in chief of *Al Ahram,* a dying newspaper with a rare reputation for veracity, owned by a Lebanese family that barely spoke Arabic, and housed in a shabby building that did violence to all of Heikal's fastidious tastes.

Immediately, Heikal began to hire talented young blood and to build *Ahram* up as the Arab world's best source of political news, an objective that was aided considerably by his friendship with the President. Heikal's editorials in the late 1950s were full of the same jingoism about "positive neutralism" and Western imperialism that filled Nasser's speeches; his editorials on the United States sometimes skirted the borderline of mendacity and occasionally crossed right over it. Paradoxically, Nasser was simultaneously using Heikal as an important pipeline to the American Embassy in Cairo.

I was press officer at the Embassy during 1957 and 1958, and occasionally I would bump into Heikal as he went in to see Ambassador Raymond Hare. Among other purposes, Heikal's mission was to persuade Washington, through Hare, to show more sympathy for Nasser's neutralism and his aspirations for hegemony in the Arab world. Hare had his own reservations about the inflexibility of John Foster Dulles' anti-Nasserism; he worked quietly to modify the policy, and by the end of the decade, with Dulles dead, Egyptian-American relations had perceptibly improved. In fact, the United States resumed aid to Egypt on a scale that was eventually to amount in value to over a billion dollars in wheat shipments, long-term loans, and credits—a feat that can be largely credited to Heikal. Over the years Heikal ran similar errands for Nasser to the British, acquiring through all of this a broad experience in diplomacy that far transcended his role as a journalist and made him ever more valuable to his master.

Not that Heikal was ever reduced to the role of Nasser's errand boy or sycophant. He fed him ideas, debated policies, and often contradicted him. He gave Nasser books on politics, philosophy, and art, tutored him on Arabic poetry, entertained him with a stream of funny stories, and urged him to favor a more liberal society. Over the years, his privileged friendship with the President permitted him to say things in *Al Ahram* which no other Egyptian journalist would dare to do. "Nasser was sometimes cross with me because of what I wrote in my column," Heikal says in conversation, "but he never made any move to censor me." Rather, Heikal censored himself; one of his greatest talents has always been in calculating exactly how far he could safely go. He ridiculed the bureaucracy for pettiness and inefficiency, attacked the intelligence services for stupidity and arbitrary arrests (on various occasions some of Heikal's closest collaborators have been jailed), campaigned for the release of political prisoners, assailed Egyptian diplomats abroad for their incompetence. "Heikal was Nasser's *alter ego*," observes Dr. Louis Awad, the distinguished literary editor of *Al Ahram* who was jailed as a Communist (which he isn't) in 1959. "When Heikal contradicted him, Nasser was in fact having a dialogue with himself."

For Nasser was a most curious mixture of incongruities, an acrobat who rode several steeds at once, an enigma who favored freedom and repression at the same time. "He invariably visualized all of his domestic problems, no matter how trifling, in terms of intrigue. He juggled human emotions, personal rivalries, ambitions, hatreds, and vendettas with intuitive skill. He played this minister off against that one, pitted the cunning of Colonel A against the pomposity of General B, and most of the time got what he wanted: a weakening of their positions and a reinforcement of his own."

The quotation is from a novel I wrote about the Middle East several years ago and the description is of a mythical Prime Minister, but I had Nasser in mind. Nasser played Heikal off against his other subordinates, just as he played the subordinates off against Heikal, for Heikal had his ups and downs with Nasser like everybody else. Nasser chastised Heikal for attacking the secret police, but permitted him to continue the attacks, which may have helped assure that the secret police never grew so strong as to threaten Nasser himself.

During my lengthy conversations with him, Heikal loyally and repeatedly stated that "Nasser believed in democracy. Yes, he created the intelligence services I have so often criticized in *Al Ahram*, but he had to do that to cope with all of the internal and external forces that were plotting against him. Many of the most repressive forces in Egypt, however, were unleashed without his knowledge, and sometimes he didn't know what the intelligence services were doing. After the defeat by Israel in 1967, Nasser was ill and preoccupied with regaining our lost territory. In late 1967 certain elements tried to assassinate me. You see, I had criticized the head of the General Intelligence Agency in *Al Ahram*. Over the years I told Nasser of these and other outrages as a friend. And he did so many things—all he could—to correct the abuses."

I remained unconvinced by this apologia, for the simple reason that I could not believe that the all-seeing Nasser was ever ignorant of anything important that happened in Egypt. Without contesting Heikal's point that Nasser often intervened to diminish the excesses of the secret police, I am more inclined to believe that he manipulated the democratic aspirations that Heikal represented as a useful counterweight in maintaining his own power. It was a kind of game between the two of them, for conversely Heikal kept playing on the liberal side of Nasser's character to reduce political repression in Egypt, and sometimes he succeeded.

Though Heikal himself prefers the most advanced methods of modern management ("within a co-operative framework," he says) to doctrinaire socialist rigorism, and though he is anathema to some of Egypt's Marxists, in the early 1960s he persuaded Nasser to release several prominent Communists from prison. Nasser had put them there in 1959, during a period of strained relations with the Kremlin. But in 1961, when the President proclaimed Arab socialism and nationalized everything in sight, Heikal arranged a marriage of convenience between Nasser and Egypt's Marxists. Not only were they liberated from jail, where many had been treated harshly, but they were given jobs in the government and in the press. The Egyptian Communist party voluntarily dissolved itself as part of the deal, and the "ex-Communists" entered the Arab Socialist Union, Egypt's only legal political organization. Heikal gathered several of the most talented leftists under the *Al Ahram* umbrella, with the exhortation, "Here is your chance to preach your Marxist views within the framework of Nasserism."

In 1965 he even gave them their own monthly magazine, *Al Tali'a*—The Vanguard—where they were permitted to propound a muted Marxist critique of Egyptian society. This gesture was quintessential Heikal. For coexisting under the same roof with *Al Tali'a* are Heikal's other subsidiary publications, the *Al Ahram Economic Review* and *International Politics*, which are edited by conservatives and which in their turn propound a muted pro-Western, free-enterprise philosophy. *Al Tali'a* is, in fact, a safety valve for Egyptian Marxists or, rather, a rest house where they write harmless manifestoes and are kept moderately happy with good pay.

In 1960, in the meantime, all of the Egyptian press had been nationalized. After vainly trying to talk Nasser out of this decision, Heikal devised a stratagem to rescue *Al Ahram* from the hands of the bureaucrats. Theoretically, the paper's ownership passed to the Arab Socialist Union, whose functionaries were eager to possess it in fact as well as name, but Heikal outmaneuvered them. He formed a co-operative, giving the real ownership of the newspaper to its employees, satisfying the technicalities of the law by leaving the license in the hands of the Socialist Union. Nasser sided with Heikal during this acrimonious dispute and once again indulged him when Heikal resolved to erect his awesome new building. Egypt was critically short of foreign exchange, but Heikal claims he never drew on its meager reserves because "we constructed the building and bought the equipment largely by relying on *Ahram*'s foreign exchange earnings from abroad." The building was attacked by some Egyptians as being too opulent for such a poor country, though Heikal compared it to the Moscow Metro and portrayed it as an act of faith in Egypt's future. Nevertheless, the building was not finished until after the 1967 war with Israel, a catastrophe that made "Heikal's Pyramid"—so the wags of Cairo called it—seem all the more extravagant.

The opulence of the building could only be justified by the quality of the newspaper itself. In this respect, *Al Ahram* has manifested a certain freedom of expression—within limits, one of them being that it never criticized President Nasser or the basic tenets of his domestic and foreign policies. During the last decade, Heikal has solicited the most talented writers in Egypt, and they have obliged him with some surprising contributions, little of it outstanding but much of it quite good. In 1967 Neguib Mafouz, Egypt's most distinguished novelist, contributed a novel in installments that obliquely pilloried the corruption of the regime. More recently, Dr. Awad, *Ahram*'s literary editor, attacked the errors of the government's educational system, and Tewfik Hakim —Egypt's leading playwright—wrote a satire on the Arab Socialist Union called "The Market of the Donkeys"; both series caused a sensation.

"We gave everybody hell," Heikal says. "We were gambling on the future of freedom in Egypt. We accepted censorship only on questions of national security, but otherwise we refused the censor many times. We said to the censor, 'If you insist on deleting this story or that one, we'll print it anyway and you'll have to confiscate the newspaper.' The censors never dared."

In my conversations with Heikal, I asked him whether he had made any effort to warn Nasser against going to war with Israel in 1967. Heikal implied that he had, privately and in print. His articles of that period, however, were ambivalent; at one moment he seemed to join in the general jingoism that called for Israel's destruction; at another, he hinted that the Army was unprepared for war. It was after the defeat that Heikal truly raised his voice for realism. He said that the defeat was Egypt's own fault—that not only the Army had failed, but the entire social and political system. He hammered frequently at this theme, eventually dismissing the idea of all-out war with Israel as suicidal for some time to come and most of the Palestinian militants as dreamers. By the summer of 1970 Egyptian policy assumed an equally moderate color, and Nasser embraced the peace plan proposed by United States Secretary of State William P. Rogers.

Not long after Nasser died in September of the same year, Heikal turned to an urgent new theme—relations with the United States. It was high time, he wrote, to stop treating the Americans as the enemy. America was too strong to be opposed head on; to do that was to tilt at windmills. What Egypt needed was not to antagonize the Americans but to neutralize them; dialogue was essential. For only then could Washington be coaxed into pressuring Israel to evacuate the Sinai—as President Eisenhower did under similar circumstances in 1957. "Am I asking for a miracle?" Heikal wrote. "The Vietnamese revolution succeeded in isolating the American military-industrial complex, and that was twenty times more potent than the power of Zionism in America. . . . The possibilities of our influencing America are small, but we must exploit them to the limit."

President Sadat was reaching similar conclusions at that time. Within a few months of Nasser's death, Heikal become one of Sadat's close advisers, and by early spring of 1971 Sadat's policies seemed to be bearing some fruit. Supremely aware of Egypt's failure to win world opinion in 1967, Heikal urged Sadat to evince sweet reason now. Israel became increasingly isolated, and sympathy for Egypt grew, even in America to a limited extent. Heikal's counsel seemed well conceived and farsighted. He calculated that even should all efforts at a peaceful solution fail, Egypt would have proved to the world—and especially to America—that she had done all she could to avoid war; if she went back to war, it was only because Israel had refused her most reasonable offers. By that time, America might be neutralized, hesitating to come to Israel's rescue in retaining territory that the rest of the world agreed she should give back.

Heikal's enemies in the Arab Socialist Union replied with broadsides in *Al Gomhouriya,* the government newspaper, contending that Heikal was a pro-American defeatist. "I sometimes find Arab folk strange for the way we are fond of rhetorical disputations, savoring words which lead us nowhere," Heikal replied coolly in his column. "My comments on neutralizing the United States have been singled out for a civil war of words."

It was worse than that: it was the beginning of a conspiracy to depose President Sadat—and to liquidate Heikal. In the eyes of the Socialist Union ideologues, and of their cohorts in the intelligence services, Sadat had come too much under Heikal's influence. Heikal was already the bête noire of the secret police, of the Russians, and of the Egyptian Communists, no matter the intellectual stable of "safe" Marxists he maintained at *Al Ahram*. A day or two after Nasser died, the secret police "bugged" his offices at the newspaper. "Now my telephone was tapped, my house, the people I met, and all my movements were placed under their surveillance," he says. "Taking over *Al Ahram* was one of their chief objectives." Whatever outer darkness his enemies were planning for him, however, it seems that Heikal was several steps ahead of them. We have, at least, seen the results of the confrontation that did come in mid-May of 1971: Sadat whisked all of his— and Heikal's—enemies off to jail on charges of trying to overthrow the government, and Heikal was left riding higher than ever.

True, the initiatives from Washington led nowhere. Both Sadat and Heikal felt cheated by what they came to feel was in effect a treacherous American endeavor to "freeze" the situation, first by fostering the illusion of progress towards a settlement and Israeli withdrawal and then—since that has yet to happen—by playing for time in Israel's favor.

My own dialogues with Heikal have extended many hours over many years, and we have talked a great deal, of course, about the Arab-Israeli problem. "The Israelis don't want peace, they want territorial expansion," Heikal says, repeating a favorite theme from his columns. "They are seeking not only to secure a homeland for the Jews in Palestine, but to establish a mini-imperialist apparatus to control the Arab world. If they persist in this, they will make the present struggle an intractable one of *them* or *us*. For in spite of themselves, they are pushing Egypt to change. They are creating a power that will defeat them.

"The future is on our side. There are now thirty-five million Egyptians, and the population of the Arab world exceeds one hundred million. Perhaps, in our present weakness and divisions, this strength of numbers doesn't mean very much. But I tell you that education, science, and technology are not an Israeli monopoly. Whatever our shortcomings, Egyptians—and the Arabs generally—are intelligent people, and we can and are acquiring education, science and technology. Perhaps I should worry about tomorrow, but I am not worried about the day after tomorrow or about the final result of our struggle with Israel.

"As for the United States, we are not giving you ultimatums, and we are not asking you to perform miracles. We are only asking that you cease being a party to the occupation of our territory. The Israelis are entrenched in our land as the direct result of the superiority provided them by the Phantom and Skyhawk aircraft and the unlimited economic aid you Americans are giving them. How can you say that the Israelis are obstinate, as you do, and then go on giving them the means to remain obstinate?"

"You might accomplish more with the United States," I said, "if you reduced the Soviet military presence in Egypt."

"We are not going to reduce the Soviet presence," Heikal retorted, "we are going to increase it. Otherwise how can we match the Phantoms that Israel has from America? If we diminish Soviet aid, we give the Israelis permanent superiority over us, on a silver platter."

"But doesn't this simply escalate the Middle East arms race?" I asked. "The Israelis successfully cite continuing Soviet arms deliveries as cause for deliveries of even more American arms to their side."

"If America has any sense, it will cease giving in to Israeli pressure. You might have reason to be concerned if we were threatening the U.S., or even Israel itself, but we're not doing either. All we're demanding is the return of our own territory. How would you Americans feel if the Japanese suddenly seized Seattle, or California, or part of the Texas desert with all its oil? Wouldn't you want it back and accept any help to get it back?"

"President Nixon is worried about the global balance of power," I said. "He's afraid that the vast Soviet military presence in Egypt might disturb that."

"I look at the problem from the viewpoint of Egypt's interests," Heikal said, "and not the global balance of power as it affects the United States. We are concerned with the independence and national security of Egypt, and only that. I say, to hell with your American strategic balance of power. I know that you landed a man on the moon, but to hell with the moon and your global strategy. I'm sorry to be so frank, but that's the way I feel."

Shortly after I had this conversation with Heikal in May of 1971, the Arab world was convulsed anew. King Hassan of Morocco narrowly escaped assassination and then shot all of the conspirators; King Hussein of Jordan massacred some more Fedayeen; the Communists of the Sudan seized power, then were overthrown in a countercoup and a shocking sequence of executions. Heikal had much to write about each of these events. He duly condemned the two Kings for their repressive regimes, but he was more indulgent towards Sudanese President Gaafar al-Nimeiry though he opposed Nimeiry's slaughter of the Sudanese Communists. Not only did he blame the Communists for much of the upheaval in the Sudan, in early August he penned a pointed admonition to the Soviet Union.

"Communism," he wrote, re-echoing a theme he has often stated down the years, "has no place in the Arab world because of basic ideological differences" and because it does not correspond to the character of the people. "President Nasser clearly condemned Communism in 1958, and there followed from that a lively controversy between Cairo and Moscow." Furthermore, "Soviet arms delivered to Cairo till now far from compensate for those which the United States has sent to Israel. . . . The Soviet-Egyptian treaty of May 1971 will mean nothing if it does not signify a common determination . . . to restore the Arab territories occupied by Israel." Translation: the Egyptians were beginning to have their doubts about the future quantity of Soviet arms and the seriousness of the Soviet pledge to help Egypt regain the Sinai by diplomacy or by war.

Nevertheless, in characteristically ambivalent fashion, Heikal exhorted Moscow to repair the conflict over the Sudan "before things get out of hand. . . . The Arabs cannot afford a dispute with the Soviet Union, particularly at this time." Such nuances were not enough for doctrinaire Marxists, and Heikal was savagely attacked—and still is—by the Communist press of Europe (*L'Unità* of Rome, for example) for "pseudo-theorizing, flagrant lying, and infamy." The attacks emphasized yet again how deeply Heikal is hated by Communists not only in Egypt but far beyond and bear witness to his own profound hostility to Communism as an internal political system.

In July of 1972 President Sadat did an about-face and expelled nearly all of the 20,000 Soviet military personnel from Egypt. He did so because of the Russians' refusal to provide offensive weapons to Egypt in its confrontation with Israel and because the continuing state of no-war, no-peace had become so frustrating that he was obliged to make a momentous gesture of this kind to appease the Army and Egyptian public opinion. Not surprisingly, Heikal was very much involved in the issues which led to this historic decision. For weeks he had been hinting to the Russians in his column that they had better produce some offensive weapons soon or face the consequences. If they failed to do so, "Egyptian friendship for the Soviet Union . . . would be undermined by overwhelming doubts as to its usefulness." The Russians were enraged and demanded that Sadat dismiss Heikal from *Al Ahram* for his impertinence. Sadat refused and—triggered partly by this open interference in Egypt's internal affairs—dismissed the Russians instead. On the eve of Sadat's announcement, Heikal unveiled what Egypt's new policy would be—a return to non-alignment. "Egypt must take its own problems in hand and do what is necessary to solve them . . . ," he wrote. "The policy of non-alignment was, and still is, a policy that carries risks, but it is better to run these risks than to hurl ourselves into the arms of a great power and thus become a dependent or a satellite." We are far from the end, however, far from knowing the dénouement of Egypt's new policy.

It would not be balanced to disregard the judgments of Heikal's severest Egyptian critics. He is very unpopular among some local journalists who do not work for him. "Heikal is a terribly complex, egotistical man," says one of his intellectual friends. "He outwits his opponents in an oblique way. He'd much rather ridicule an enemy in his newspaper than get him sent to prison. He's a conjurer, a manipulator of men, but always for a purpose. He's one step ahead of the rest of Egypt—especially on the issue of internal freedoms—when he should be ten steps ahead. He's so shrewd, though. If he were ten steps ahead he would long ago have lost his job—he might even be in jail."

"Heikal is a democrat in an autocratic way," adds an embittered leftist writer. "He's for a liberal society only so long as it strengthens his personal position. It's true that he's brought the best talent to *Al Ahram,* but then he turns them into his puppets, all echoing their master's voice." A prominent Palestinian intellectual observes: "Heikal was the measure of Nasser's arrested development. He still writes like an adolescent. His style is sentimental, syrupy, and hopelessly overdone—that might have been good Arabic twenty years ago, but it's distasteful now. Did you read his articles when Nasser died? He had oceans heaving, the heavens thundering, the earth quaking!"

The charge of an overdone style cannot be leveled at Heikal in *The Cairo Documents*. Here the style is simplicity itself, and if elsewhere Heikal can be accused of intruding his "I," in this book he is almost too self-effacing, given his importance as Nasser's most intimate counselor. When I read the original manuscript of *The Cairo Documents,* I found most of it interesting and some of it fascinating. The chapters on Dulles, Eden, Khrushchev, Chou En-lai, Ludwig Erhard, and Che Guevara are especially vivid. Khrushchev's letter to Nasser is priceless, the Chou chapter contains surprising revelations, parts of the Erhard chapter are hilarious, and to my mind the concluding chapter, on Che Guevara, is the most moving in the book.

The book conveys the flavor of Khrushchev's bumptious character as it must have been; it confirms the impression of many Europeans themselves about Sir Anthony Eden (now Lord Avon) who in Nasser's pithy phrase was "like a prince dealing with vagabonds." It neglects to mention some of the provocations that caused John Foster Dulles to act towards Nasser as he did, but the quotations from the letters to Nasser of Presidents Kennedy and Johnson shed much light on the way those two men dealt with the outside world. Kennedy's letters reflect little credit on him for his naïve use of trite Cold War language, and with respect to his intervention in Cuba he was obviously not telling the whole truth. Johnson's obtuse and fatuous letters to Nasser could serve as models of how *not* to talk to a leader of the Third World. At the same time, unconsciously perhaps, Heikal portrays a Nasser who could often be impulsive and reckless in his own right.

In fact, after reading the manuscript I asked Heikal why he had not given greater stress to Nasser's miscalculations during the events that led to the Six-Day War and why he had not mentioned the impassioned Egyptian press which contributed so much to the mood that helped to produce the explosion. "Wait till my next book," he told me. "It's about the Six-Day War." It is to be hoped that in that future work Heikal will treat such essential questions with the same kind of candor he has applied to the characters of Anthony Eden and Lyndon Johnson.

The Cairo Documents is, of course, Heikal's version of Nasser's relations with world leaders, seen very much from his own and Nasser's points of view. One cannot, after all, criticize an author for not having written a different book, and he is entitled to tell the story as he himself witnessed it. Other writers of different persuasions have been and will be writing of the same events from their perspectives, and while they may be less friendly to Nasser, they are not necessarily more accurate. The major virtue of Heikal's narrative is that it is based on Nasser's own correspondence, conversations, and encounters with world leaders who include some of the most renowned men of our time. The book is not a formal biography of Nasser, it does not tell or pretend to tell the entire story, it is not written so much for the professor as for the public, but taken for what it is and on its own terms it is a rare and valuable document. Moreover, the American edition contains further material and information that Heikal has added to clarify various points of interest for the trans-Atlantic audience.

Heikal's greatest contribution to the already copious literature on Nasser, it seems to me, is that in this book he presents his hero through Egyptian eyes, with an Arab's voice, and not with the usual Western voice, however well informed, to which we in America are so accustomed. Here we see some of the crucial conflicts of our time—the nationalization of the Suez Canal and the war that ensued, for example—from Nasser's not disinterested perspective, and that perhaps is why the portraits of Dulles and Eden are so devastating. After reading Eden's account of the same events, one is left to compare, to wonder, and to smile. Of this much I am sure: Eden's account is hardly more disinterested than Heikal's.

A final observation about Heikal and I am done. The most universal criticism of him centers on the quality of *Al Ahram* itself. It may be the best newspaper in the Arab world, but while it is leagues ahead of *Pravda*, it is still leagues behind *Le Monde*. Several of Heikal's own subordinates admit this and lament that till now they have not really been free to embark upon a searching critique of Egyptian society and its government. If we are to believe Heikal, this may be more their fault than his. "Our censorship laws hold chief editors responsible, nor ordinary journalists," he says. "But Egyptian journalists have not been writing frankly because of fear. Censorship has been in force in Egypt since early in World War II, and a new generation of journalists has grown up under its shade. I'm not afraid of the *visible* censor in Egypt, but of the *invisible* censor implanted by the habit of thirty years. We must first defy the censor in ourselves."

And yet, whatever Heikal's encouragements to write freely, his subordinates cannot forget that Egypt is still an authoritarian country and that every now and again a journalist is sent to jail. True, they have been encouraged to pillory the secret police and President Sadat's enemies, but when will they be allowed to criticize Sadat himself—in the manner that American newspapers call Richard Nixon to account?

Many of these critiques of Mohamed Hassanein Heikal may be valid to a greater or lesser degree. Nevertheless, he remains in sum a strong force for good in Egypt. He has matured immensely since Nasser came to power, particularly since the defeat by Israel more than five years ago. Heikal's realism, his love of quality, his devotion to the rule of law are rare enough intangibles in the Arab East, and if Egypt ever truly emerges from its backwardness,

Heikal will deserve much credit. His cunning has served him well in the treacherous labyrinth of Egyptian politics; above all, he has learned how to survive. He may be the cleverest man in the Arab world.

Cairo-Paris, 1972

Mr. Sheehan, a journalist and novelist who has known Egypt and the Middle East intimately since 1956, has adapted and expanded his introduction from an article that originally appeared in the New York *Times Magazine*. He served as press officer at the American Embassy in Cairo in 1957–1958 and subsequently at the American Embassy in Beirut. He has returned to the area many times on assignment for the New York *Times Magazine*.

Publisher's Note: Footnotes for clarity and identification have been added by the publisher throughout the text.

THE CAIRO DOCUMENTS

I

Nasser: Lion of Egypt

Gamal Abdel Nasser, President of Egypt and leader of the Arab people, lay on his bed in his big, cool room behind the green shutters of his modest house in Cairo.

He had been stricken with a heart attack, his second, earlier in the afternoon. Now, as the time came up to five o'clock, he waved aside his doctor's protests and reached across to switch on the transistor radio that stood on his bedside table. The familiar tune of Cairo Radio announcing the news filled the room. He lay back, listened to the headlines, then switched off and said: "I did not find what I expected."

A few minutes later he was dead and the world will never know what he expected to find. The world itself had found in him one of its most controversial statesmen and the Arabs had chosen him as the symbol of their lost dignity and their unfulfilled hopes.

The international events that culminated in his death had rocked the world, one leading to another with great speed and ever-increasing danger. There had been the series of hijackings,[1] the outbreak of open warfare between King Hussein and the Palestinian forces, Syria's incursion into Jordan, and the threat of intervention by the United States and Israel—with detailed plans made—for an attack on Jordan.

Through all these events President Nasser had worked unceasingly for peace. He differed from both King Hussein and the guerrilla leader Yasir Arafat.[2] When he met Hussein at Alexandria on the eighteenth of August, 1970, five weeks before his death, he felt that the King was underestimating the Palestinian resistance and was mistaken when he said that he could finish them off in a matter of hours.

Similarly, when he met the guerrilla leaders he thought they were mistaken when they told him they could finish the King in seven hours.

He told both sides: "You have to exist together, neither can get rid of the other and this is a fact of life you both have to accept."

He said to the King: "You say you can eliminate them. All right, if you say you can, you can. But the price will be too high. How can you rule over a country after a civil war which will cost you twenty or thirty thousand people? You will rule over a kingdom of wandering ghosts."

[1] Palestinian guerrillas from the Popular Front for the Liberation of Palestine hijacked several planes from the U.S. and Western Europe to obtain release of other guerrillas held in Israel and several Western European countries and to dramatize the Palestinian problem. One plane was flown to Cairo and burned on the runway; three others with their passengers were taken and held at the "Revolutionary Airport" in North Jordan.

[2] (Also spelled Yasser) Leader of Al Fatah, largest Palestinian guerrilla organization.

And he said to the guerrillas: "Don't think that you can face a modern army. If he decided to liquidate you, then he could. So don't overestimate your power. You must try to co-exist."

His efforts to bring about peace in Jordan resulted in a summit meeting in Cairo attended by ten Arab presidents and kings. Their meetings had all the contradictions of the Arab world, set against the background of the fighting. President Nasser wanted desperately to avoid the danger of polarization by the different groups and so he played the role of mediator and conciliator throughout the eight days of the meetings.

It was often difficult. Yasir Arafat had been smuggled out of Amman wearing a borrowed Kuwaiti cloak and headdress so that he could attend the summit. He arrived, filled with enmity for the King. And then the King himself telephoned and asked to come to the conference in order to refute the report given by President Nimeiry[3] of Sudan that blamed Hussein for the continuing bloodshed. Some were opposed to his taking part.

President Nasser argued that King Hussein should come because the aim of the summit was to bring an end to the killing.

But President Muammar el Qaddafi of Libya exploded at that: "What's the use of getting him? He's crazy. He's mad."

King Feisal of Saudi Arabia immediately objected: "How can you say that about an Arab king?"

Qaddafi replied: "But where is his father? Isn't his father in an asylum in Istanbul?[4] He's mad. Certainly he's mad. It's an inheritance in that family. They are all mad."

King Feisal appealed to President Nasser to intervene with Qaddafi: "How can we accept this? One of our colleagues calls an Arab king, who is going to take part in our discussions tomorrow, mad?"

[3] President Gaafar Muhammad al Nimeiry of Sudan.
[4] Hussein's father, King Talal, abdicated in August 1952 and lived in seclusion in Istanbul until his death in July 1972.

President Nasser started to smile but Qaddafi said: "Yes, by God, he is mad and we should get some doctors here tomorrow to send him to an asylum so that we can tell if he is mad or not."

Nasser intervened, laughing: "It seems to me that we are all mad. I suggest that we get some doctors to see us and decide who is mad and who is not."

King Feisal said: "Well, all right, my brother. But I want to be the first to see the doctors. Maybe they will discover that I am mad and then I will be spared the agony of taking part in such discussions."

When Hussein arrived for the meeting, he had two officers with him. They were all armed. Yasir Arafat had a revolver at his waist, and President Qaddafi was wearing sidearms too.

Arafat pointed at Hussein and shouted: "You see this criminal! First he kills us and now he comes here." He was calmed down. But King Feisal looked around and said: "My God, we are living in an arsenal, and with all those tempers . . ." He did not want to sit next to anybody carrying a revolver, but they kept the weapons just the same.

It was a tense meeting, but in typically Arab fashion the men who had been ready to kill one another in the morning were kissing one another in the evening. President Nasser had won Hussein and Arafat's agreement. They would stop the shooting. Everybody was astonished. There had seemed to be too much passion, too much basic disagreement, and to the outside world failure seemed inevitable. But Nasser, with statesmanship and infinite patience, persuaded his quarreling brothers to sign an agreement.

It was the last service he was to render the Arab people. The sustained effort, work, and worry had cost him dear.

He was already a sick, tired man. He had suffered with diabetes since 1958 and, as a result of the disease, had developed an extremely painful arteriosclerosis condition in his upper legs. The doctors asked him to give up smoking, and when he did, he said:

"I put out my last cigarette and promised never to light another. I felt that I had just parted with a dear friend. Smoking was the only luxury I enjoyed and now that too is gone."

He took a course of hydrotherapy treatment in the Soviet Union and for a time he felt much improved, but he could not keep to the rigorous program that had been laid down for him by the doctors. They said that he should avoid physical and emotional strain. "How can I do that?" he asked the doctors. "These are my entire life." His colleagues constantly urged him to rest, but he would not and on September 11, 1969, he had his first heart attack. Nobody was told except about seven people who needed to know. It was announced that he was suffering from a bad case of flu and would be away from his office for six weeks. Even his wife was not told, but she began to suspect when she found engineers installing an elevator in the house.

It was decided to call in outside help. A secret message was sent to Moscow and Dr. Yevgeni Shazoff, the Soviet Deputy Minister of Health, who was also a prominent heart specialist, brought a team of experts to Cairo. Their diagnosis was identical with that of the President's own physician. Dr. El Sawy Habib and Dr. Shazoff told him that he could not take any more hydrotherapy treatments in Russia for at least five years. Thus he realized that he would have to bear with his heart trouble as well as the constant pain in his legs.

He thought of resigning, but did not because he felt the Egyptian people would take his resignation as an admission of defeat. So Nasser worked on, hard and long. He had always thought that he would not be spared to enjoy a long life. When asked if he would write his memoirs to occupy himself when he retired he replied: "People who live the way I live do not live long."

He emerged from the summit conference an exhausted man. He told his friends that he was going to soak his legs in warm water and salt, an old farmer's remedy, to relieve their pain, then he would sleep for a whole day, and then he would talk about taking a vacation.

First of all he had to say good-by to the men who had shared the summit with him. When President Qaddafi tried to leave quietly so that Nasser would not be bothered more than necessary, Nasser insisted on driving out to the airport to escort the Libyan leader to his aircraft.

The last of the leaders to go was the Sheikh of Kuwait. President Nasser promised his wife that he would be home early to have lunch with his children and with Hala and Gamal, his grand-daughter and grandson. Then he drove out to the airport again, saying, with unconscious prophecy, that he was going for "the last farewell." He felt unwell at the airport, and as the Sheikh boarded his aircraft the President asked for his car to be brought over. Normally he walked to his car. He asked his secretary to call Dr. Sawy to his house. His family was waiting for him to join them for lunch and they noticed how very tired he was. He talked with them for a while and then went up to his room saying that he could not eat anything.

Dr. Sawy arrived and Mrs. Nasser left the room. In deference to her husband's wishes, she never remained in the room when there was anybody else with him. Dr. Sawy examined the President and, recognizing the signs of another heart attack, called for Dr. Mansour Fayez and Dr. Zaki el Ramli, the specialists who had been treating him since his first attack. The men who had been formed into a committee to run affairs of state during his first attack were also called. When the specialists arrived, they carried on the treatment begun by Dr. Sawy. The heart equipment that had been installed in the house was made ready and the committee began to gather.

The President lay on his bed in his blue pajamas and just before five o'clock his pulse began to steady and his heartbeat became nearly normal. He began to talk with the three doctors. Dr. Fayez told him that he needed a long leave, but Nasser insisted that he wanted to go to the front to see "our boys" before going on holiday.

Dr. Ramli and Dr. Fayez left the room and it was then that Nasser reached over to switch on the radio set. When he failed to hear what he expected, Dr. Sawy again urged him to remain quiet and he replied: "Doctor, thank God, I feel better now."

They were his last words. His eyes closed and his arm fell limply to his side. Dr. Sawy called his colleagues and they started to work frantically on the President.

The men waiting outside sensed the urgency and came into the room and watched in complete disbelief as the doctors fought for their leader's life. After his previous attack they had soon found him sitting in a chair eating his favorite white cheese, but now he lay lifeless on his bed, moving only when the electric shock machinery sent three charges quivering through his body. It was hoped that the shocks would start his heart beating again. But nothing would ever restart Gamal Abdel Nasser's heart. It was broken.

As the hopelessness of the doctors communicated itself to the men standing round the room, they began to display the first signs of the great wave of grief that would roar through the Arab world.

Vice-President Hussein el Shafei turned to face Mecca and knelt in prayer. Anwar el Sadat, who was to succeed Nasser, stood by the bed, turned his face to heaven, and recited verses from the Koran. I could not believe it. I watched the doctors and muttered: "Oh God, it is impossible."

The people there all knew of his bad health but nobody had expected him to die like this. The fear of assassination was always present in their minds. Nasser was the man at the very heart of the turbulence in the Middle East. He had made many powerful enemies and there were many men who would have liked to remove him from the scene. He was careless about personal security; he did not object to others making security arrangements for him, but he was always going to the people, going into the crowds, and it was difficult to protect him. He would shrug the danger aside, saying: "I have put my soul on my palm and I am going out with it."

Now God had taken his soul, peacefully. Still the men around the bedside could not believe what they saw. General Mohammed Fawzi came in and urged the doctors to go on with their work. Nobody really believed the truth until Dr. Sawy covered his face with his hands and wept uncontrollably.

The doctors pulled Nasser's blanket over his face and left to break the news to his wife. She came into the room, took down the blanket again, and kissed him as the men filed out and left her alone with him.

A meeting was immediately called of the High Executive Committee of the Socialist Union and the Cabinet. It was held in the Cabinet Room at the Koubbah Palace where ministers who had been visiting the troops at the front arrived still wearing their combat uniforms. His chair was empty while they decided what to do, but his presence was everywhere in that room. It was arranged that his body should be moved to the infirmary of the Koubbah Palace for three days and then he should be given a State funeral.

The radio stopped ordinary programs and broadcast only verses from the Koran. The people sensed that something important had happened but none of them suspected that Gamal Abdel Nasser had died. Then Vice-President Sadat told the world the news in a short broadcast. The effect was both instantaneous and fantastic.

People poured out of their houses into the night, making their way to the broadcasting station on the banks of the Nile to find out if what they had heard was true. It is strange that since time immemorial the Egyptian people are always drawn to the Nile at moments of extreme emotion and that night the methods of modern communication coincided with their age-old feelings. First, little groups were to be seen in the streets, then hundreds, then thousands, then tens of thousands, and then the streets were black with people until it was impossible for anybody to move. A group of women outside the broadcasting station were screaming: "The Lion is dead! The Lion is dead!" It was a cry that came to echo round Cairo and it spread through the villages until it filled Egypt. That night and in the days to come he was mourned with a wild and passionate grief. Soon people began to move into Cairo from all parts of Egypt until there were ten million in the city. The authorities stopped the trains running, for there was nowhere for the people to stay and food supplies were running short. But still they came, by car, by donkey, and on foot.

Thousands came from other Arab countries, by jet and by ship. It became a mass migration of sorrow.

The news sped round the world, taking shock and sorrow with it. In Amman all fighting stopped. The King's tanks unloaded their guns, the guerrillas came out of their trenches shouting his name, and in death Nasser achieved what he had struggled so hard to do in life. In Beirut men brought out their guns and fired mourning barrages of shots into the heavens. In Tripoli, President Qaddafi locked himself into his room and wept and did not come out until the second day.

The Syrian Defense Minister—now President—Hafez el Assad cried and said: "We used to act like children and blundered and we knew he was there to correct our faults and protect us against their consequences."

Even in Tel Aviv Mrs. Golda Meir, the Israeli Premier, said: "It is a bad joke." President Richard Nixon, who was due to board the aircraft carrier *Saratoga* for maneuvers in the Western Mediterranean—the Americans wanted the Sixth Fleet's guns to be heard in Cairo—canceled the maneuvers.

Somebody unknown composed a ceremonial song in Egypt. Its refrain was "Farewell, Gamal. Beloved of the millions, farewell." It ran like fire through the streets. Everybody was singing it. It had the soul of Egypt in it; the chant could have been composed for the funeral procession of Ramses II.

The grief of the people took charge. Five divisions of troops were moved in to control the mourners, but the crowds were so enormous that the troops were swept away. Only at the headquarters of the Free Officers movement in Liberation Garden, where his flower-decked coffin rested on a stand covered in green silk, were the troops able to keep the way clear. It was there that the visiting heads of state paid their last respects to the President.

Many of them had difficulty getting there. Premier Aleksei Kosygin had to be taken from the Soviet Embassy by boat because the crowds were so dense. He was overwhelmed by the people and their sorrow. He looked at them and said: "You must restrain your grief." It had been planned that heads of state would be taken to the Nile Hilton to watch the funeral procession, but many of them never got there.

Nothing could restrain the people. Three flags were torn from the coffin and at the Railway Square the President's body had to be taken from the gun carriage, which was in danger of being wrecked, and put on an armored car. Eventually, after a tumultuous seven-mile procession, the President's body reached El Fateh Mosque. This was a mosque in which he had taken a great deal of interest, built in an area of particular personal associations for him. Close by was the apartment where he lived at the time of his coup, a little farther on was the army headquarters which the Free Officers took over that dramatic night, and not far away was the house in which he lived and died as President.

He is buried now beneath a marble tomb inscribed with the verse from the Koran that was broadcast by Anwar el Sadat when he announced Nasser's death:

O ye tranquil soul,
Return back to your God willingly and you are accepted,
Return back to my house among the faithful.

On the twenty-seventh of January, 1971, an Egyptian delegation that was touring Eastern countries to explain why the cease-
fire on the Suez Canal could not be extended indefinitely met
Premier Chou En-lai in his office in the Forbidden City in Peking.

He welcomed the delegation. It was led by Dr. Labib Shoukair,
who was Speaker of Parliament, and Dr. Mohammed Abd el
Salam el Zayyat, the Minister of State for Parliamentary Affairs.
He sat them down and they exchanged official greetings but Chou
En-lai immediately launched into the question of Nasser's death.

"Can you answer a question which I want to ask and which is
puzzling me?" he asked. They said: "Yes, by all means."

"This is my question," said Chou. "Why did Gamal Abdel
Nasser die?"

The delegation was puzzled, but he persisted, "When was he
born?" They replied: "The fifteenth of January, 1918."

"And when did he die?"

"The twenty-eighth of September, 1970."

"Then," said Chou, "he died at the age of fifty-two years, eight
months, and thirteen days. Is this possible?"

The delegation, still puzzled, replied that he had died because
it was God's will.

"Let's not blame God for what we do," said Chou. "There must
be a reason. Gamal Abdel Nasser was young, fifty-two years is
young. I am seventy-two and I am still working and, as you can
see, I am in good health. I cannot conceive how he died in this
way. He was a head of state, leader of the Arab world, with the
best of medical attention available to him. How could you allow
him to die?"

The delegation fell silent. They had no answer to Chou's question. He had his own: "I am going to give you the explanation. He died of sorrow, he died of a broken heart.

"And it is the fault of the Soviet Union. They deceived him. They pushed him into a situation and then they left him. They allowed his heart to be broken."

The delegation protested that they had not been deserted by the Soviet Union and pointed out that the Russians were giving them arms.

"Selling you arms, you mean," said Chou.

The delegation argued that such was not true, that the Soviet Union had replaced all the arms lost in the battles of June 1967 at no cost to Egypt, and it was only the new arms which were being paid for.

"How can you buy?" said Chou. "You should not buy. It is inconceivable that the first Socialist country should be reduced to being an arms trader."

Chou's argument, of course, had all the overtones of the Sino-Soviet quarrel, which he pursued in a Chinese way. The facts of the situation are different and far more complicated. Really to understand the way in which Gamal Abdel Nasser lived and died one must examine the condition of the world in which he worked and fought. He was caught up in the processes of historical change that moved so rapidly after World War II. The old empires were crumbling. The French and the British, who had shared Asia and the Middle East between them for so long, were retreating everywhere. The old colonial authorities could no longer rule as they had. Nationalism and new ideologies swept the once-subject peoples. It was a time of turmoil.

Two new powers were already contesting for influence in the Middle East. The United States of America and the Soviet Union sought to fill the vacuum left by the British and the French. By the end of the war the Americans were already quarreling with

Britain over rights and oil concessions in the Middle East. The struggle had begun.

The United States had become a world power, but the Americans had little experience in this role and they placed too much reliance on undercover work in their fight for influence and prestige. At one stage the Central Intelligence Agency affected developments in the area more than the State Department did.

The role of the other new power, the Soviet Union, was more complicated for the Soviet Union is two things—it is a big power and it is an ideology. People in the Arab world were intrigued by the Communists. They wanted to know what the Communists had to say. Egypt had no diplomatic relations with the Soviet Union until after Russia entered the war. There were no copies of the *Communist Manifesto* in Egypt and the few Arabs who were Communists were persecuted. They meant nothing to the masses who were content with the teachings of Islam, but some intellectuals looked on them as martyrs and wondered what it was they had to say.

The old political parties all over the Arab world were bankrupt of ideas and influence because the world was changing and they were not prepared for change. So there was a vacuum of power and the idea of Communism was potentially attractive because it had proved itself in the war against fascism as the foundation of a society knit into a strong fabric.

When the *Communist Manifesto* was smuggled into Egypt it caused a sensation. Intellectuals read it and thought they had come upon a key that could open all the political and social doors. President Nasser himself was attracted to the ideas of Communism but finally rejected it as a way of life on two grounds: nationalism and religion. He used to argue with the Communists in this fashion: "I accept the fact of a material world. But then, how was life created? Maybe I am ready to accept the theory of evolution and development. But then I want you to tell me how the earth was created, how the universe was made, and until you can do that I am going to believe in God."

As a power, Russia was traditionally interested in the Mediterranean for its warm-water ports. As Chairman Nikita Khrushchev used to say: "You are our backyard."

That was the international situation when Gamal Abdel Nasser came onto the political scene. The old order was disintegrating. Two powers were departing and two new protagonists had arrived, one using undercover work to achieve its ends, the other using ideology.

In the Arab world it was a time of conflict. The Arabs were trying to find a sense of direction but were torn between different routes. First there was the Islamic road, whose supporters argued that Islam was the only way and that all Islamic countries should move together.

This was Iraqi Premier Nuri Said Pasha's argument for joining the Baghdad Pact.[5] He said the Arabs could get the Turks and the Pakistanis to fight for them. There were historical precedents for such an argument. One hundred years after Napoleon's brief stay in Egypt in 1798–99, which opened Egypt's eyes to the world, the Egyptian political leader Mustapha Kamel struggled against the British occupiers. But he was not fighting for Egyptian independence. He was fighting for a return to the Ottoman empire—an Islamic empire. There was a great sense of belonging to one vast Islamic nation among those who wanted to travel this road, but they were opposed by the believers in Arab nationalism, those who argued that if all the Islamic people were included, it would bring in people from Africa and Asia and as far away as the Philippines.

They insisted that the real bonds of their unity and develop-

[5] An anti-Communist pact formed in 1955 and signed by Iraq, Turkey, Britain, Iran, and Pakistan, with the U.S. as a non-signing associate.

ment could not come from the world-wide believers in Islam but had to stem from Arab nationalism.

The ideas of these Arab nationalists were first expressed in Lebanon and in Egypt. The Lebanese intellectuals argued that development based exclusively on Islam would exclude too many people who were vital parts of the Arab world. The Copts of Egypt and the Christians of Lebanon, for example, would not be able to join a totally Islamic way of life. Instead, the intellectuals argued for an Arab entity with common pillars of geography, history, culture, and language to serve as the framework on which the Arabs could build and move into the future.

So the original contradiction was between Islam and Arab nationalism.

The second came when some of the Arab states started to get their independence. They had fought for their freedom in different atmospheres against different imperial powers. The Egyptians fought the British in the context of their mood. The Syrians fought the French in the context of their mood. They were different confrontations. The British were more flexible than the French. The British did not retaliate against the Egyptians by bombarding Cairo, whereas the French twice crushed Syrian uprisings by shelling Damascus, once in 1925 and again in 1944. There are different moods, different accents even in imperialism.

This led each country to winning its freedom in a different way, and because of these differences a contradiction developed between those who wanted complete national independence and those who had a sense of belonging to Arab nationalism as a whole.

This conflict was intensified by the different ways in which the countries set out after they had achieved independence between the two World Wars. The Lebanese thought that free enterprise was best for them, while Egyptians adopted a sort of socialism and Saudi Arabia remained a traditional monarchical society.

There were two other great influences on the Arab world at

this time. The first was the attack of Jewish nationalism as expressed in Zionism. The second was the impact on Arab society of the development of the oil fields and the vast wealth that flowed from them.

This wealth created an upheaval in the Arab world. The extravagance of some oil-rich sheikhs was frightening in its vulgarity and its irresponsibility. They could be seen driving Cadillacs with goats sitting beside them. One man would twiddle a rope of pearls through his toes, another had millions of pounds in notes pinned to his clothes and kept his country's treasure under his bed.

Some men, a few, became inordinately rich, but the majority of people remained miserably poor, many living on the borderline of existence. This new wealth and the way in which it was used put up barriers in the Arab world where there was supposed to be unity. It put up new kinds of class barriers that proved to be a force to be reckoned with, for the men with the money tried, and often succeeded, to buy influence and power.

With all these conflicts the whole Arab world was in turmoil. And nowhere was there more turmoil than in Egypt. Centuries of exploitation by foreigners, of oppression on behalf of absentee landlords and stockholders, and of persecution by petty officials had bitten deep into the Egyptian soul. There was a yearning for freedom, for dignity, for the right to be proud of oneself and one's country.

But there seemed little chance. King Farouk was in his palace and one half per cent of the population was getting 50 per cent of the national income. Corruption had fed on World War II and grown to fantastic proportions. The political parties had collapsed with no sense of direction and no sense of purpose. There was nothing to be proud of and there was no dignity.

The depths to which Egypt had fallen are demonstrated by the fact that in the latter years of the war and immediately after, the country was run by three women. They were Lady Killearn, the young, Italian-born wife of the British Ambassador; Mme. Nahas, who was also young and was married to the elderly Nahas Pasha, leader of the Wafd party and Lord Killearn's choice as Prime Minister; and the King's mother, Queen Nazli.

The ruling forces in Egypt at that time were the British Embassy, the Palace, and the Wafd party, and in each one there was a dominant woman. They were powerful and supreme.

Nothing affronted Egyptian pride more than the events of the fourth of February, 1942, when Lord Killearn issued an ultimatum to King Farouk demanding that Nahas Pasha be made Prime Minister. The King refused, whereupon Lord Killearn called out a British armored force and rolled tanks up to the gates of the Abdin Palace. Under threat of the tanks' guns, the King was forced to abdicate.

The effect on the Egyptians was devastating. Once again an Egyptian ruler had been forced to obey the dictates of a foreigner. Once again they had been made to eat dirt. But it had an electrifying effect on young officers of the Army, and one of them, Gamal Abdel Nasser, became determined that never again would Egypt be humiliated in such a fashion. The start of the Free Officers movement as a cohesive effort can be dated from the moment when the first British tank trained its gun on King Farouk's palace.

The Free Officers talked of little else but freedom and the restoration of their country's dignity and Gamal Abdel Nasser plotted his revolution.

At the same time, another revolutionary force was gaining support in Egypt: the Moslem Brotherhood, the extreme, militant movement of Islam.

At one stage Nasser was attracted towards the Brotherhood just as he had been towards Communism. But the Brotherhood's methods of bombing and assassination were not to his taste. The one assassination attempt in which he was involved was a failure, and the screams of the intended victim's wife as the shots rang out induced such revulsion within him that he could not sleep. He was relieved beyond measure when he learned that all the bullets had missed, and he vowed: "Never again."

It was this revulsion that saved King Farouk's life on the night he was overthrown in 1952. Many of the Free Officers wanted to kill him. "Let's try him and hang him," they argued. But Nasser said: "If you are going to hang him, why bother to try him?" He argued for nine hours for Farouk's life, pleading not only for Farouk but for the others who would inevitably die as a result. "In all my reading of history," he told the others, "I have learnt the same lesson over and over again: bloodshed will lead to bloodshed."

In the end he prevailed, and Egypt was saved from terror. But such niceties were not for the Brotherhood. They had been using assassination as a political weapon. They bombed cinemas and night clubs. Murder became commonplace. Egypt had become a volcano of repressed feelings, bubbling over into violence.

That was the world that Gamal Abdel Nasser stepped into on the night of the twenty-second of July, 1952, when the Free Officers seized power. The Middle East was undergoing a revolutionary change with the old empires collapsing and new powers moving in. Arab states were trying to find their roads to independence and beyond. And Egypt was ripe for revolution.

These were the historical conditions that formed Nasser's destiny, that made him into the symbol of lost dignity and hopes unfulfilled. They laid on his shoulders a burden too great for any man to bear. They formed his life and they brought about his death.

When the people ran into the streets that night crying, "The Lion is dead," all Egypt echoed with the grief of the cry, for among the Arabs the protector of a family is known as "the Lion" and these were people grieving for the man who had become the spiritual expression of the Arabs, the protector of their honor and their dreams.

The Lion's life had three stages: the Lion free, the Lion chained, the Lion wounded.

The first stage of freedom lasted until the Suez invasion in 1956. Unwittingly, the attacks by the British and French and the Israelis made him into a world figure. Instead of destroying Nasser, Prime Minister Sir Anthony Eden's folly gave him international stature and thrust him outside the borders of Egypt. He was never again to be concerned solely with Egyptian affairs.

He was always a rebel, a characteristic which stemmed almost certainly from his reaction to the stern traditionalist views of his father who, as a post office clerk in Upper Egypt, was a minor member of the Egyptian bureaucracy.

He adored his mother, an Alexandrian and a person quite unlike his father in temperament. As a young boy he was sent to school in Cairo where he stayed with his uncle. He wrote long and loving letters to his mother and could not understand why she did not reply to him. When he returned home he found that she had died and that his father had remarried. He was only eight. His world had fallen apart. From that moment on, he was a confirmed rebel.

Nasser was sent to his mother's family in Alexandria to complete his education and it was there that he first became involved in politics. He saw a demonstration in the street that was being broken up by the police. Not even knowing what the demonstration was about, he joined the fight. It was enough for him that it was against established order. He was arrested and spent the night in jail where he found that his companions were members of the Young Egypt party. He joined on the spot and soon served the party by running copy for its magazine.

His arrest did not ease matters between himself and his father.

There was always friction between them, and when he graduated from school he set out to find a career that would keep him away from home. He tried to join the police and passed all the necessary examinations until he came before a committee headed by a general with the title of Pasha. This committee was to inquire into his social status.

The General asked: "What does your father do?" When Nasser replied, "A clerk in the post office," the General said, "My son, you are not fit to be here . . ."

Nothing could be more calculated to increase the young rebel's hatred of the established order. After that disappointment he studied law for some six months and was doing well. But it meant living at home, and so he abandoned his studies and entered the Military Academy, where, within the military framework of discipline, he found the freedom to develop his thinking, to read, and to plan for the future.

It is one of the paradoxes of Nasser's life that while he was always a rebel, he remained a conservative in his personal life. Some of the traditional upbringing against which he rebelled had entered his soul. He was taught to believe that Hell was a very terrible place but that all children automatically went to Heaven. So awful was the prospect of Hell that when he was seven he and another boy decided not to risk going there and made up their minds to commit suicide. They went to the post office and stole some wax that Nasser's father was always warning him was poisonous. They ate it and lay down to die. But the nearest he got to Heaven was a stomach-ache and the nearest to Hell was a beating from his father.

That original simplicity stayed with him all his life. He was never interested in women or money or elaborate food. After he had come to power the cynical old politicians tried to corrupt him but they failed miserably. His family life was impeccable. He always tried to lunch with his wife and their three boys and two girls. Often they would sit and eat his favorite dish—white Egyptian cheese—while they watched films—his only relaxation.

As for money, millions of pounds were sent to him in donations. He used it for Egypt's benefit, and when he died there were £2,500,000 in his public account but only £610 in his personal account.

His taste in food was for the traditional Egyptian dishes of meat, vegetables, and rice and was simple enough to be something of a burden to his traveling companions. Once when he and a delegation were sailing to Yugoslavia on what had been King Farouk's yacht, his immediate entourage found that they were eating the usual dull foods while lesser members of the delegation were being given beautifully prepared meals. So they arranged with the chef to serve them something special. When the meal arrived in all its glory, the President looked at it and said: "It is very colorful. Just like the advertisements in the American magazines."

He started to taste some caviar, but while his companions were beginning to enjoy their meal, he slowed down. At that moment a waiter arrived with a tray of the usual simple food. The chef knew that Nasser would prefer his normal meal.

On another occasion, during the austerity that followed Suez, his ministers were struggling to find items to cut from the import list. Nasser asked to see the list and immediately struck out asparagus, champagne, foie gras and a dozen other luxuries saying: "Things which I do not know about, the ordinary Egyptian would not know about."

But that came later, after he had been chained by events. What mattered to him as a cadet at the Military Academy and afterwards as a young officer serving in the Sudan was the reading that he could do. He was intensely interested in history, especially in the unification of Germany and in the French Revolution. The novels he read about the revolution had a marked effect on his later conduct. He was so impressed by A Tale of Two Cities and its story of the Terror that reigned in Paris that it probably saved the Egyptian people from much bloodshed after their own revolution because it made him so conscious of the terror that can follow all revolutions.

He was also fascinated by *The Scarlet Pimpernel*, by the hidden, underground character who led the resistance without appearing in person. He wrote a novel himself about the popular resistance to the first British invasion of Egypt at Rosetta in 1807, in which the hero was an Egyptian Scarlet Pimpernel.

One can see the effect that this had on Nasser's actions when he overthrew Farouk. He remained in the background. He was the hidden, underground leader. He put up General Mohammed Naguib as a popular façade.

When World War II started, the young officers in the Egyptian Army were all discussing how they could win freedom. A few of them thought that they could best do it by collaborating with the Nazis along the lines of "My enemy's enemy is my friend." Nasser never agreed with this argument, and he served with an infantry battalion that helped protect the British rear during the battle of El Alamein. Then came Lord Killearn's humiliation of the young King Farouk, and Gamal Abdel Nasser, always a rebel, put his feet firmly on the road to revolution.

He remained, like the Scarlet Pimpernel, always clandestine, unknown except to his colleagues among the Free Officers, and it is a tremendous tribute to his ability that the organization remained undiscovered. For any man in that time of general doubting to gather a hundred other men of different characters and temperament about him and give them the confidence to carry out their mission was an incredible achievement.

Another substantial influence on Nasser's life came in 1948 during the first Arab war against Israel, when he was one of the men who were cut off by the Israelis at Faluja but who fought on bravely without surrendering. He would talk across the front line to the besieging Israelis and their talk was of how the Jews forced Britain to give up the Palestine Mandate.

Out of that experience he also acquired a new feeling for the Arab nation. He returned convinced that the different Arab states were one people with one culture and, particularly, one language. His thinking expanded outside the borders of Egypt and he began to think not only of Egyptian nationalism but of the condition of the whole Arab world.

All these influences, the reading, the experience, the humiliations—both national and personal—came together on the night of the twenty-second of July, 1952, when Colonel Gamal Abdel Nasser put on his uniform, kissed his wife, gave his brother all the money he had (£30) to look after his family in case anything went wrong, and walked out to overthrow the King and change the history of the world.

He did not go in for many subtleties. The value of his uncomplicated method of thinking and acting was demonstrated that night. Many of his colleagues wanted to carry out a classical coup d'état, occupying the Abdin Palace and all the principal offices. But Nasser said: "Take control of the army and we will have won." And so they concentrated on occupying army headquarters and the radio station.

When that was done, the revolution was virtually complete. "By taking over the army," said Nasser, "we took over the stick with which the King was threatening the people." If the rebels had tried to take the Palace, the Palace Guard would have been forced to open fire and there would have been bloodshed.

The Free Officers had been forced to carry out their coup earlier than expected because one of them had at last broken the long and effective conspiracy of silence and talked to his brother who was in the Air Force and who in turn warned the King's men. Nasser once again took an uncomplicated approach to danger. He argued that it was too late to turn back and if they failed then at least the people who would follow in their footsteps would know that they had done their best for Egypt.

As it happened, Nasser's men arrested the generals when they arrived at a crossroads outside the dusty Abbasseya Barracks. They had been summoned to a meeting at General Headquarters to plan the crushing of the revolution.

There was one moment of danger for Nasser when he was arrested by his own men on his own orders. Because most of the Young Officers were of junior rank, he had issued an order that all officers of the rank of colonel and above were to be arrested. During the night, the 13th Battalion had been delayed in coming into Cairo. So, in his colonel's uniform, he drove out to discover what had happened to them. He met them at the outskirts of Heliopolis and they, seeing his badges of rank, promptly arrested him. Luckily, after some time, he heard the voice of one of his friends and shouted out to him. He was recognized and released.

It was later that night that he saved King Farouk's life. If he had killed Farouk he would immediately have become the most popular man in the Arab world. But he was still being the rebel. He did what he believed was right. He saved Farouk and then he presented General Naguib to the people as the leader of the revolution.

Naguib was very popular and he took all the glory while Nasser stayed in the background, always thinking, always appearing to the people as a grim man. He was much misunderstood.

It is strange that the man who came to be loved by everybody started off with such misunderstanding from the people. The theme that ran through his speeches at that time was: "I will never beg for applause. I will never beg for popularity." He offended everybody. The mood started to change when the people saw that Naguib was flirting with the old politicians. But the real change came, as it did so often for Nasser, with a single dramatic incident.

He was shot at six times while he was making a speech in Alexandria. But he did not flinch, just stood there, braving the assassin as the bullets whistled past him. He spoke to the people as the shots rang out: "My fellow countrymen, stay where you are. I am not dead, I am alive, and even if I die all of you is Gamal Abdel Nasser. The banner would not fall."

It was an act of extreme courage and was a turning point in his career. From then on the people began to warm towards him.[6]

And with the people's support he was very much the freed Lion. His fight with the British over the evacuation of the Canal Zone, his turndown of the Baghdad Pact, his quarrel with Sir Anthony Eden, his dream of building the Aswan High Dam, his decision to nationalize the Suez Canal were all expressions of the rebel spirit. He felt free to do as he wished.

Then, in 1956, came the Suez invasions, and Gamal Nasser won a smashing international political victory. He destroyed the last pretensions of imperialism in Egypt and became the undisputed leader of the Arabs and a world statesman.

But the very magnitude of his victory and the responsibility it laid upon him meant that the old days of the Lion Free had gone forever. He was now the Lion Chained, fettered by the power that the events of Suez thrust upon him. The whole Arab people had risen in his defense. Pipelines were cut, Western Europe was starved for oil. The Arab world was in a state of change with Nasser as the symbol and the embodiment of that change. His popularity was such that he spontaneously became involved in the internal politics of every Arab country. The Nasserite party that grew up in each one caused jealousy and dissension. Some of these parties were of dubious value and he used to say rather wistfully: "You know, I can control whom I choose, but I cannot control who chooses me."

[6] Publisher's note: Naguib was removed in April 1954 and Nasser became Premier. He was elected President in June 1956.

That was his explanation to King Saud of Saudi Arabia who was extremely jealous of him at that time. Practically all his friends among the Arab leaders were jealous and all his enemies were furious. He had come to have a constituency outside the jurisdiction of the Egyptian state as he depended on the support of wide masses of the people contrary to the wishes of their ruling classes. The only way he could influence that constituency was by example and so he fought for Arab rights, not just Egyptian rights, wherever he could.

This led to quarrels with Britain and America and even with the Soviet Union.

He realized a dream that appealed to every Arab; he joined Egypt with Syria in the United Arab Republic and seemed to have laid the foundation stone of a wider Arab unity. But what had started out so brightly ended in disaster when Syria revoked the union. Then in 1962 he was dragged into war in the Yemen, which at first seemed an easy affair but turned out to be very hard indeed.

He was blamed for all the troubles in the Middle East but his answer to that was: "I am not acting, I am reacting." He told Selwyn Lloyd, then Britain's Foreign Secretary, "If you think that I have got buttons on my desk and I push them and there is a revolt in Iraq, or a coup d'état in I don't know where, or a bomb explodes there, or a demonstration here, you are giving me super-human powers which I do not possess. Don't exaggerate my importance."

So this was the period of the Lion Chained, bound by events outside his control, when he no longer had the freedom to be a rebel. Now he was the symbol of the Arab world and as a symbol he had to fight the rest of the world on behalf of Arab nationalism. It was a confining role, and it led directly to the last stage of his life—that of the Lion Wounded.

Gamal Abdel Nasser was bound by the ideas of Arab unity and he felt a moral, political, and ideological obligation to the Palestinian people. He had a duty toward all those people who had lost their land and their homes, who had been forced out by the Zionist reign of terror. But he hated war. He hated it from a personal point of view and a national point of view. For instance, he did not form the Fedayeen until after the Israeli raid on Gaza on the twenty-eighth of February, 1955, in which thirty-seven Egyptians were killed. This raid was an expression of Premier David Ben Gurion's policy of "forcing peace," of trying to make the Arab nations come to terms with him by force of arms.

Nasser was once again obliged to react. At that time Egypt had not started to receive arms from the Communist bloc and was not equipped to fight a war, but the country, faced with Ben Gurion's policy of massive raids, had to defend itself and so the Fedayeen were organized as a form of defense short of war.

His personal experience of war at El Alamein and at Faluja had taught him to hate it. Whenever he inspected young soldiers and the senior officers were taking pride in the troops' performance, he would say, "Yes, it is pleasing to see those boys, but I can't enjoy it like other people because I always feel that one day I am going to have to give the order to those young boys to go and die."

The start of his quarrel with the Syrian Baath party in 1959 came when the Israelis began to divert the waters of the Jordan and the Syrians wanted him to mount a limited operation against the Israeli engineering project some four miles over the border. President Nasser opposed them in the Council of Ministers, arguing in the first place that: "It is easy to start a war but it is not easy to end it." His second argument was that the idea of a limited war was a fallacy. "I am willing to carry out a limited war," he said, "but only if one of you gets me Ben Gurion's assurance that he too will limit it. For a war to be limited depends on the other side."

However, despite his hatred of war, he was still the Lion Chained, still the symbol of Arab unity and resistance, so that when the crisis came in 1967 he was forced once again to react on behalf of the Arab people.

The events that followed left him the Lion Wounded. He never recovered.

He saw defeat coming. He foresaw that the Israelis would start the war by striking at Egypt's airfields, and he constantly warned the Air Force to be on their guard against a surprise attack. Yet when the attack came, just as he had predicted, they were caught unprepared. At General Headquarters on the first morning of the war he felt the atmosphere of panic and from that moment he lost confidence. He tried to bolster his generals' morale, urging them to fight on until, as at Suez, the international forces of world order would come to their aid and force the Israelis to abandon their onslaught.

Events moved too quickly. The generals decided to evacuate the Sinai and took their decision without consulting him. When he heard of the evacuation he wept for the first time in his adult life. He went to General Headquarters and tried to halt the retreat. But it was too late. The Egyptian Army had been defeated.

With the defeat came humiliation. He decided to resign and was quite prepared to stand trial for his responsibility. He was ready, almost eager, to give himself to the people.

"If the people find me guilty," he said, "and hang me in Liberation Square, then I think they have got the right."

But the people moved the other way completely. When he made his speech accepting responsibility, announcing his withdrawal from political life and saying that he was ready for any decision the people might make, the people begged him to stay. He was astonished. He was quite prepared to be hanged; instead the whole

Arab world once again rose in his support. They begged him to stay on. They felt that he still represented their will and they wanted him to lead them on to correct the effects of defeat.

Nasser accepted their verdict. But he was building on ruins. And he had to take harsh decisions. He was obliged to remove Field Marshal Abdel Hakim Amer, one of his closest friends, and all the old generals of the Army. Alone now, he began to feel that there was a conspiracy against him. And despite the support of the people, he felt humiliated. There was a deep scar on his soul.

For the first time in his life he needed sleeping pills. He had been gifted with the ability to sleep soundly. Even during the Suez crisis in 1956 he was able to go to bed and fall asleep whenever he needed to. On the night when the British invasion fleet approached, he went to bed leaving orders to be wakened only when the first landings were taking place. But after 1967 he lost this ability. He was ill. He talked of resigning. He still felt his humiliation, his responsibility, and the continuing burden of being the expression of the Arab spirit. He was both chained and wounded. The wounds would not heal and on the twenty-eighth of September, 1970, President Nasser died.

And his people cried to the heavens: "The Lion is dead, the Lion is dead!"

The Lion was dead but his achievements have lived on. He tied Egypt to the rest of the Arab world and he tied the Arabs to the contemporary world and its ideas. He did not realize the total Arab unity that he dreamed of and worked for, but he crystallized the need for it. During his time this unity proved impossible to achieve. But after him it has become impossible to ignore.

He had changed the face of the Arab world. He had changed the colors on the map. The red of Britain and the green of France no longer fill the boundaries of the Arab countries—the colonialists have gone. And he broke the feudalistic pattern of Arab life.

In Egypt he provided the stability that enabled him to bring about change. No Egyptian government based on the old, weak, party system could have given the country the stability to embark on major projects like the High Dam and the electrification of the country. Such governments were always too unstable, too frightened to undertake vast programs needed to change the face of the country. Nasser gave Egypt that stability of government which permitted the fundamental changes embodied in his programs of land reform, industrialization, and worker participation in the economy.

André Malraux pronounced the proper eulogy for Nasser, not long after our President's death and it is quoted at the end of this book. But first, to the beginning.

II

On the Brink with Dulles

Gamal Abdel Nasser and John Foster Dulles, the two men who were to have more effect on the modern history of the Middle East than any others, met just once, at dinner in the American Embassy in Cairo on May 11, 1953. It was a simple dinner: soup, sole *meunière*, saddle of lamb, and an ice cream dessert. There was no drinking, in deference to the Moslem guests, but the Americans had enjoyed a glass or two of whiskey before Nasser arrived.

However, it was not a simple occasion. United States Secretary of State Dulles had come to Cairo with two objectives. The first was to try to arrange peace between the Arabs and the Israelis. The second was to further his plan to encircle the Soviet Union with military and political alliances, a plan that he pursued with a religious fervor and which was the mainspring of all his actions in the Middle East.

On the Egyptian side, General Naguib was still titular head of the revolution but, by now, ten months after King Farouk had been deposed, it had become obvious that Nasser was the man who held the power. And what Nasser wanted were arms to defend his country against the threat of Israeli aggression.

So the two men, the gray-haired champion of the West and the young soldier of the nationalist revolution, sat down to break bread together with widely different hopes for what might stem from their meeting. Dulles set out to charm Nasser and told him a series of stories about international politics and the bargaining that was going on between the various powers. Nasser was impressed. He found Dulles obstinate, dogmatic in his hatred of Communism, but also a man who had an unexpected sense of humor and the ability to listen and to be receptive. One episode that night particularly impressed Nasser.

When Dulles had arrived at Cairo Airport that morning he had made a statement in which he had said how glad he was to be in Egypt, a country of great civilization. It was impeccable, exactly the right thing for a visiting statesman to say. But then he went on to say that General Naguib was "one of the outstanding free world leaders of the postwar period." Again, for someone like Dulles, this was the standard thing to say. What right-thinking man could object to defending the Free World? But Nasser soon tackled him about it: "I did not like your statement today."

Dulles looked up in astonishment and protested that it was made in friendship. Nasser then explained that the phrase "the Free World" had unfortunate connotations for Egypt "because we have been occupied by the British to secure the communications of 'the Free World' and so for us 'the Free World' has come to mean imperialism and domination, and when you used that phrase this morning it created a bad effect."

Dulles took the point immediately, called one of his aides, and issued another statement more amenable to Egyptian feelings.

The Secretary of State's visit to Cairo was made at a time of growing American involvement in the Middle East, an involvement that was looked on with hope by many people in the area. The whole picture of the United States at that time was a glamorous one. Britain and France were fading, hated empires. The Soviet Union was five thousand miles away and the ideology of Communism was anathema to the Moslem religion. But America had emerged from World War II richer, more powerful, and more appealing than ever. Hollywood was churning out war pictures in which the Americans were the heroes and the others were the villains. Refrigerators, television, all the new instruments of the new life seemed to be coming from America. So the United States wore an aura of success and glamour, shining out above the tarnished failure of the old imperialists, and people were receptive to the idea of the Americans playing a major role in the Middle East.

On their part, the Americans were vitally concerned with the Middle East oil, staging posts on their world-wide system of aerial communications, the Cold War, the need to fill the vacuums left by Britain and France, the growth of Zionism—all were factors in leading the United States into an area made turbulent by the ferment of Arab nationalism and its expression in the Egyptian revolution.

One ironic symptom of America's growing importance in Egypt at that time is that on the night of the revolution, the leaders of both sides, Nasser and King Farouk, sent messengers to the American Ambassador, Jefferson Caffery. Here is the story:

There was an obvious possibility that the British Army would intervene from the Suez Canal Zone on behalf of the old regime. There was a precedent for this because there had been serious discussions on whether or not to intervene during the Fire of

Cairo[1] only five months before the coup. Sir Ralph Stevenson, the British Ambassador at that time, was against intervention but General Sir George Erskine, the British commander in chief, was for it. In the end the British did not intervene, but it was a contingency Nasser had to take into account.

He took military precautions first of all, sending a brigade to block the road to Suez. A defense line was improvised and more troops were held in reserve to cope with a possible British attack. A political effort was needed to march with the military precautions. Nasser wanted the world to know that the revolution was an internal affair, that it was concerned solely with Egypt and would not affect the interests or the safety of foreigners living in Egypt. So at three o'clock in the morning of the coup he decided to send a message to the American Ambassador explaining the aims of the revolution.

There was a snag. None of the young officers knew Caffery and the difficulties of delivering the kind of message they wanted to give the Ambassador at that time in the morning—and be believed —were obvious.

Then Ali Sabry said that he knew the American air attaché. So Sabry[2] was bundled into a car and rushed to the attaché's house, and within half an hour Caffery had Nasser's message explaining that the revolution was an internal affair and warning against any British intervention.

As it turned out, the British had no knowledge of the revolution until it was too late for them to intervene even if they had wanted to. By noon that day the Egyptian people had given their support

[1] On January 25, 1952, anti-British riots broke out in Cairo after a skirmish between Egyptian police and British troops. Before Egyptian police could restore order, a considerable part of the modern quarter of Cairo was burned and destroyed.

[2] Then a major, later Minister for the Presidency of the Republic.

to the young officers and any military move by the British would have been useless.

At the same time, King Farouk, in a state of panic, also sent a message to the Americans. The way in which he sent it was typical of the man who sent it.

When the King was a boy there was a young Italian mechanic working at the Palace called Antonio Polli who mended Farouk's electric train when it refused to run. They became friends and later, the King created a post for him, private secretary for the private affairs of the King, giving him the title of Bey. He was responsible for arranging the King's gambling, his nights out, and his escapades. Polli became a powerful man and at one stage was virtually the ruler of Egypt. After the revolution he opened a restaurant and it was said that he had turned from private royal services to public popular services. But on that night he sent his assistant, Eli, to Ambassador Caffery with a message from the King that said that the King thought the situation was developing dangerously and asked if there was an American destroyer near Alexandria that could take him to safety if it became necessary.

Caffery passed on Farouk's request to Washington and later, after the danger to the King's life had passed, informed the revolutionary authorities of the reply. He told the young officers that Washington had said that there were no destroyers near enough, but had instructed him to do everything possible to ensure the King's safety. That was on the second day of the revolution. Nasser had already won his battle to save Farouk's life and the King had been ordered to leave the country. The King, still seeking American protection, telephoned the Ambassador and asked Caffery to stay with him until he left. So the American went to the Palace, remained there while Farouk packed, and went with him to his ship.

So there were connected events that were highly symbolic of America's position and influence at that time. Her diplomatic

representative was the last man to see off the remains of the old
regime and the first in contact with the new.

The United States immediately began to capitalize on this connection. They increased the number of diplomats at the Embassy
—some of them belonged to the Central Intelligence Agency
(CIA), but that was not known at the time—and they showed
every good will toward the reborn Egypt. The riches and strength
of the New World were going to help one of the world's oldest
countries emerge from the cocoon of colonialism.

It was in this atmosphere that Nasser took the step from which
so many other things have devolved: he asked the Americans for
arms.

Their first reaction was surprise—and surprising when they
pointed out that the two countries already had an arms contract.
A secret agreement was produced, one concluded with Farouk's
government after the Fire of Cairo in February 1952, in which
the Americans agreed to supply Egypt with $5,000,000 worth of
weapons.

There was an agreed shopping list. But when Nasser went
through that list he discovered that it was not what he wanted at
all. Farouk's government, worried by internal security after the
Fire, had ordered armored cars, machine guns, and other weapons
suitable for controlling the populace. What Nasser wanted was
tanks and aircraft, artillery and ships, to secure the frontiers of
the country. He told the Americans that one of the reasons for
the revolution was that Egypt had a weak army, and that the Army
had fought a losing battle in Palestine in 1948 with bad ammunition, ammunition that was bought at fantastic prices in Europe
and that killed more Egyptian soldiers than it did of the enemy.
He argued that the revolution was spearheaded by elements from
the Army and that although it was a popular revolution, it was
the Army that led it, and with the background of the ammunition
scandal of 1948, the officers were determined to have a strong

Army. They needed to be strong psychologically and also practically so that Egypt could be defended.

Nasser also told Caffery that if the Americans *did* sell arms to Egypt, it would be an act that would enhance the prestige of the United States; and he gave his personal assurance that the arms would only be used in self-defense.

In October Egypt was asked for a new list of requirements to replace the old one and this list was subsequently given to the American military attaché. The principal items were equipment for one armored division with its tanks, transport, artillery, and anti-tank guns, and three squadrons of jet fighters.

William C. Foster, the American Deputy Secretary of Defense, arrived in Cairo on the fifth of November and Nasser was invited to dine with him and to discuss the arms question at the American Embassy. It was a good dinner. Foster became expansive, studied the "shopping" list, noted the items that could be sold, discussed the method of payment—in installments, some of it in Egyptian cotton, and he said that if relations between the two countries prospered, then America might waive some payments. By the end of the evening Foster was suggesting that an Egyptian mission should go to America to tour military bases, talk to the men responsible for supplying arms, and arrange for deliveries. Some time later Caffery said he thought Foster had become too expansive and had exceeded his authority. But we did not know that.

All seemed to be going well. The mission was formed, headed by Ali Sabry, and left in November 1952 for what everybody expected would be a successful expedition.

During Farouk's regime the Americans, along with the British, French, and Turks, had suggested to Egypt a defense pact—the Middle East Treaty Organization, to be called by its acronym METO. It was immediately dubbed the "Me Too" pact and did not get very far, and when it was revived it was renamed the Middle East Defense Organization, or MEDO. However, despite its lack of success, the idea of treaty organizations to surround the Soviet Union with bases was of prime importance to the Americans, and while our arms mission was in America the idea of an Islamic military pact was again floated.

The man who put up the idea was Major General George H. Olmsted, director of the foreign military assistance program. He told the mission that the potential of an Islamic pact would be great. It would contain three capitals: Ankara, capital of the most modern Islamic country, Karachi, capital of the most populous Islamic country, and Cairo, capital of the most prestigious Islamic country. He went on to say that such a pact, apart from defending the Middle East, could have an enormous impact on Moslems in the Soviet Union and China. Then he shocked everybody by talking about how a "fifth column" could be created in those countries. It was quite astonishing, because it was completely outside the context of the mission.

He pushed aside a curtain covering a big map on the wall of his office. The map was full of pins and flags. He took a pointer and started to demonstrate what the markers stood for, and then he pointed to an area where there were few pins and said: "Gentlemen, we ought to put some pins and flags here. There is a vacuum here." And he was talking about the area covered by the proposed Islamic pact. It was a most extraordinary performance. He wanted to fill up his map with flags and pins.

However, everything seemed to be going well with the arms mission. Ali Sabry discussed Egypt's requirements with General Omar N. Bradley, chairman of the Joint Chiefs of Staff. Subcommittees were formed to discuss technical details. Nasser was so confident of the mission's success that he told Egyptian Army units he visited that they were going to get new weapons from the United States and that the first shipments would be arriving soon. Then, one day, as he was talking in this fashion to an officer, telling him that he was waiting for the first shipment, the officer said:

"I'm afraid that Ali Sabry himself will be the first shipment."

Nasser told Caffery that story and asked: "What's going on? What's happening to Sabry?" He was reassured and about the same time Ali Sabry sent a message to Cairo saying that everything was going smoothly. Sabry asked for modifications to be made to the military airfields so that they would be ready for the jets.

But time went by, Christmas came and still nothing definite had happened. No arms had arrived. The mission began to be disillusioned. They were told that no decision could be taken because there was a change in presidential administration—Dwight D. Eisenhower was about to take over from Harry S Truman. Nothing could be done until the new President had taken office. But, they were assured, the Egyptian request was already on the desk of the new President and it would be one of the first things he would decide.

So Ali Sabry returned to Cairo in January. There were some doubts about the ultimate success of his mission, but the general feeling was that as Egypt had already waited for two months, it could afford to wait a week or so until the new President took office.

It was at this stage that Dulles came into the picture, bringing with him his missionary fanaticism, dedicated to the containment of Communism. He judged the Middle East situation so important that he came to Cairo only four months after taking over the State Department. It was then that he sat down to dine with Nasser. They talked for two hours after dinner. Nasser immediately brought up the subject of arms, and Dulles offered the first explanation of why President Eisenhower had delayed sending Egypt the arms it needed.

He said that Prime Minister Sir Winston Churchill had telephoned the newly elected President and urged him not to sell arms to the Egyptians and so start his presidency by providing weapons that might be used to kill British tommies who had served under Eisenhower during the war. This plea, said Dulles, affected Ike deeply. He had asked for the list that Nasser wanted. When he studied it he saw there mainly small arms, bazookas, and machine guns, the type of weapons that could be used in guerrilla warfare against the British in the Suez Canal Zone. It seemed that Churchill's fears were justified. So Eisenhower decided to do nothing. He did not refuse the arms outright. He just kept the application in the "Pending" file.

It was not until much later that it was discovered that he had been given the wrong list. What he received was *Farouk's* list for internal security, not Nasser's list for national defense.

Dulles went on to say that he would look on the Egyptian request with favor and at the same time he would try to help solve the problems that existed between Britain and Egypt. He then moved to the subject that interested him most: the anti-Communist pact. He talked about the need for collective security pacts and in particular about MEDO, the Middle East Defense Organization. He stressed how important it was for Egypt to take part in this organization.

Nasser asked why he should join? Who was the pact going to be defense against? And Dulles replied: "Against the Soviet Union."

Nasser was astonished: "Why? The Soviet Union is more than a thousand miles away and we've never had any trouble with them. They have never attacked us. They have never occupied our territory. They have never had a base here, but the British have been here for seventy years."

Dulles said: "All right, but under the pact the British, who would stay here in the base, would belong to the pact and they would not be allowed to raise the British flag. They would be under the flag of the pact."

It was naïve thinking, which Nasser pointed out: "If I went and told my people that the British status here is going to be changed from occupiers to partners by a change of flag, they will laugh at me.

"They will lose faith in me and other people will rise from the underground and win the confidence of the people. If I stop leading my people as a nationalist, then the Communists are going to lead them. They would use my partnership in pacts with you to say that I am a stooge.

"How can I go to my people and tell them I am disregarding a killer with a pistol sixty miles from me at the Suez Canal to worry about somebody who is holding a knife a thousand miles away? They would tell me, 'First things first.' People must first own their independence before they are really interested in defending it.

"We are not ready to discuss pacts or any security measures unless we do it of our own free will."

He argued that if he entered into a pact before the British evacuated the Canal Zone, it would look as if he was being forced into it by the pressure of the eighty thousand British soldiers in the Suez Canal bases. This was an argument that gave Dulles some hope. He felt that after the British had evacuated the bases, then Nasser might be talked round to joining a pact.

Nasser also admitted the need to defend the country against Communism: "But what is the way for us to defend ourselves against Communism? I don't think the Communist attack is going to come across our frontiers because we have no frontiers with the Soviet Union. But it will come through internally. So what we really need to defend against Communism is our internal front and not our frontier." And he warned Dulles: "I think you are complicating the football game. Colonialism is played out and now the match is between two teams—Communism and nationalism. And if you insist on playing, you are going to spoil the game for the others."

Dulles was fascinated by these arguments. They had obviously not been put to him before and towards the end of two hours of argument and discussion he said he thought there had been a breakdown in communication. It is probable that he then took the decision to replace Jefferson Caffery.

It was certainly true that there had been a breakdown in communication. Caffery was over sixty-five and had spent most of his career in South America and Europe; it seemed that he found it difficult to deal with young Arab officers. He had assigned a young man, William Lakeland, a counselor at the Embassy, to be the liaison with the officers. Nasser used to have dinner at his house; they would discuss relations between their two countries, and Nasser was under the impression that Bill Lakeland was an important man. At the dinner with Dulles when Nasser explained that he had already conveyed his feelings to the Embassy on certain subjects, the Secretary was puzzled because he had not been told. When he queried Nasser, his guest would reply: "Yes, I told Bill . . . ," "I told Bill about it . . . ," "as I said to Bill. . . ." After some time Dulles could stand it no longer and burst out: "For heaven's sake, who is Bill?"

Poor Bill. He was down the room by the door trying to hide, trying to cover his embarrassment. His true status had been discovered.

That dinner was of far-reaching importance. Dulles was influenced by the strength of Nasser's arguments against Egypt's joining a mutual security pact and afterwards Dulles drew back from wholehearted support of the Baghdad Pact. He became convinced of the need to ease the path of Britain's withdrawal from Egypt. He became even more determined to try to make peace between Israel and the Arab nations. And he decided to replace Jefferson Caffery.

But the immediate result desired by Nasser did not come about. There were to be no American arms for Egypt. In fact, the only guns ever to be supplied by the United States were the matched

pair of silver-plated .38 Colt revolvers that Dulles had brought
with him to present to Premier Naguib.

When Churchill heard about these pistols, he made another
telephone call to President Eisenhower. This time he protested
the symbolism of the guns. It was a bad sign, he said, and would
encourage the Egyptians.

Events moved quietly for a time after Dulles returned to Washington. It was a time of diplomacy. He decided that the Arab
countries were best left to their own affairs for the time being and
concentrated his efforts on the "Northern Tier" countries of Turkey, Iraq, and Pakistan.

In January 1955 President Eisenhower replaced Caffery with
Henry Byroade, the State Department's Assistant Secretary for
Near Eastern Affairs. Byroade was a charming young man with
a military background who had served in China and seemed an
ideal choice. He started well and made a good impression on
Nasser, by then Premier of Egypt. But then everything went wrong
for him and his service in Egypt was both personally and politically unhappy.

In July 1954 Egypt and Great Britain reached an agreement
under which Britain would evacuate the Suez Canal Zone within
twenty months and finally leave Egypt after 72 years of occupation. This agreement and the continuing good will being displayed
by America toward the Egyptian revolution did not please the
Israelis. They wanted the British Army to remain in Egypt, for
the British were both a distraction to the Egyptians and a buffer
along the Suez. And the Israelis did not want the United States
to remain on good terms with Egypt.

So Ben Gurion, ostensibly living in retirement in the desert,
concocted a terrorist campaign with the aid of a group of senior
officers in Israel's Defense Ministry. It was done without the
knowledge of Pinhas Lavon, the Minister of Defense, and his

name was forged on the orders authorizing the plot. Its object was to convince Britain and America, by blowing up American and British installations in Egypt, that Egypt was not to be trusted and that Nasser could not control the country. The Israelis smuggled in an Army Intelligence officer who organized a group of young Egyptian Jews to do the dirty work. But the plot was both evil and amateurish in concept and execution. It failed miserably. The plotters were arrested. Two were hanged and the Israeli agent committed suicide in prison.

However, the effects were far-reaching. Lavon resigned in protest but Ben Gurion's group put him back into power at the Ministry of Defense, partly to cover up their complicity in the plot. The Israelis put a tight security lid on all news of their disaster. But it stank. And soon afterwards Premier Moshé Sharett, unable to restrain Ben Gurion, resigned in despair and Ben Gurion took his place. Thus, the notorious "Lavon Affair."

While all this was going on, the CIA was as busy in Cairo as it was everywhere else in the Middle East. One day Nasser and the Revolutionary Command Council were discussing the building of a radio tower for the world-wide communications of the Ministry of Foreign Affairs and the intelligence services. Nasser was told that some equipment had already been bought. When he protested that there was no money budgeted for it, he was told that the money was coming from the special American fund. Nasser was astonished; this was the first he had heard of any special fund. He was then told that the CIA had passed three million dollars to General Naguib when he was Premier.

The money had been handed over by an American agent in a big bag stuffed with hundred-dollar bills. It was actually given to an officer in the Egyptian Intelligence Service who acted as a liaison man between the Egyptian and American intelligence services. The transaction was carried out at the American's house in the fashionable Cairo suburb of Ma'adi and the Egyptian officer took the bag to General Naguib's office where it was put in Naguib's safe.

When Nasser heard this, he was furious. He drove immediately to the Council of Ministers and demanded an explanation from Naguib who was then Premier. Naguib insisted the money had nothing to do with the CIA but had been sent by President Eisenhower who made funds available to some heads of state so that they could go outside their budget in order to defend themselves and their countries against Communism. Nasser demanded that the money should be locked in the safe of the Intelligence Service and ordered that none of it could be spent except by permission of the Revolutionary Command Council.

Eventually the tower was built. Originally planned as a simple, functional tower with radio antennae on top and cables passing down through the central core, Nasser decided to build a folly as a monument to the CIA. He used the Americans' money to build the concrete lattice-work tower with a revolving restaurant on top, which dominates the Cairo skyline today. It was heavily criticized when it was built because nobody could understand why money was being wasted on it. The communications part of the building was serious and essential, but the restaurant and frivolous architecture were intended as an insult to American intelligence.

Nasser remained angry with the Americans over this incident. He considered it an attempt at corruption. Even during an Arab summit conference to solve the civil conflict in Jordan, just before he died, he stood on a balcony of the Nile Hilton and, looking at the Tower of Cairo, said: "No, don't talk. Beware. We are being watched."

"By whom?" I asked.

"The CIA," he said and pointed at the tower.

The effect of discovering this money was to make Nasser much more suspicious of the United States and he ordered a complete survey of all American activities in Egypt. This in turn made the

Americans suspicious of Nasser's intentions. From Egypt's point of view, it was like trying to deal with two Americas, one the America of Secretary of State John Foster Dulles and the other the America of his brother, Allen Dulles, director of the Central Intelligence Agency.

The next turning point in Middle East affairs came in February 1955 when the Israelis raided an Egyptian army camp at Gaza and killed thirty-seven Egyptian soldiers. This attack was ordered by Ben Gurion just one week after his return to power as Minister of Defense and it set the pattern of his policy of massive punitive raids.

It came at a time of dissension in the Arab world. The Iraqis had joined the Baghdad Pact while Nasser was bitterly opposed to it, believing that it was an attempt, led by Britain, to suck in the other Arab states and isolate Egypt. Before, in January 1955, there had been a meeting of Arab prime ministers in Cairo which had collapsed in disarray. So when the Israelis struck at Gaza, Nasser came under great pressure. He had little support from the other Arab nations. He was threatened by the Baghdad Pact. He was disturbed by the CIA's machinations. He had to get arms from somewhere. He had to equip his army to face the threat posed by Ben Gurion.

Nasser tried to buy obsolete arms from World War II dumps in Belgium. He got a few pieces from Italy. He tried in Sweden, Switzerland, and Spain. He tried to get the British to release the eighty Centurion tanks that the Egyptian government had contracted to buy before the revolution and which had already been paid for. The British sent sixteen and said they would deliver the rest if Egypt would stop attacking the Baghdad Pact.

At the same time our Intelligence Service began to get information about the Israeli arms purchases from France that had started in 1954.

It is often said that the French gave arms to Israel because of

Egypt's support for the Algerian revolution. This is not true. The French started to supply arms to Israel before the Algerians rose against them, and Egypt's decision to help the Algerians was taken so that, in Nasser's words, "We will make them need their arms in Algeria so that they will not be able to give them to Israel. We will oblige them to use them far away from us so that they will not be used against us."

It was vital, therefore, for Nasser to obtain arms from somewhere, anywhere. Henry Byroade arrived in late February 1955 to take up his post as American Ambassador two or three days after the Gaza raid, and at their first meeting, Nasser told him how essential it was for Egypt to get guns and tanks and jets, and he asked Byroade to pass this message urgently to Secretary Dulles.

But Dulles was not at all happy with Nasser at that time because the Premier had announced his intention of going to Bandung, Indonesia, for the conference of non-aligned nations, and Dulles saw this as a betrayal of his anti-Communist crusade. Non-alignment was a dirty word to Dulles. He tried to convince the Premier that he ought not to go. But he did not succeed.

Nasser arrived in Rangoon with Prime Minister Nehru of India on their way to the conference and there to greet them at the airport was Burma's Prime Minister U Nu and China's Chou Enlai. Nehru introduced Nasser to Chou and the two men struck up an immediate rapport. Later, when Nehru, Nasser, and U Nu put on Burmese national dress and went off to watch the water festival, Chou stayed behind but asked to see Nasser when he returned from the festival that afternoon. They met in a room in what had been the governor-general's residence but what was now a government guest house. It was a big old-fashioned colonial room with fans in the ceiling and half shutters on the door. Chou was already there, chain-smoking, impassive in his high-collared tunic, when Nasser arrived.

They talked first about the Bandung Conference, and Chou

spoke of the situation in Indochina and China's relations with the United States. Premier Nasser talked about the Middle East, and then they discussed areas of possible co-operation between the two countries. To demonstrate the vast possibilities of the Chinese market, Chou told Nasser that China could take all the cotton that Egypt produced simply by ordering every Chinese to lengthen his coat by about two inches.

Nasser then said that where he really wanted co-operation was in obtaining arms. Did Chou think that the Soviet Union would sell arms to Egypt?

That was the first overture of the arms deal. Chou promised that he would ask the Russians, adding that he knew they thought highly of the Egyptian government. The situation had changed because both the Soviet Union and China had been very suspicious of the revolutionary leaders and the Soviet Union in particular had attacked them violently, branding them as a bunch of fascists who were trying to suppress the freedom of the popular masses. But the Soviet attitude had altered in view of Nasser's opposition to imperialism and to the Baghdad Pact, which was aimed at the Soviet Union.

But Chou warned that if the Russians did agree to sell arms to Egypt, it would create many complications with the Western powers.

Nasser said that he was ready for all complications because the only course left open to him was to obtain arms from the Soviet Union. He pointed out that after the revolution he had cut the Army's budget and had used the £70 million he had confiscated from King Farouk to build hospitals, schools, and roads. But, he said, we cannot defend ourselves with hospitals or schools, all we are doing is getting them ready for the Israelis to occupy.

Chou did as he had promised, and after Nasser had returned from Bandung, the Chinese leader sent word that the Russians had agreed and that if Nasser approached them, they would be ready to do a deal.

Soon afterwards, on May 18, 1955, Nasser found himself alongside Daniel Solod, the Soviet Ambassador, at a party in the Sudanese Mission. They shook hands and the Premier said: "I wanted to see you." Solod replied: "I have been instructed to ask for an audience with you, sir."

That audience took place on May 21 in the Premier's office and that was how the arms deal started.

In May, June, and July there were discussions about it at a house in Ma'adi. The Soviet Union sent Colonel Nimoshenko to Cairo as a military attaché, but his real function was to discuss Egypt's requirements. They were practically the same—just a few more—as those on the list which had been given to the Americans.

The Russians were not yet ready to appear as a party in the deal, for this was the time of the Geneva Summit[3] and the Russians felt that if they supplied arms openly, it would be taken as a deliberate breach of the spirit of Geneva. And so, from August onwards, the talks were conducted by the Czechs in Prague. The lists were prepared and prices agreed upon.

However, before all that happened, Nasser gave the Americans one last opportunity to supply the weapons he needed. On May 22, one day after his discussion with Solod, he asked Byroade to see him and told him that he had a firm Russian offer of arms. At that time Nasser would still have preferred Western arms. He felt that the Egyptian Army was not accustomed to Russian arms. There would be a language barrier. Egypt did not know what was in the Russian arsenal. And there would be political repercussions, especially from the conservative regimes in the Arab world.

[3] Conference in Geneva, Switzerland, July 18–23, 1955, attended by the heads of state of the major powers: President Eisenhower, Prime Minister Eden, Premier Faure of France, and Premier Bulganin and Party Chairman Khrushchev of the Soviet Union.

Byroade reported what Nasser had said to Washington. But there was no official reaction. Dulles thought Nasser was bluffing. Byroade also told the retiring British Ambassador, Sir Ralph Stevenson, of his conversation with Nasser and when Sir Ralph called on the Premier to say good-by, he said that he had been told that Egypt was contemplating buying arms from the Soviet Union. He gravely warned Nasser "as my last act in your country" that it would be very dangerous and would lead to many difficulties.

The news of the talks in Prague began to leak out. The Israelis were first on to it and then the Americans began to get wind of what was happening. Suddenly they began to hint about giving Egypt arms. They again asked for a list of requirements and said they were ready to look favorably on an arms deal. But by that time it was too late; everybody felt that it was just a maneuver, a ploy to upset the discussions in Prague.

However, despite Nasser's warning and all the indications that we were going ahead with the deal, Dulles refused to believe it, still convinced that Nasser was bluffing. He was quite fanatic about it. It seems probable that when he received Byroade's report, the Americans contacted the Russians and asked if it was true that the Soviet Union was going to give weapons to Egypt. The Russians of course said no. And Dulles believed them.

When he eventually came to see that Nasser had done precisely what he had said he would do, he was shattered. The report that finally opened Dulles' eyes came from an Egyptian who was in the CIA's pay. This man had a talk with a highly placed Egyptian, and he concluded from the discussion that the deal either had been or was about to be signed. He telephoned the top CIA agent at the Embassy, James Eichelberger, and told him the news. Eichelberger reported to Washington and then the explosions started. At three o'clock in the morning a very agitated Eichelberger telephoned me and pleaded, asking me to beg the Premier not to fall into a Communist trap. Tell the Premier to "keep his pants on," he said, there was a special messenger on his way from Washington.

This special messenger dispatched by Dulles—the two Dulleses in fact—was Kermit Roosevelt who had been mixed up with CIA operations in Iran and was now involved with the Middle East. When I reported all this to Nasser he decided to announce the news of the agreement. His reasoning was that he could not refuse to see Roosevelt, but he did not want to be interrogated, did not want to be asked if the news was true or not. So he decided to pre-empt Roosevelt.

He looked around for a forum from which to make the announcement and discovered that the Army's public relations department was holding a small one-room exhibition of photographs. So the Premier went to this exhibition, where there were about seventy people, looked at the photographs, and then stood up and announced that Egypt had signed an arms agreement with Czechoslovakia. This was actually an agreement with the Soviet Union but effected through the Czechs. That was on September 27, 1955. The agreement was a week old, but no arms had yet arrived.

The Egyptian Ambassador to Washington, Dr. Ahmed Hussein, was on holiday in Cairo at that time, and when he heard the news he rushed to see Nasser without an appointment at nine o'clock the following morning and asked him if the story he had read in the newspaper was true. Nasser said it was and Dr. Hussein became very excited. The Americans not long before had organized the overthrow of Arbenz's left-wing government in Guatemala and Hussein just kept on repeating: "Guatemala, Mr. Premier, Guatemala."

Eventually Nasser replied: "To hell with Guatemala."

But Hussein persisted: "How can I go back to Washington and meet Mr. Dulles?" Nasser became angry at that and said: "You don't have to go back if you don't want to."

Kermit Roosevelt arrived in Cairo the same morning bearing the news that Dulles was furious. He told Byroade that Dulles was

behaving like an agitated ox and was determined that the deal had
to be stopped. Dulles, he said, wanted Nasser to cancel the deal,
and if it was not canceled, then the United States was going to
take four measures. It would: (1) stop all aid, (2) stop all trade,
(3) break off diplomatic relations, (4) blockade Egypt, preventing
any ships arriving with arms. Dulles thought all this was necessary
because the arms deal was a jump by the Communist powers over
the Northern Tier. It destroyed his pattern of pacts.

Roosevelt was persuaded by Byroade to be diplomatic when he
met Nasser that night. And when they met he said: "Mr. Premier,
you are buying arms from Czechoslovakia. Let me tell you the
result of collaboration between Czechoslovakia and the Soviet
Union." And he started to tell the story of Jan Masaryk. But he
did not put Dulles' four threats to Nasser.

The talks went on for two days. It was impossible to reach a
solution. Nasser would not be moved. On the third day Roosevelt
was told that Dulles was sending another envoy, George Allen,
the Assistant Secretary of State, who would be bringing an important letter with him. But before Allen arrived there was an incident
that made Byroade's life very difficult. He already had the feeling
that his mission was a failure, that Dulles had lost faith in him.
He had been sent as a special emissary with special powers to a
special spot and special results were expected from him. But it
was impossible for him to achieve those results. Egypt has been the
graveyard of so many diplomats' careers. During Roosevelt's discussions with Nasser, Ambassador Hussein, who had been so upset at the possibility of another Guatemala, tried to introduce a
cordial note by arranging a dinner party at the house of his father-
in-law at Giza, close by the Pyramids. Roosevelt was there, so was
Eric Johnston, a special representative of President Eisenhower
who had been trying to solve the problem of the head waters of
the Jordan, and Byroade. The Premier arrived with Field Marshal
Amer and Wing Commander Baghdadi, a member of the Revolu-

tionary Command Council. The Premier asked for an orange juice, Byroade was drinking whiskey. Nasser had only taken one sip when Byroade started to talk and immediately everybody sensed disaster. Byroade, shaking with emotion, said: "Mr. Premier, one of my men was beaten nearly to death today in Suez." Nasser said that he had heard of the incident and asked, "Why did he go to Suez?"

Byroade replied that Mr. Finch, the man who had been beaten, was the labor attaché; it was his job to be in touch with the labor movement and so he had gone to Suez to study the situation in the oil industry.

The Premier, who knew all the details, said that unfortunately Finch had behaved in such a way people thought he was a spy.

The American Ambassador denied this. "He was no spy and yet he was beaten." And then he added, bitterly: "I am sorry, I thought we were in a civilized country."

Nasser was enraged. He stubbed out his cigarette, looked round for Amer and Baghdadi, said "Let's go," and walked out.

The others were appalled. Relations between Egypt and the United States seemingly had been destroyed with a few hysterical words. It was a frightful situation.

Johnston and Roosevelt started to go after Nasser to apologize and bring him back. But he refused. And the dinner party, designed to promote friendship, broke up in disaster.

As a result of that incident, Roosevelt and Johnston sent a cablegram to Dulles advising him to recall Byroade. Poor Byroade was dismayed. He asked me to see him. When I arrived he was in a desperately depressed mood. There were tears in his eyes and he said he had lost control because Mrs. Finch had telephoned him and she had been terribly upset about the beating of her husband. The Ambassador wanted to know if the Premier would receive him again because he was supposed to go with Allen to introduce him to Nasser. At Roosevelt's request I had already asked Nasser about this and he had said that if Byroade wanted to come he could. He thought Byroade had made a mistake, but the incident had ended when he left the party. There was not going to be a vendetta.

Now the news agencies were full of stories from Washington saying that Allen was carrying an ultimatum to Nasser. So the Premier, still very much the Lion Free, called Roosevelt while Allen was still airborne and showed him the agency dispatches. He told Roosevelt that if the stories were true and that Allen gave him an ultimatum, he would ring the bell on his desk and have the Chief Chamberlain of the Presidency show the American out, and then he, Nasser, would go outside and tell the reporters that Egypt had broken off diplomatic relations with the United States. He was not going to be threatened.

This was the atmosphere into which George Allen was flying. Roosevelt, Johnston, and Byroade decided to avert catastrophe if possible. They drove out to the airport and sent a message through the control tower asking Allen to say nothing to the correspondents who were waiting for the customary airport statements. As they drove from the airport, they briefed him, advising that as the situation was so tense he should not give the written message to Nasser but should adapt to the situation and give some of the points in the message verbally, but on no account should he deliver an ultimatum.

Allen was convinced by their arguments. He kept his letter in his pocket and nobody knows what was in it because he never showed it to anybody. But it seems certain that it contained the same four points that Roosevelt had been told to put to the Premier.

Allen had a long discussion with Nasser. He got nowhere. He said that Dulles was annoyed. The Premier said: "Well, he is annoyed, but my people are threatened." Allen said that if Nasser would cancel the Communist deal, the United States would look favorably on supplying arms. And Nasser replied: "It's too late."

So Allen failed, and left. And one hour later a cablegram arrived for him from Dulles insisting that he must deliver the written message. But that, also, was too late.

Dulles was furious with Byroade, furious with Johnston, who never had permission to take part in the negotiations, furious with Roosevelt, and furious with Allen. He began to think that Nasser had some strange power over his men. Later, after Johnston and Roosevelt had submitted a joint report on the problems that could have arisen, he calmed down a little and accepted the fact that there was nothing he could do about the arms deal without making affairs worse still for the United States. The situation had, however, been dangerous for Egypt throughout these negotiations because no arms had arrived and an American blockade would have made things very difficult. The first shipment was docked at Alexandria ten days after the official declaration of the agreement. The CIA got to work immediately.

They talked a sailor from one of the first arms ships into defecting. The captain of the ship reported that the man was missing and the Egyptian authorities traced him to the American Consulate in Alexandria. But by the time they picked up the trail it was too late. The defector had already been put in a big bag marked "Diplomatic Papers," loaded onto an American plane and flown off to the United States.

Despite Dulles' anger and frustration with Nasser, he never gave up his efforts to obtain a settlement between Egypt and Israel. Shortly after the arms deal, he conceived a piece of secret diplomacy, and early in 1956 he sent Robert Anderson to Cairo bearing a letter from President Eisenhower. This was a letter entirely different in character from the one that had remained in George Allen's pocket. The burden of its message was that the United States wanted to solve the Palestine problem and arrange for peace between Egypt and Israel. Anderson had a series of meetings with the Premier at a house in Zamalek where Nasser put to the American his argument that the basis for discussion should be the United Nations Partition Plan of 1947. Anderson traveled several times between Cairo and Tel Aviv. There were many problems and many plans for overcoming them, but one of the biggest stumbling blocks—and it remains a valid argument today—was that there is no direct land transportation route between Egypt and the rest of the Arab world to the east.

One of the plans to clear this block had been put up by the Americans two years before the Anderson mission. It was an ingenious technical solution based on American road-building expertise. The idea was to give part of the Negev Desert to Egypt and part to Jordan, with both parts meeting at the road leading to the port of Elath on the Gulf of Aqaba, which would remain in Israeli hands.

The crux of the plan was that the Americans would build a complicated overpass system by which the Israelis would use an underpass connecting them with Elath while Egypt and Jordan would be connected by an overpass built over the Israeli road.

The Americans put an enormous amount of work on the scheme. The United States Army, the CIA, and the State Department produced dozens of detailed engineering drawings for building this overpass in the desert. These drawings were shown to Nasser who examined them with interest and then destroyed the whole scheme. "The Arabs," he said, "will be on the overpass and the Israelis will be on the underpass. Well, all right, suppose an Arab was on the overpass one day and felt the call of nature and it landed on an Israeli car on the underpass . . . What would happen? There would be war."

Nasser always referred to that meeting as the "pee-pee discussion." He felt that the Americans were too concerned with superficial and artificial ways of settling problems, and he could not take these gimmicks seriously. Anderson did his best, but he was doomed to failure, principally because the Israelis had no intention of going back to the borders laid down by the partition plan.

At the same time another piece of the Middle East jigsaw puzzle was falling into place. In April 1956 Chairman Khrushchev and Premier Bulganin were paying their renowned visit to London, and there Eden told the Soviet leaders that if they continued to send arms to Egypt they would cause many complications, and he suggested that they should complete the one deal that had already been arranged and then stop.

Khrushchev replied that the Soviet Union would be ready to stop all further arms deals if it was part of a general embargo agreed to and supervised by the United Nations.

Eden argued that Britain had treaty obligations in the area and that, for instance, the British were supplying arms to Turkey and Iraq under these obligations. But Khrushchev would not accept this argument. His point of view was that even the countries that had treaties with Britain had to be included in a United Nations embargo.

Nasser knew about the argument because Khrushchev sent him a full résumé of the talks. The Russians were so keen to cultivate their relations with Egypt that they informed Nasser of everything concerning their foreign relations that involved the Middle East. This report worried Nasser because when the United Nations imposed an arms embargo during the Palestinian War in 1948, we were not able to get arms while the Israelis could and did. If the Soviet Union joined in another United Nations embargo, Egypt's supplies would again be cut off.

How could Nasser get round such an embargo? Communist China was the answer. It was not a member of the United Nations so it would not be bound by any embargo. Chou En-lai, who had set up the first arms deal, was a friend. If other sources were cut off, China could provide the loophole. So in the spring of 1956 Nasser extended diplomatic recognition to Communist China.

Once again Dulles was furious. We kept hearing that "the Secretary is mad." We heard it so often that eventually it became a catch phrase: "The Secretary is mad." Nasser began to think he really was mad.

Dulles responded to the recognition of Communist China by authorizing the French to supply the Israelis with more and better types of Mystère fighter planes under the tripartite agreement between Britain, France, and the United States that was supposed to maintain a balance of arms in the Middle East. In his turn Nasser asked the Russians for MIG-17s instead of the MIG-15s that had formed the core of the first arms deal.

There was no official second deal; it was incorporated in the first. But when Dulles heard about it, we heard once again that the Secretary was mad.

All this time Nasser had been working to turn his dream of building a high dam at Aswan into reality. Egypt had approached the World Bank for the necessary financing. But the Bank could not undertake such a vast project on its own; it had to go to its major participants for help and that was how the United States and Britain became involved.

The negotiations began to gather pace late in 1955, and when Ahmed Hussein returned to his post as Ambassador in Washington after the announcement of the arms deal, he had a long and far-ranging talk with Dulles. The talk took place on October 17, 1955, and in his dispatch to Nasser dated the following day Hussein reported to Nasser on their conversation. "I explained to Mr. Dulles," he wrote, "that it was essential Egypt should have the support of the United States in building the High Dam. I told him that despite the fact the Russian government had offered us better conditions than those offered by the World Bank to finance the project, we still preferred to deal with the World Bank.

"I told him that a decision could not be delayed much longer because Egypt regarded the Dam as its most important economic project, and that every delay would cause trouble for the Premier and the government with the Egyptian public. And that it is not in the Bank's interest for him [Dulles] to delay his decision to finance the Dam much longer because this would create pressures on the Premier to accept the Russian offer."

Hussein went beyond his mandate when he told Dulles that the Russians had made an offer. They had not. It was a card he played on his own initiative.

It was, as it turned out, prophetic.

Dulles did not commit himself to anything in this conversation with the Egyptian Ambassador. Hussein reported that Dulles said he was highly disturbed by the arms deal and he warned Egypt once again about dealing with the Russians. "But," said Dulles, "the United States would not deal vindictively with Egypt."

In November 1955 Dr. Abdel Moneim el Kaissouni, Egypt's Finance Minister, went to London and Washington for talks on the project with the British and American governments and the World Bank. When he saw Dulles in Washington, Dulles asked him to take a message to Nasser saying that the Soviet Union was helping Egypt with arms and that meant death but the United States was going to help Egypt with the High Dam and that meant life.

He said he hoped Nasser would take this into consideration and think about the difference between the nature of the two types of aid and then decide who were Egypt's true friends.

But Nasser got the feeling that the Americans, through the size and expense of the project, thought that they could get a firm grip on Egypt and that the very duration of the project would give them time either to offset the growth of Soviet influence in Egypt or to topple him from power. There was at that time a great deal of anti-Nasser propaganda being directed at Egypt from secret radio stations by both the CIA and the British Intelligence Services and Nasser had no illusions about the West's wish to replace him with a more amenable character.

It was estimated that the High Dam would cost $1 billion of which $400 million would have to be in foreign currency. The Bank offered to put up half of this if the British and the Americans would put up the other half.

What Egypt needed was a loan for the $200 million from the United States and Britain. Not a grant, not aid, but a loan. However, the Americans and the British discussed it privately and in December they announced that they would give Egypt a $70 million grant to cover the first year's operation.

President Nasser's reaction to this was that he could not possibly start a project which was going to take ten years with only enough money for one year's work. It meant that if there was a change of policy after only one year, he would be left with a huge heap of rocks and nothing accomplished. But Dulles insisted that he could not go to Congress and get a long-term obligation. There was an annual budget for aid and it had to be voted on every year. Moreover, said Dulles, the building of the Dam would outlive three Congresses and no Congress could bind a succeeding Congress.

President Nasser was completely opposed to this plan of action because when each year's aid came up for discussion, it would give the American government an opportunity for pressure, for dictation. He learned that his suspicions were justified in January 1957 when King Saud of Saudi Arabia visited the United States and Dulles told him that he had decided to help with the Dam because the project was a long-term one. It would have tied Egypt to America for ten years, and in that time Nasser would either have learned the danger of co-operating with the Soviet Union or he would have fallen from power.

At the same time Egypt was having problems with the World Bank. There were three main points of disagreement. Because of the large amount of money involved, the Bank wanted the right to supervise Egypt's foreign indebtedness—another point that appealed to Dulles: he thought this would preclude the buying of any more Communist arms. Nasser objected, arguing that it was a political tie and not an economic tie. The second point of disagreement was over the rate of interest. The Bank was asking for the market rate of 5.5 per cent and Nasser thought that this was too high, especially on such a long-term project. The third was that the Bank wanted to send Egypt a letter of intent to finance the Dam while we wanted a letter of commitment.

Eugene Black of the Bank came to see Nasser twice and they smoothed over the difficulties, coming to an agreeable compromise. They exchanged letters that gave the Bank the right to be given information about the economy and to advise on necessary steps but did not give it the right to supervise the economy. The rate of interest was fixed at 5 per cent, and Mr. Black agreed to send a letter of commitment rather than intent.

So Egypt ironed out its differences with the World Bank, something it was never able to do with the United States.

When President Nasser made an analysis of events later, he came to the conclusion that Dulles was serious for possibly one month at the beginning of 1956 about helping to build the High Dam. For a time there was a rather peculiar campaign in America to exaggerate the importance of the Dam. In January there was what appeared to be an inspired (or "planted") story in *Newsweek* which said that Egypt's very existence depended on the Dam. It seemed as if the Americans wanted to boost its importance to offset the propaganda value of the Russian arms coup. Also, over-stressing its importance may have had some propaganda value at a time when Secretary of State Dulles was briefly interested in selling the United States Congress on the idea. Conversely, many Americans might have thought of a dam for Egypt as just one more "give-away" or "hand-out" in foreign aid.

If it was not essential to Egypt's survival, it had a particular importance. For centuries Egyptians had felt encircled and imprisoned by the desert. The dimensions of the High Dam as seen when it was first widely discussed in 1953 meant a great benevolent invasion of the desert, a way to push it back. One and one half million acres could go under cultivation—one quarter of all the land that Egypt had cultivated in 4,000 years. Now, we had the hope of making such a leap in less than a generation.

This was a tremendous vision, new land for a people who had always survived by farming. And it was *the* vision for a country longing to industrialize. It meant the possibility of electrical power on a legendary scale: 10 billion kilowatt-hours a year. Egypt would have 50 per cent of all the electrical power in the continent of Africa. Even the sheer dimensions of the Dam were an exhilarating challenge. It would be seventeen times the size of the Great Pyramid, people said.

Nasser frequently remarked: "In antiquity, we built pyramids for the dead. Now we will build new pyramids for the living."

At the end of May 1956 Ahmed Hussein asked for permission to come home to explain the difficulties that Dulles faced with Congress. Before he left Washington he met Under Secretary of State Herbert Hoover, Jr., who was acting for Dulles. Hoover was an engineer and he had been responsible for rousing Dulles' interest in the Dam. Apart from insisting that Egypt would have to accept all the monetary conditions laid down by the United States and Britain, Hoover asked for two more things. The first was that Egypt would make a declaration saying that there would be no more arms deals with the Soviet Union.

He said that this was necessary so that the Egyptian economy would not be affected and Egypt would be able to pay its debts instead of mortgaging its cotton for arms. This was a theme that kept on recurring, but it was a false theme. As a matter of fact, we were not exporting too much cotton to Russia. Nasser insisted that we keep a balance of export, with a third going to the Communist bloc, a third to the non-aligned bloc, and a third to the Western bloc. The first arms deal did not cost more than £80 million with repayments spread over twelve years. So Egypt was paying not more than £7 million a year. That was not mortgaging Egypt's cotton.

The second thing that Hoover asked was for Nasser to exercise his leadership in the Middle East and conclude peace between the Arabs and the Israelis. He said that if Premier Nasser wanted to build the High Dam, it would be better if he first of all removed the reasons for tension and war in the area.

So American policy was becoming clearer. In exchange for help with the Dam, Egypt would have to curb its relations with the Soviet Union on the pretext that the arms deals were imposing too great an economic burden; and if Egypt was going to dedicate its efforts to the High Dam, then Egypt would have to conclude peace with the Israelis.

Hoover went on to say that the United States was under severe pressure not to help the project from its big friends in the area, meaning Britain and France, and from its small friends in the area, meaning Turkey, Iran, and Iraq.

The British had already turned implacably against Nasser. His policies of attacking the Baghdad Pact and fostering Arab nationalism in the other Arab countries were directly opposed to British interests throughout the Middle East. Eden, obsessed with memories of Munich, was already referring to him as a "dictator." The French were furious with him for his support of the Arab nationalists in North Africa. The "small friends," for their part, saw danger to their regimes from Nasser's policies of support for nationalism.

Hoover said there was also strong opposition from three lobbies in Washington. The cotton lobby of the South was opposed to the High Dam because it opposed any expansion of cotton production in Egypt. The Israeli lobby was opposed to any aid that would strengthen Egypt. And the China lobby, led by Senator William Knowland, was enraged by Egypt's recognition of Communist China. Dulles was under pressure from all sides to back out of his commitment.

All this came as no surprise to Nasser. He knew by April 1956 that the Americans were going to renege on their pledge. He knew because he had been provided with all the top secret minutes of the meeting of foreign ministers of the Baghdad Pact in Teheran in the middle of March. An Iraqi Minister took complete notes, photographed the documents, and, when he passed through Beirut, gave them to one of our men there, saying that he had a package he wanted delivered personally to Nasser. He wrote a note to go with it that said he was passing this information to the leader of the Arab nationalists out of loyalty to Arab nationalism and opposition to the conspiracies against it.

Initially, there was some hesitation about accepting the validity of these documents. But events began to prove them accurate. They spoke for themselves, and further reports from the same man were a regular source of vital information until the Baghdad Pact collapsed after the revolution in Iraq in 1958.

On June 23, 1956, Nasser was elected President.

Ahmed Hussein came back from Washington to make his report on the High Dam negotiations and called on the new President during the first week in July at the little seaside town of Burg el Arab where Nasser was resting before going to Yugoslavia for the Brioni Conference with President Tito and Prime Minister Nehru—another non-aligned conference that would make "the Secretary mad."

There was a family party for lunch the day Hussein arrived and after lunch the men went off to talk business. Nasser, dressed in sports shirt and shorts, drove the party in a Chevrolet down to a cabin on the seashore. Looking out to sea over the beach, they started to talk. Hussein spoke of the Washington scene and Dulles' difficulties with Congress. But Nasser stopped him: "I'm not going to go into details, but Ahmed, I have concrete evidence that even if you went back and accepted all their conditions, they will not give us the Aswan Dam."

Hussein demurred: "No, Mr. President. The problem is that Congress . . ." and he went on for an hour explaining Dulles' problems.

Eventually the President said: "Well, all right. I shall give you the opportunity to prove something for me. Go and tell Dulles that you have accepted all his conditions and watch his reactions."

Hussein was astonished: "You don't want to amend any of the conditions?"

"No," said Nasser, "I give you carte blanche. Go and tell him that we have accepted everything. But don't humiliate us. Because we are not going to get the High Dam."

Hussein was a puzzled man.

He went back to Washington through London while President Nasser went to Yugoslavia. When Hussein got to London he made a statement: Egypt would accept all the Western propositions for the High Dam and "it hopes, depends and asks for" the help to build the Dam.

The President heard about this statement over the radio at about midnight on a train crossing Croatia. He was very angry indeed. He felt that Egypt had been humiliated, that Hussein ought not to have made a statement before seeing Dulles and he hated that phrase "it hopes, depends and asks for."

Strangely enough, at that moment the train stopped at a small station and there was a crowd of people there shouting: "Tito, Nasser, Tito, Nasser. . . ." The President was not dressed. He was in his pajamas and he did not want to see the people; he was not dressed properly and he was angry. But he was told the people had been waiting for him for a long time. So he put on his shirt and stood at the window and waved. He had his shirt on top and his pajama trousers down below. Then, when the train pulled out, he put on his pajama top again and went on talking about Ahmed Hussein.

Dulles also learned of Hussein's statement and he felt he was going to be put on the spot. He would find it very difficult if the Ambassador arrived and told him officially that Egypt had accepted all his conditions.

President Eisenhower was convalescing, playing golf, after an attack of ileitis, and so Dulles telephoned him and said that the Egyptians "were not playing ball" and that he proposed to withdraw the High Dam offer. And Eisenhower reportedly said: "Whatever you think, Foster, whatever you think." That was on July 18.

The next day Ahmed Hussein arrived at the State Department for a meeting with Dulles. One minute after he had walked through the door of Dulles' office, Lincoln White, the State Department spokesman, issued a statement to waiting reporters announcing the withdrawal of America's offer of aid. That was before the discussion between Dulles and Hussein had even started.

It was a most unfortunate meeting between the two. Hussein cabled his account of it to Nasser, a pained dispatch. Before Hussein had even opened his mouth, Dulles said: "Mr. Ambassador, we are going to issue a statement. I am sorry, we are not going to help you with the Aswan Dam." Hussein, remembering what Nasser had told him, was speechless. Dulles went on, reading the statement that White had already distributed which said that the United States had decided to withdraw its offer because Egypt's economy could not sustain such a project. Hussein began to protest that this was an insult. But Dulles continued, according to Hussein's report, arguing in a sarcastic fashion that "we believe that anybody who builds the High Dam will earn the hatred of the Egyptian people, because the burden will be crushing.

"The Egyptian people," he said, "could not take up the burden of building such a big project. It is more than Egypt's resources can bear, especially with the arms commitments. We don't want to be hated in Egypt, we are leaving this pleasure to the Soviet Union if they really think they want to do it." He said that he did not think the Russians had sufficient resources for the project and if they did undertake it, the satellite countries would revolt against it because the Russians would be helping Egypt while refusing them the help they had asked for.

The fact is that although the American newspapers had picked up Hussein's diplomatic ploy of mentioning Russian aid, there had been no contact with the Russians at all on this subject and there was none for some time.

Ironically, Dulles came back to this theme during a discussion he had with Dr. Mahmoud Fawzi, Egypt's Foreign Minister, during the Suez crisis debates at the United Nations. Fawzi reported in a dispatch to President Nasser that Dulles had told him: "The High Dam is an operation which is going to exhaust the Egyptian economy and it would have raised the hatred of the Egyptian people against the Americans because the Egyptians would feel that they had been deprived of so many things because of the United States. So we do not object to the Russians building the dam."

"He thought," reported Fawzi, "that anyway Egypt could finance the High Dam through the revenue from the Suez Canal and this is the best solution because it would mean that no one particular nation would finance the High Dam."

Nasser was told later that Dulles regarded his withdrawal of aid as his master coup. He was once told, when complaining that he could not follow Nasser's moves, that Nasser was a good chess player. His move, he thought, would mean checkmate.

That night President Nasser was flying back from Brioni with

Nehru in an Egyptian official plane. Nehru was to spend two days in Cairo. The two men were sitting at the front of the aircraft, taking some refreshment, waiting for the lights of Alexandria to appear. Nasser's Air Force aide-de-camp came back from the cockpit with a radio message. It was a résumé of Dulles' statement. The President read it, excused himself to Nehru without telling him what was in the message, then brought it back to show Dr. Fawzi and myself.

"This is not a withdrawal," he said. "It is an attack on the regime and an invitation to the people of Egypt to bring it down."

He sat by himself for some fifteen minutes and then went and showed the message to Nehru. The Indian leader read it and said: "Those people, how arrogant they are." But Nehru did not feel the strength of the storm that was brewing.

It was about midnight when we landed at Cairo Airport. The ambassadors were there to greet Nasser and Nehru according to protocol, even Byroade. He was dreadfully embarrassed. Everybody had heard the news. The President shook his hand. It was Byroade's last humiliation before leaving Egypt.

The President drove home. The next day, Nehru cut his visit short. The storm signals had become apparent. But before he left, Nasser had already decided on his reply to Dulles' insult.

He was going to nationalize the Suez Canal, for so long the symbol of foreign domination, and he planned to use its revenues to build the High Dam.

That decision was taken between ten and eleven o'clock on the morning of Saturday, July 21.

The High Dam at Aswan had become the symbol and the background for one of the political struggles of our generation—leading to the nationalization of the Suez Canal and the Suez war. Though there were questions about whether it would ever be built, or maintained, the Dam exists, and if it has not yet realized every dimension of the great dream, it brings Egypt ever closer to it. We have re-claimed and cultivated 550,000 new acres. Important new chemical industry clusters around the Dam. Electricity is being generated to the point where within four years of this writing, every village in Egypt will be electrified. Such changes make a deep imprint on the social structure of society as well as on its agriculture and chemistry. With much more water available, we now, for example, export rice, a commodity that in the past we could grow in quantity sufficient only to feed ourselves. The experience of building the Dam provided our technicians with valuable new knowledge, which they are employing as entrepreneurs and builders through-out the Arab world. Light and power flow. Nasser, Dulles, others are gone—but the Dam stands.

III

Eden and Suez

Sir Anthony Eden, like Dulles, met President Nasser just once, at the dinner table. It must be rare for two men to sit down to break bread together who were so completely opposed in every way as these two. Every aspect of each man was completely the opposite of the other's. Heritage, upbringing, appearance, dress, experience, outlook, loyalties, and ambition, everything conflicted. The dinner was not a social occasion, it was a confrontation between the ultimate representatives of two inimical ways of life, a confrontation that was both personal and national and that ended in tragedy.

It was held at the British Embassy on February 26, 1955, when Eden, then Foreign Secretary and Deputy Premier to Sir Winston Churchill, visited Cairo on his way to a Southeast Asia Treaty Organization (SEATO) meeting in Bangkok. Nasser hated going to that building. For seventy years it had been the real center of power in Egypt. It was the symbol of colonial domination. The fate of Egypt was always made there and Nasser felt the humiliation of Egypt's colonial subservience when he walked through its gates.

His feelings were shared by many Egyptians. They remembered with anger how Russell Pasha[1] would ride through Cairo in a white uniform astride a white horse to strike fear into the city. They remembered the bitter insult of the ceremonies to mark the beginning of Ramadan being held in the British Embassy under the auspices of the Christian Ambassador. It is extraordinary that in all the years the British spent in Egypt they never got to know the real people of Egypt. Hundreds of thousands of British soldiers passed through the country in two world wars but they only got to know two classes. The officers got to know the upper class and the tommies got to know the prostitutes and were subjected to the pickpockets, shoeshine boys, and the pimps on the streets of Cairo. The only time they encountered the real Egyptians was during demonstrations against the British.

This lack of contact was emphasized in official relations and it was one of the paths that led to Suez. The British government made two grave errors of judgment. They preferred to deal with the desert tribes rather than with the city intellectuals and middle class and they preferred to deal with the royal families rather than with the people.

The British trusted the Bedouin, romantic as they were about people like Lawrence of Arabia, Gertrude Bell,[2] and Glubb Pasha,[3]

[1] Sir Thomas Wentworth Russell, British Commandant of the Cairo Police from 1917 to 1946.

[2] Gertrude Bell (1868–1926), Oriental Secretary to the British High Commissioner of Iraq. Born in England, she spent most of her life in Iraq and was closely associated with the Iraqi monarchy which was supported by the British.

[3] John Bagot Glubb, an Englishman who commanded the Arab Legion in Jordan from 1939 to 1956.

but they did not trust the intellectuals of Cairo and Alexandria. They were infected with the euphoria of Arabism and put their faith in the ruling families who, in their turn, like King Abdel Aziz of Saudi Arabia, thought that "God is in heaven and the British on earth."

Naturally, the British were delighted to do business with men like that and they had their own way of dealing with the difficult people—the students and politically inclined members of the middle class. They showed them the "red eye."

In Egypt the red eye is the eye of fury and this was Lord Killearn's motto for dealing with Egypt. He showed the red eye to demonstrators and he showed it to King Farouk when he surrounded the Abdin Palace with tanks on that infamous day in February 1942. It was not a policy which endeared the British to the Egyptian people.

So it was against this background that Nasser, the revolutionary dedicated to removing the last vestiges of colonialism from his country, sat down to eat with Eden, the conservative dedicated to preserving his country's waning power, in a building which was charged with symbolism for both.

Nasser was dressed in his colonel's uniform. Eden was elegant in a dinner jacket. Nasser, as was customary, had left his wife at home. Eden was accompanied by his wife Clarissa, lean and fashionable in a long evening dress.

Eden astonished Nasser by greeting him in Arabic and then going on to talk about the Koran and Arab poetry and literature. He told Nasser that he once thought about becoming an Arabist and devoting his life to Arab affairs, but had found politics more exciting. Nevertheless he had something in him of the British officers who used to sit cross-legged with the desert sheikhs in their tents and discuss poetry in perfect Arabic. He too was a believer in the Bedouin and not in the cities. And that was an important factor in the development of his policies towards Egypt and Nasser.

He mentioned his memories of Cairo and spoke about the 1936 treaty between Britain and Egypt when the Egyptian leaders were shipped to London to sign the treaty at Lancaster House. It was an eternal treaty, a more sophisticated version of the treaties the British signed with the Sheikhs of the Persian Gulf which were supposed to last until "the crows grow white and the earth is no longer filled with dust." These Egyptian leaders had a group photograph taken wearing their tarbooshes. Eden, who had signed the treaty as Foreign Secretary, told Nasser that he kept a copy of that photograph at his home along with the special set of stamps that were issued to commemorate the occasion.

It was a glamorous performance. He was the star of Western diplomacy who knew all the answers, talking to an unknown colonel with an uncertain future. There were those there who felt that Eden was showing off, trying to impress his young wife.

Nasser, on the other hand, wanted to talk business. He told Eden how pleased he was that Britain and Egypt had signed the agreement under which Britain was to evacuate the Canal Zone and said he hoped that this would lead to a new chapter in the story of Anglo-Egyptian relations. He pointed out that he had already paid dearly for the agreement and might yet have to pay for it with his life. But nevertheless, he said, he would keep the agreement in the hope that the new chapter would be opened.

He added that the only thing that could affect the new relationship was Egypt's suspicion of the British efforts to push the Baghdad Pact. Eden asked him why he was against the Baghdad Pact and Nasser explained, as he had to Dulles, that he could not enter any defense pacts with the big powers. But Eden did not behave like Dulles. Where Dulles was receptive, Eden was bored. He acted as if he had heard it all before. And when Nasser had finished he said: "I am acquainted with all those arguments."

He wanted to know why Nasser, given that he did not want to join the Pact, was attacking people like Nuri Said and the Hashemite royal family of Iraq who did believe in it. Nasser insisted that he was not attacking these people personally but that he thought the idea of the Baghdad Pact was leading to the division of the Arab world and to the isolation of Egypt. Iraq would join, then Syria, Lebanon, and Jordan and then possibly the Gulf States. Egypt would be left alone to face the Israeli danger, and the whole concept of Arab unity would be endangered. He started to talk about the idea of Arab unity and Eden said that he knew enough about Arab unity—after all, it was he who initiated the idea of the Arab League. He was referring to a speech he made in 1942 in which he said that Britain looked with sympathy on the efforts of the Arabs to build a political bond and that Britain would help them after the war.

Nasser argued that in making this speech Eden had proved that Britain had not invented the idea of Arab unity but was responding to a current of nationalism that was already in flow.

The argument continued. Eden said that Egypt could refuse to join the Pact if its government so desired, but he still could not understand why Egypt should impose its thinking on the rest of the Arab countries.

Nasser replied: "We are not imposing our thinking on them. We are merely explaining our point of view, and the support we are getting comes from the fact that our point of view corresponds with what the masses feel."

Eden then said he thought Nasser's explanation was debatable, he maintained that Britain was in a better position to know the real feelings of the Arab people, and he knew that the people wanted to defend themselves against Communism.

In reply Nasser used the same strategic argument he had used with Dulles, that the proper defense of Egypt against Communism had to come from inside the country and not from pacts concluded outside the country and aimed at the encirclement of the Soviet Union.

But he could not shift Eden. The British Foreign Secretary was completely convinced of the correctness, the justice, and the strength of his own line of thought. He insisted that there was nothing that Nasser could do to stop the Baghdad Pact and that Britain was not worried by Nasser's opposition to the Pact. Britain, he said, would be ready to negotiate with Egypt concerning Egyptian problems, but he would not accept the Egyptian stand concerning the over-all Arab situation. He also made the point during the discussion that nobody should be left in any doubt about the importance of Arab oil to Britain, both strategically and economically.

The confrontation ended coldly and Nasser said afterwards that Eden behaved like "a prince dealing with vagabonds." Eventually the prince lost his throne because of those vagabonds.

Eden passed through Baghdad on his way back from Bangkok and from there came word that he had encouraged Nuri Said to go on with the Pact, telling him to stand firm and pay no attention to Nasser's opposition.

So Egypt went on attacking the Pact, and despite what Eden had said this opposition began to have an effect. Syria refused to join and it became clear that the Pact was getting nowhere. Later, when an Egyptian mission went to London to arrange for a shipment of the Centurion tanks that Farouk's government had ordered, the mission was told that there would be no more deliveries unless Egypt stopped attacking the Baghdad Pact. Eden had begun to realize that he could not just brush Egypt aside.

When Eden became Prime Minister of Great Britain on April 6, 1955, Premier Nasser set up a special committee to study what the effects of his appointment would be on Egypt's relations with the British. The committee was composed of several ambassadors and some other experts, with Dr. Mahmoud Fawzi as its chairman.

The committee thought that Eden would be his own Foreign Secretary and came to the conclusion that he intended to play a

very important role in the Middle East because that was the area
where he could leave his fingerprints on history. All the other
areas had been claimed. Churchill had arranged for Britain's special
relationship with the United States and had organized the defense
of Europe through the North Atlantic Treaty Organization
(NATO). The Americans had taken over South Asia. Only the
Middle East was left.

Eden, the one-time Arabist, was interested personally in the
Middle East and the area was of vital importance to Britain strategically and economically because of its oil and communication links.
So, the committee said, Eden was bound to become involved in
the Middle East.

After this initial report the committee was asked for a more detailed assessment of Eden's intentions. They decided that he would
move in three directions, first of all, organizing the oil sheikhdoms
of the Gulf to forestall the Americans. There had already been a
clash between British and American oil interests at the Buraimi
oasis where the British-backed troops of the Sultan of Muscat had
kicked out the Aramco oilmen, who were backed by Saudi troops,
and confiscated their equipment.

When Eden called on Eisenhower to discuss Western problems,
he was astonished to find maps of Buraimi spread in front of the
American President who refused to talk about anything else before
they had discussed the Buraimi problem.

Nasser knew about this because the Americans told King Saud
and Saud sent Nasser the report he had received from the Americans. This meant, said the committee, that Eden would have to
tie up the Gulf States first of all. Then he would carry on with trying to get recruits for the Baghdad Pact among the Arab countries.
And then his third drive would be on Egypt, either to influence it
or to isolate it.

So, over-all, it was felt that Egypt was going to have a rough
time with Eden, and that therefore, with the new Prime Minister

taking such a great interest in the Middle East, it would be advantageous if better relations could be established with Britain.

Egypt's opposition to the Pact was hitting hard by now. Nuri Said was complaining to the British and the British were complaining to the Americans, so Nasser was delighted on both counts when in August of 1955 Selwyn Lloyd, who had been appointed Foreign Secretary, told the Egyptian Ambassador in London that Britain would stop all further efforts to pull Arab countries into the Pact if Egypt stopped its propaganda against the Pact.

In November 1955 Eden made his famous speech at Guildhall in which he suggested a solution for the Arab-Israeli dispute based on new borders for Israel between the actual armistice line and the partition line of 1947. This speech was received with satisfaction in the Arab world. And Nasser issued a statement saying that it contained constructive elements that could be the basis for discussion.

However, Egypt was receiving information that Eden was vacillating over decisions and that he was not in good health. At the same time there were the beginnings of doubt in the Tory party about his leadership and there were critical articles about him in the British press. Reports said that he could be convinced by one thing one day and by the opposite the second day. There was proof of his unpredictability a month after his Guildhall speech when, despite Selwyn Lloyd's pledge, Field Marshal Sir Gerald Templer, the newly appointed Chief of the Imperial General Staff was sent to Amman to bring Jordan into the Baghdad Pact fold.

The Turks and the Iraqis had been working on this move for some time. At Nuri Said's instigation, King Feisal of Iraq wrote to his cousin, Jordan's King Hussein, and said they should stand together, that Jordan should join Iraq because they were facing an alliance of the new republics of Syria and Egypt and their old tribal enemies in Saudi Arabia.

Then the Turkish President, Celal Bayar, visited Amman after a Baghdad Pact meeting to prepare the scene for Jordan's entry. Britain promised Jordan arms and Templer flew to Amman to get Hussein's agreement to join the Pact.

Hussein went to a meeting of his Cabinet and asked it for unanimous approval of his decision to join. But they would not agree. There was a split in the Cabinet. Demonstrations against joining were organized throughout Jordan. There was bloodshed, practically a civil war. The government fell. The King was obliged to back down. And Templer went home to London, his mission a disastrous failure.

Nasser had been kept fully informed on the situation by certain ministers of the Jordanian government who were bitterly opposed to the Pact. But at the beginning he refused to believe that negotiations were going on for Jordan to join because Eden had promised there would be a moratorium on persuading Arab countries to join. When he learned that Eden had broken his word, he lost all faith in the British Prime Minister. He felt that Eden was no longer to be trusted.

The Templer mission therefore marked the start of a period of all-out propaganda against the British, the Baghdad Pact, and all their other policies in the Middle East. It was a time of absolute confrontation through propaganda.

During this period Selwyn Lloyd came to Cairo. He arrived on March 1, 1956, to see Nasser. It was a fateful encounter.

The Arab world was still boiling against the British after the Templer affair. Their stock had gone down. But Nasser, who had brought off the arms deal with the Soviet bloc, was riding high. He had never been so popular. Selwyn Lloyd met the Premier in the Tahira Palace, the Palace of the Pure, and he gave Nasser his word that Britain would renew the moratorium on the Pact if Nasser would calm the propaganda attacks. Lloyd explained away the Templer affair, saying it was done under pressure from the Turks and the Iraqis and that Templer just happened to be there because he was arranging for arms to be sent to the Jordanians.

They sat together in a salon at the Palace, which is an official guest house, and the Premier explained to Selwyn Lloyd his position from the very beginning, telling him what he had told Eden almost exactly a year before and recounting how Eden had said that he could do what he liked but the Baghdad Pact was going ahead and there was nothing Nasser could do to stop it. He reviewed the whole problem of Anglo-Egyptian relations. He also talked about the arms deal, arguing that it was not the nationality of the arms that mattered, it was the fingers on their triggers that gave the guns their passports.

They talked for two hours and Selwyn Lloyd was very diplomatic. He suggested that it was time for both countries to start again, to "open a new page." At nine they went in to dinner with their colleagues and sat down to the first course. It was interrupted when a British Embassy official arrived with an urgent message for Humphrey Trevelyan, the British Ambassador. One of the chamberlains went into the dining room and whispered to Sir Humphrey; the Ambassador excused himself to talk to the messenger who gave him a piece of paper. Sir Humphrey read it and was visibly perturbed, but he went back to the dining room and said nothing.

Sir Humphrey showed Selwyn Lloyd the message as they were driving back to the Embassy in the ambassadorial Rolls-Royce. It said that Glubb Pasha had been dismissed by King Hussein and was leaving Jordan that same night.

The British Foreign Secretary was thunderstruck. He had been talking with Nasser about Jordan and Glubb's position there, and Nasser had said to Selwyn Lloyd that he should not believe the reports of people like Glubb if they told him that the people of Jordan were for the Pact. "I know the people," Nasser had said, "and they are against it. People like Glubb are out of touch and their days are numbered."

Now, having read of Glubb's dismissal, Selwyn Lloyd was certain that Nasser had known what was going on and had been laughing at him all evening.

Lloyd, naturally, was angry and despondent at what he considered a cynical deception. The truth of the matter was that Nasser had no idea that Glubb was about to be dismissed and he did not know about it until nearly nine o'clock the next morning when Tom Little, one of the newspapermen covering Selwyn Lloyd's trip, telephoned me with the news and I was able to contact Nasser just as Selwyn Lloyd was arriving for another meeting before flying off to Bahrein. Selwyn Lloyd had considered canceling that meeting but went on with it despite his certainty that Nasser had made a fool of him.

When Nasser heard the news he was certain that Glubb's dismissal had been forced by the British as a sign of the change in British policy—at that time I had no details of the manner of the dismissal.

"What an intelligent move," he said. "So they really are sincere in their talk about starting a new page."

The British officials' Rolls-Royce arrived while Nasser was still getting the news over the telephone. He cut off the call, so pleased with the news that he did not notice that Selwyn Lloyd was upset. They sat down and Lloyd asked immediately: "Mr. Premier, have you heard what happened in Amman yesterday?"

Nasser, delighted, smiled and said: "Yes, I think that was a brilliant move on your part." For Nasser could not believe that Hussein would have dismissed Glubb except on British orders.

Selwyn Lloyd was astonished: "Brilliant from our side?"

"Yes," said Nasser, still not realizing what was going on. And Selwyn Lloyd asked angrily: "What's brilliant about it?"

"Wasn't it you who took the decision?" asked the Premier.

It was an extraordinary conversation. Selwyn Lloyd thought that

Nasser was teasing him, humiliating him, and he replied: "I don't know who took it; but it is the result of agitation."

Then, for the first time Nasser began to realize that Selwyn Lloyd believed that he had engineered the whole business. He protested that he had heard about Glubb's dismissal only that morning and that he had been certain Selwyn Lloyd was responsible for it. He began to laugh at the irony of the situation. And, of course, Selwyn Lloyd thought Nasser was laughing at him.

Selwyn Lloyd was miserable. He said: "I don't know where we are going to go from here, Mr. Premier." It was then that Nasser protested that he was not omnipotent and did not have buttons that he could push to bring about revolutions. Nevertheless, said Nasser, he intended to adhere to what he and Selwyn Lloyd had agreed the night before.

Later, Nasser said that Selwyn Lloyd looked like a puzzled fish that morning. "I was not able to convince him of my innocence and at the same time I was unable to stop myself from laughing at what had happened and the way he looked."

What had happened in Amman was that King Hussein, who found himself in a very dangerous position after the Templer affair, had been talked into dismissing Glubb by some of his officers who were jealous of the British general and who suggested his being fired to Hussein as a means of restoring the King's popularity. Some of these officers had been affected by Nasser's ideas, but they were loyal to the King and the dismissal of Glubb was a completely Jordanian affair. Hussein himself was jealous of the power that the British general enjoyed in Jordan. And so he set out to make himself King in fact as well as in title.

Several days later Nasser talked to Sir Humphrey Trevelyan and explained once again that he had no previous knowledge of the affair, and the Ambassador said that he believed him and he went on to explain how Selwyn Lloyd was convinced that Nasser had set out to humiliate him. Once again the Ambassador said that despite the misunderstanding, Britain wanted to stand by the moratorium on the Pact.

But by that time the situation was irretrievable. Selwyn Lloyd had been involved in a hostile, dangerous situation in Bahrein. He was stoned by demonstrators chanting Nasser's name. His car was stopped and he was forced to take shelter from the demonstrators before being rescued by the police. The chants of "Nasser . . . Nasser . . ." from the crowd, following on Glubb's dismissal, convinced Selwyn Lloyd that Nasser had deliberately set out to wreck his mission. He thought that Nasser was playing a cat-and-mouse game with him and that Bahrein was the final act of the cat attacking the mouse.

The situation hardly improved for him when he went on to meet his allies in Karachi.[4] They were all furious with Britain and the United States because the Western countries were offering to put up money for the High Dam and their attitude was that it was obvious that the only way to get aid from the West was to oppose the West and behave like Nasser. One can imagine the effect of Selwyn Lloyd's report to Eden after this mission. The British were angry.

The Americans were also frustrated with Egypt's policies at this time, and when Nasser revealed in April 1956 that Egypt would recognize Red China, they too became angry.

The result was a stepping-up of the propaganda war against Nasser. The British and the Americans between them had nine radio stations working against him. British newspapers were full of hostile articles against him. The *Daily Telegraph* published one article headlined THE MASTER PLAN OF NASSER. Nasser read this article, cut it out, wrote "a good plan" on it and sent it to the head of the Egyptian Intelligence saying: "If they are accusing us of doing all that, then we had better do it."

[4] The Turks and the Iraqis, not members of SEATO and therefore not in attendance, conveyed their feelings through the Pakistanis.

Ahmed Hussein, in another of his dispatches from Washington, reported to Nasser on May 8, 1956, that "Dulles told me that Henry Luce had told him that Winston Churchill had told him if Nasser was going to make Britain lose the Middle East's oil, then Nasser must go. Dulles added that Britain was doing all they could to convince the United States of the dangers of Nasser's policies to the West and its friends."

Hussein went on to say that in his judgment this was correct because "a certain Mr. Hall, a Counsellor at the British Embassy in Washington had called Nasser 'Public Enemy Number One' in a public lecture. I told this story to Dulles and I told him George Washington was 'Public Enemy Number One' when he was fighting British Imperialism."

There were plots against Nasser by the Free Egypt movement. Exiles worked against him. Leaflets were smuggled into the country and the CIA laid the ground for a change of regime. Nuri Said was involved in it and Nasser learned later that two possibilities were discussed, a take-over by Nahas Pasha and the old Wafd party or the replacing of Nasser by General Naguib.

Egypt countered this activity by an intensification of its own propaganda war, with all the media attacking Britain and the United States and their friends in the Middle East. Sir Humphrey Trevelyan, writing about this period in his book *The Middle East in Revolution,* said: "We were on the road to open hostility."

Many important developments stemmed from the tragedy of Selwyn Lloyd's mission, but probably the most important was that he, personally, but in all innocence, started the chain of ideas that led to Nasser's decision to nationalize the Suez Canal.

During their conversation before dinner in March 1956, Selwyn Lloyd had talked about the importance of the Middle East to Britain and in particular the importance of the Suez Canal from which the British troops were being withdrawn. Britain, said Selwyn Lloyd, considered the Canal an integral part of the Middle

East oil complex, which was vital to Britain. Nasser's reply was to point out that the oil-producing states took 50 per cent of the profits from their oil but that Egypt did not get 50 per cent of the profits from the Canal. If the Canal was an integral part of the oil complex, then surely Egypt ought to be treated on the same basis as the oil producers.

Negotiations were going on at that time between Egypt and the Suez Canal Company, which was exploring the prospects of renewing its concession then due to end in 1968. A committee had been set up by the Ministry of Industry and Commerce to study the situation and some people said that Nasser got the idea of nationalizing the Canal from this committee, but that is not true at all.

When Nasser gave his instructions to the Egyptian negotiators, he remembered his talk with Selwyn Lloyd and told them that as the Canal was part of the Middle East oil complex, then Egypt should get the same percentage of revenue as the oil-producing states.

There was one more link to be forged in the chain of ideas started by Lloyd—that connecting 50 per cent with 100 per cent—and it came white hot from the furnace on Friday, July 20, the day after Dulles—and consequently Eden—had withdrawn the offer of aid for the High Dam.

Preparations were being made for the celebrations of the anniversary of the revolution, and when I telephoned the President on the morning of the twentieth he said that the theme of his speech would be that Egypt would build the High Dam even if we had to build it with shovels. He was still very angry. Dulles and Eden, he said, were deceiving us all the time. They pressed us for peace with Israel, they pressed us for pacts, they pressed us to extend the Suez Canal concession, and all they wanted to do was to increase their own influence.

"But," he said, "we are going to build the High Dam by ourselves and we will do anything to make it possible."

I asked him if he remembered his idea of keeping half the revenue of the Suez Canal, as the oil-producing countries retained half their oil revenues, and using that money to build the Dam.

He replied, in a tense voice: "But why only half?"

Later that day he asked for an assessment of British military forces in the area. Egypt had good friends in Cyprus. We had helped the EOKA[5] rebels, giving them arms and money and facilities. They had returned the help by taking photographs inside the British radio stations set up on Cyprus for propaganda attacks against Nasser. These photographs showed both the inside of the studios and the announcers' faces, so we knew who they were. Now Egypt's Intelligence Service asked the EOKA rebels to report on what forces the British had on the island. They also asked Egypt's friends in the labor movement on Malta for a similar report. Egypt had contacts with all the rebels in the area.

That night Nasser sat down and made his estimation of what would happen if he nationalized the Suez Canal. He wrote it in pencil on six sheets of paper folded lengthwise. It was done in the fashion of an Army staff paper. It was headed: "If I were Eden" and it was based on everything that had happened between himself and Eden since their dinner seventeen months before, set in the context of the whole history of Anglo-Egyptian relations.

President Nasser told me all about it over the telephone. His assessment covered fourteen points, which, according to the notes I made at the time, were as follows:

1. Eden will behave in a violent way.
2. The violence will take the form of military action. He will be violent because he feels his position is weak. Violence

[5] National Organization of Cypriote Struggle.

is not strength. What can he do? A full invasion? Unlikely.
Maybe he will try to force his way through the Suez Canal,
by getting battleships into the Canal. I have planned what
to do in such a situation. Very simple. I will get a convoy
taken in the other direction and meet them face to face so that
they will block the Canal. Can they make a *marche en
arrière?*

3. The possibility of violence will be 80 per cent. It depends on how many troops the British have ready for quick
intervention from the Mediterranean, Aden, Cyprus or
Malta.

4. Most probably Eden will try to pull France with him,
or maybe France is going to pull Eden. But certainly France
may participate in any operation against us.

5. The United States will remain silent, giving their blessing under the table. After all, they are responsible for all
this. Can somebody study the effects of the coming American
elections?

6. The position of Russia will be decisive. Shall we tell
them? Shall we surprise them? If we tell them will that mean
asking their permission? If we surprise them that means they
will feel no obligation.

Or maybe if we told them they would try to dissuade us
with all those very cautious calculations of theirs. . . . Better
not to tell them. Estimation of their position: direct interference in the case of invasion? Out of the question. Political
support? Yes.

The position of India, Ceylon and Pakistan. Can we contact them after the decision? . . . Australia? A hopeless case
. . . What would be the position of the rest of the Commonwealth? What pressure can they exercise on the British Government?

7. United Nations. Refer this to Dr. Fawzi.

8. The possibilities of the success of intervention. Very difficult. But what are possibilities? Could they attack Alexandria via Libya? That would need big forces because they would be obliged to carry on to Cairo. Could they bombard Alexandria from the sea like Admiral Seymour in 1881? Completely impossible. World public opinion would not permit it and anyway it would not lead to any result. Landing, occupying the Canal? . . . Possible. We need to reinforce Eastern Command.

9. Evacuation of Sinai. Talking with Hakin [Marshal Amer]. Keep only necessary troops.

10. Israel. Participation of Israel in this operation to be ruled out. Eden would not accept. Israel may try but Eden will refuse. He will prefer to keep it European.

11. National Guard. Where should it be concentrated? Put the question to Kaml el din Hussein [Commander of the National Guard].

12. The appropriate time for intervention? It must be immediate. It must appear as a direct reaction. If Eden delays, the pressure against him will increase.

13. Can we gain time? Prepare letters to Tito, Nehru and Sukarno.

14. Would Israel take the chance alone and attack Syria or Jordan? Message to Syrians and Jordanians . . . better keep quiet. We need a detailed estimation from the Committee of Estimations of the Intelligence.

Conclusion and Summary. Peak danger time . . . 80 per cent at beginning of August, decreasing each week through political activities. How can we make the political situation swim? Fawzi can do that. He is an expert in floating things. Second week in August, danger 60 per cent. Third week, 50 per cent. Fourth week, danger 40 per cent. End of September, danger 20 per cent.

Can we gain two months by politics? If we succeed we shall be safe. So much will depend on Fawzi.

Such were the jottings I made as he spoke.

Everything depended on the reports of British strength. Nasser waited impatiently for those reports to come in. On Tuesday, July 24, he attended the opening of an oil-pumping station at Mostorod on the pipeline from Suez to Cairo. He had thought of announcing the nationalization of the Canal on this occasion, but not all the reports had arrived. Instead he attacked the Americans, told them that they could choke on their fury and that Egypt was going to build the High Dam even if we had to build it with our own nails.

Until then he had told no one about his plans. But at the opening of the pumping station he heard Mahmoud Younes, the engineer in charge of the pipeline, talking, and decided to choose him to head the nationalization project.

After the ceremony he asked Younes to call on him later in the day. Then he broke the news to two or three people from the Revolutionary Command Council and asked them to prepare a situation report on what they thought Eden would do.

When Mahmoud Younes arrived at the President's house, Nasser told him what he had in mind and asked him to prepare a complete plan for the take-over of the Canal administration, to cope with any trouble, and to keep the Canal running. He wanted this plan the following day.

That night the President had enough information to convince him that the British did not have a sufficiently powerful force in the area to mount an invasion and that it would take them two months to assemble such a force. The President said: "All I need is one month, so this is long enough for me." The President was to make a speech on July 26 at the celebrations marking the anniversary of the abdication of King Farouk, so when Younes appeared with his completed plans for the take-over of the Canal administration Nasser told him to go to Ismailia and listen on the radio to the speech he was going to make in Alexandria on that evening.

Younes was to listen for President Nasser to mention the name De Lesseps, the French builder of the Canal. That was the code-word for Younes to put the plan into action.

If the President did not mention De Lesseps, then Younes was to do nothing and wait for further orders. Younes had picked a team of military engineers and civilians to help him with the take-over and they had their orders in sealed envelopes. Their instructions were to open the envelopes when the President started his speech in Alexandria. Inside they would find another envelope and they were only to open that when they heard the name De Lesseps.

Before Nasser made his speech, he called the Cabinet to a meeting at the house in Alexandria in which he used to spend the summer. The house stood on a cliff overlooking a body of water called Stanley Bay after a British Colonel Stanley who once commanded the barracks nearby. And there, just two hours before his speech, he broke the news to all his colleagues. Many of them were very perturbed by the danger of what he was about to do. But he insisted that there was no point of discussion. He had made up his mind and he was going to take the responsibility. In fact, the meeting ended without a formal decision. It was Nasser's show.

He had explained his thinking to them, said that this was the only way we could build the High Dam by our own resources, that this was our reply to Dulles' insult, and that it was our right to own the Canal.

He had told them also that the British could not intervene for at least two months and he estimated that he only needed one month to ensure success. One member of the Cabinet raised the possibility of Britain using Israel to mount an invasion. His reply was that this was impossible because it would destroy Britain's position in the Middle East and that Eden knew the Middle East better than to make such a mistake. It was, he said, a taboo that Britain could not touch.

He was also asked about the possibility of French intervention. He agreed that there was a possibility but argued that they were completely occupied in Algeria and if the British needed two months that meant the French also needed two months. He was completely convinced that he needed only one month of quick political action showing Egypt's good intentions to the rest of the world and all would be well.

While the President was talking with the Cabinet, a lawyer had been locked in another room of the house preparing the text of the decree of nationalization. The President wanted the text of a legal declaration so that he could announce it officially at the end of his speech. The lawyer finished it just before the President set out to make his speech. It was not even typewritten and Nasser did not sign it until after he had made his speech.

He drove to Manchia Square in Alexandria, the scene of two previous turning points in his career. It was there that he first joined in a demonstration against the British as a schoolboy and it was there that he was shot at on October 26, 1954 in an assassination attempt, when his behavior under fire won him tremendous public popularity.

He had no speech written. He had scratched some notes on the back of an envelope before meeting his ministers and he had no time to expand them because there were so many people waiting for him in the streets. He was forced to stand up in an open car and acknowledge their salutes.

Then he spoke, giving the background of the situation, talking about recent events, telling the people how we had been deceived and exploited by the imperialist powers and in due course he mentioned the Suez Canal and De Lesseps.

The President was so worried that Younes and his team would miss it that he kept on repeating the Frenchman's name. It was "De Lesseps" this and "De Lesseps" that until he had repeated the man's name about ten times and people began to wonder why he was making such a fuss about De Lesseps, for the Egyptians had no real love for him.

Mahmoud Younes moved immediately when he heard that name the first time. He had been listening to the President's speech over his car radio, and at the word "De Lesseps" he switched off the set and took over the Ismailia headquarters of the Suez Canal Company at gun point. ("I'm sorry," he said to Nasser later, "I missed the rest of your speech.")

The governor of the Eastern District, which had only been formed a month previously, as the last of the British troops moved out of the Canal bases, had been ordered to put himself at Younes' disposal, and they took over the Canal installations while the police occupied the Company's offices in Cairo.

It was a well-planned and well-executed operation. By the time the President had finished reading his declaration of nationalization, the Canal had been taken over.

Later, Younes told the President how he carried out the operation in his "Report on the Operation of the Suez Canal," in which he said: "I chose very few people to help me because I believed that secrecy was the most important element in ensuring success.

"Only three of my assistants knew what we were really doing. The rest were told that we were doing a secret job and that they should not ask for any details. There were four groups, one was left in Cairo to take over the administration, one went to Port Said, another to Suez and I led the main group at Ismailia. . . ."

Younes had gathered his group together when the time came to explain their orders and he felt that many of them were shocked by what they were being asked to do. "I am sorry, sir," he reported to Nasser, "that I found myself obliged to tell them that I had the authority to shoot anybody who behaved in a way which would reveal the secret. That declaration, sir, had the desired effect. Because every one of them felt that he was liable to be killed even if he behaved in a way which only seemed to be suspicious.

"They were really nervous and I think they were very relieved when they heard you on the radio leaking the secret yourself."

The people went wild with excitement. The Canal had always stood as a monument to the exploitation of Egypt. Thousands of Egyptians had died digging it. The Suez Canal Company was a state within a state. It had its own ciphers and its own flag. We had a motto, one that said we want the Canal "for Egypt and not Egypt for the Canal," but the wildest dream of most Egyptians had been that we might not renew the concession when it ran out in 1968. And now Nasser had nationalized it. It belonged to Egypt.

The way in which Nasser announced the take-over, the violence of his speech, and the insults he hurled at Britain and the United States surprised Eden, but there was no reason for his surprise because the insults were deliberately calculated as a reply to the insulting fashion in which Dulles withdrew his offer of help for the Aswan High Dam. President Nasser belonged to the Beni Mor village of Upper Egypt. They are "the Bitter Ones" and they are Saiedis (peasants) to whom revenge is sacred.

Gamal Abdel Nasser took his revenge on the night of July 26, 1956, in the Manchia Square of Alexandria. That same night Anthony Eden was giving a dinner party at No. 10 Downing Street in honor of King Feisal of Iraq.

A number of British politicians and military leaders were at the dinner. Hugh Gaitskell and Sir Hartley Shawcross had been invited from the Labour party, and, of course, Nuri Said Pasha was there with his King. (My account of what took place at that dinner party comes from the report Nuri Said made to his Cabinet when he returned to Baghdad and which was immediately passed on to President Nasser by our friend in the Iraqi Government.)

Nuri Said and Eden met with a small group of advisers in the Prime Minister's office before dinner and talked about the Middle East. Eden was very pleased with himself. He had expected trouble from the Tory party's 1922 Committee of backbenchers over his Middle East policies when he had met the committee earlier in the evening. But the meeting had gone his way. The committee had thanked him "for the way in which he was carrying out his heavy responsibilities."

The conversation with his dinner guests turned to what Nasser's reactions would be to the withdrawal of aid for the High Dam. Eden was convinced that Nasser had been checkmated by this move and that there was nothing he could do.

Somebody else suggested that Nasser might start an adventure against the Israelis to restore his prestige in the Arab world, but they agreed this would do Nasser more harm than good.

They went into dinner at about eight-thirty, still talking about the Middle East in general and Nasser in particular. King Feisal listened to the politicians talk. They wondered who they could get to replace Nasser once he had been toppled. Eden was bitter in his condemnation of President Nasser but he remained convinced that he was finished.

Toward the end of the dinner a secretary came into the dining room and handed Eden a slip of paper. The Prime Minister read it and turned white with rage. He told his dinner guests that Nasser had announced the nationalization of the Suez Canal, then he lost his temper and demanded furiously: "How can he do it . . . how can he do it . . . ?"

He asked Nuri Pasha for his advice, and Nuri, according to what he told his Cabinet, said to Eden: "You have only one course of action open and that is to hit, hit now, and hit hard. Otherwise it will be too late." Nuri then gave a very clear assessment of the effects of the nationalization on the Arabs. Nasser's popularity would soar.

Eden, however, was completely convinced that Egypt could not run the Canal and that its administration would collapse overnight. But another message was brought in giving the news that the Egyptian authorities had ordered all the foreign experts who ran the Canal to remain on duty.

Eden seized on this as his chance to take action against Nasser. The Egyptian leader, according to Eden, was going to imprison British and French and other foreign subjects. This was a good enough reason for intervention.

While everybody was still sitting at the dinner table he called a meeting of the Inner Cabinet. Selwyn Lloyd, Lord Salisbury, and Lord Home were already there and he summoned the others, along with Field Marshal Templer and Lord Mountbatten. He asked Andrew Foster, the American chargé d'affaires, and the French Ambassador, Jean Chauvel, to call on him. He also arranged to see Jacques Georges-Picot, the director general of the Suez Canal Company, who happened to be in London.

The dinner party broke up in some confusion. Eden had a lot to do. He was in no mood to continue and so his guests went without their dessert.

As the guests left, Eden went into a series of meetings with his Cabinet colleagues and military leaders. Nuri Said was the man who summed up the thoughts of Britain's friends in the Middle East when he advocated striking at Nasser, "for if he is left alone he will finish all of us."

That prophecy came true two years later when the people of Iraq rose in revolt on the fourteenth of July and three days later Nuri, dressed as a woman, was caught trying to escape and shot himself to death in the streets of Baghdad.

On July 26, 1958, the anniversary of the nationalization of the Suez Canal and Eden's interrupted dinner party, an Iraqi came to Cairo and presented Nasser with a carefully wrapped cardboard box. This Iraqi, who knew that Nuri Said had been with Eden on that night, had come to Cairo for the anniversary celebrations and had brought a special present for Nasser.

He gave the box to the President, saying: "It is something that you will like," and he insisted that Nasser should open it. "With pleasure," said the President. He opened the box and saw it was filled with cotton wool. "What's this?" he asked. And the Iraqi replied: "It is one of Nuri Pasha's fingers. It has been well taken care of; we have preserved it in alcohol."

President Nasser was furious. Nuri Pasha had been no friend of Nasser's. He had been one of the main architects of the Baghdad Pact, a supporter of the old regimes and the colonialist power of Britain. He had once gloated over an Israeli attack on Gaza. And he had approved of the withdrawal of aid from the High Dam. In return, he had been bitterly attacked by Nasser as a lackey of the imperialists and an enemy of the Arab revolution. But this gift was shameful, obscene. President Nasser ordered that Nuri's finger should be buried with all decency in a Cairo cemetery.

Later Nasser got a much more welcome present from Iraq. All the Baghdad Pact's confidential documents were loaded onto a special plane and flown to Cairo. They proved extremely interesting.

There was turmoil in London following the take-over of the Canal. Eden wanted to launch an immediate military operation, ignoring the legalities of the situation. But he was stopped in the first place by Mountbatten and Templer, who refused to agree to an airborne strike unless the paratroopers could be followed up with a main force invasion within twenty-four hours. They remembered the disastrous British paratroop attack at Arnhem in 1944, and they were very aware of the tanks and the MIG fighters Egypt had received from the Soviet Union.

Eden was restrained in the second instance by a report from

the Foreign Office that in the event of the Canal being cut Britain had oil reserves for three weeks of normal consumption but only one week if a major military operation was to be launched.

Third, Georges-Picot, anxious about the safety of his employees, had sent a signal to his resident director in Cairo, telling him to order the employees to work for the Egyptian authorities but to make a daily protest about being forced to work. This meant that the Canal operated as usual, the foreign employees were able to make their protests and were not harmed, and Eden had no excuse for mounting an operation to rescue them.

He was a very frustrated man. He promised that he would never allow Nasser to keep his hands on Britain's neck. He was urged to take action by the majority of the House of Commons and the press, who were now referring to Nasser constantly as a dictator in the same context as Hitler and Mussolini. But there was little Eden could do. As Nasser knew, Britain did not have the forces in the area to mount an invasion and, as time passed, the reasons for invading were being eroded. A recruiting campaign around the world soon produced enough canal pilots so that when Georges-Picot eventually withdrew his men there was a smooth take-over. The Canal continued to operate as efficiently as it had always done, observing the Constantinople Convention of 1888.

As Eden's position weakened—he was coming under fire in Britain for the failure of his Middle East policies—his temper grew more and more brittle. Nasser knew about his outbursts because from the time of nationalization until the invasion started, the CIA leaked constant reports on Eden's physical breakdown and the effect of his illness on his stability. In this roundabout, devious way, the Americans warned Egypt that Eden was in a highly unpredictable condition and in a state of mind that made him ready to undertake the most dangerous of gambles. At first Nasser was suspicious of these reports. He thought that they were being planted by the CIA to make Egypt frightened of continuing its propaganda attacks on Britain. That may well have been so, but the reports were confirmed by Egypt's embassies and its friends in Britain. So whatever devious reasons lay behind the CIA's actions, they were certainly accurate.

Nasser, on the other hand, became more and more relaxed. He stayed on in Alexandria after his speech and had a few days holiday. His popularity was enormous. He was cheered through the streets when he went to talk at the University of Alexandria. The people were still wildly excited. They felt that the soul of Egypt had returned after seven thousand years.

On Sunday, July 29, Eden met with representatives of the French and American governments. Dulles, who had heard the news of the take-over while on the beach at Lima, was still in South America, so the United States had sent Robert Murphy, a senior official of the State Department, to hold the fort, and France had sent its Foreign Minister, Christian Pineau. The meeting had been set up to explore what the three countries could do about Suez.

It was obviously of great importance and Nasser wanted to know what was going on. The Egyptian Embassy in London was isolated, there was little news coming from it. But the news agencies were full of stories about the meeting and so the President telephoned me to find out what the agencies were reporting from London. However, Murphy's plane had been held up and the meeting delayed.

I promised to phone him back when the news came through. But he replied: "Don't bother. I am going to the movies. Why should I strain my nerves? I shall learn about it soon enough when they issue a communiqué." And he went to the Metro Cinema to watch Cyd Charisse in *Meet Me in Las Vegas*.

Eden's nerves, however, were severely strained. Ahmed Hussein in Washington reported in a dispatch dated August 3, 1956, a conversation he had had with a Baghdad Pact ambassador who had been told by Dulles that "he was worried by the mood which Eden had got himself into and that this problem became apparent to him when he attended the London Conference. He felt that Eden would stop at nothing in order to harm Nasser and that is why he was asking them as Moslems to talk to the Egyptians and tell them that they should compromise and not give Eden the chance he was waiting for.

"Dulles feels that Eden will use force if he does not reach a solution which he considered satisfactory.

"I asked the Ambassador," wrote Hussein, "what those satisfactory conditions were."

But Dulles had not said. The only suggestion he had to make was that the Egyptians should compromise.

Britain and France took a number of economic measures against Egypt. The nation's assets were frozen and the transfer of Suez Canal Company funds to Egypt was forbidden. The United States followed suit—"Pending determination of their ownership and the existing situation."

Britain and France also stepped up their military preparations, calling up reservists and transferring planes and ships to Malta and Cyprus, all of which was faithfully reported to Cairo by EOKA and our Maltese friends.

Dulles had flown back from Peru and spent two days in London talking with Eden and Pineau, and from these talks emerged the idea of calling a conference in London of twenty-four maritime nations, composed of the signatories to the 1888 Convention and others who had become major users of the Suez Canal.

The conference met on August 16 at Lancaster House in London. But there were two user nations missing: Greece, which did not want to get involved because of its special interests in Cyprus and Egypt, and Egypt itself.

Nasser was ready to attend the conference. His Comet aircraft was prepared for the journey and his party's passports were put in order. He did this despite the violence of the British press attacks on him. They called him a dictator. This was nonsense. Egypt was not Germany, and Nasser was not Hitler.

He was being advised by Nehru and Tito to go and he also saw the conference as another way of gaining the time he needed to make his take-over secure. Then, several days before the President was due to fly to London, he received a dispatch from the Embassy in London that reported that during a television appearance Eden had made a violent personal attack on him, saying: "Colonel Nasser is the enemy, we have no quarrel with the Egyptian people." And then he held up a piece of black paper with the comment: "This is Nasser's black record."

When Nasser read this dispatch he said: "This man is acting. He has turned from being a Prime Minister into an actor."

This report, taken in conjunction with the reports about Eden's health, temper, and unpredictability, determined the President not to go to London. He sent Ali Sabry instead, with orders to stay in the Embassy and act as an observer.

This did not mean that Egypt was not represented at the conference. We had our friends there, particularly the Indians in the person of V. K. Krishna Menon who spoke passionately on Egypt's behalf, and the Russians, represented by Foreign Minister Dmitri Shepilov.

Dulles was the mastermind of the conference and he talked through a lawyer's solution that was adopted by eighteen of the conferring nations—the exceptions being the Soviet Union, Indonesia, Ceylon, and India—and that called for the setting up of an international management body to run the Canal.

It was never a feasible project, but it appealed to Dulles' legal mind and so a committee of five was set up to explain the proposal to President Nasser. Dulles was asked to lead this mission but refused, and it was headed instead by Robert Menzies, the Australian Prime Minister. It was composed of the Foreign Ministers of

Iran (as an Asian nation), Ethiopia (as an African nation), and Sweden (as a European nation) and Deputy Under Secretary of State Loy Henderson representing the United States.

They arrived in Cairo on the second of September and stayed at the Semiramis Hotel overlooking the Nile. Twice during the following day they met the President and explained to him what had happened at the London conference and gave him their mandate. They told him they had come to explain the declaration of the eighteen powers. They stressed the importance of the Canal to the maritime nations and expressed the hope that an agreement could be reached.

The President gave a dinner for the mission on September 5 at the Manial Palace, which before the revolution had been the palace of King Farouk's uncle, Crown Prince Mohammed Ali. It is surrounded by a marvelous group of old trees, and at dinner Menzies talked ecstatically about these trees, saying how beautiful they were. He exercised all his charm and amused the President.

Menzies asked Nasser: "Have you ever met Churchill?" Nasser replied: "No, but I admired him."

"Have you ever heard him talking?" asked Menzies, and again Nasser said: "No."

"Do you know," said Menzies, "I have the reputation for being the best imitator of Churchill."

And throughout the dinner Menzies kept whispering in Nasser's ear and everyone thought that they were talking important business about Suez when in fact Menzies was imitating Churchill's speech. He also imitated Bernard Shaw and General Jan Smuts. He was not talking seriously, but he set himself out to charm Nasser, and the President, indeed, found him very likable.

They had their third set of talks the following day, Thursday, September 6. Menzies pressed the arguments for an international administration to run the Canal. But Nasser refused on the grounds that this would be a new form of imperialism. Menzies asked how this could happen.

Nasser explained that if, after nationalizing the Canal, he then brought in an international administration, that administration would need protection and that protection would have to come from outside. And, once again, Egypt would be subject to occupation by foreign troops.

Menzies would not accept this argument and insisted that an international administration would solve all the problems. Nasser's reply was: "You think that an international administration would end the trouble, but I think that an international administration would be the beginning of trouble."

Menzies leaned forward over the desk, his thick eyebrows bristling, and growled: "Mr. President, your refusal of an international administration will be the beginning of trouble."

Nasser immediately closed the files on the desk in front of him and said: "You are threatening me. Very well, I am finished. There will be no more discussions. It is all over."

Menzies grew red. The Ethiopian Foreign Minister tried to calm the situation. He said that Mr. Menzies had expressed himself badly but it was not meant as a threat. Speaking for his country, an African country, he had not come to threaten, and he had not come to impose a solution on Egypt that Egypt would not like. The Swedish Foreign Minister also tried to ease the atmosphere, and Loy Henderson too argued that what Menzies had said was not meant as a threat. Menzies himself, by now terribly embarrassed, apologized: "I'm sorry, I did not mean to convey a threat to you."

But the President would not be mollified. He was angry: "To tell me that my refusal to accept an international administration will be the beginning of real trouble *is* a threat and I will not negotiate under threat."

That was the end for the Menzies mission. It was an abject failure. It was doomed anyway, doomed by its originator Dulles who, at a press conference in Washington on August 28, had told the world that "the Suez Canal is not a primary concern to the United States." He thus rendered Menzies powerless and President Eisenhower added to Menzies' discomfiture at another press conference on September 4, soon after Menzies had arrived in Cairo. "We are committed," said Eisenhower, "to a peaceful settlement of this dispute, nothing else." When Nasser heard of this, he said: "That man puzzles me; which side is he on?"

It was obvious that the Americans were backing down. Eden was beside himself with fury. And Nasser rode high.

All the other attempts to bring pressure on him also failed. There was a second London conference which proposed setting up the Suez Canal Users' Association (SCUA), a fantasy organization promptly denounced by President Nasser and equally promptly scuttled by Dulles who, at yet another press conference, said that he never envisaged SCUA shooting its way through the Canal. Some days later he denied that SCUA had ever possessed any teeth.

Then, on October 5, the Suez question came before the United Nations Security Council. The Council met for nine days in private, then continued in public, and in the end unanimously adopted the six principles on which a settlement could be based. These principles, which had been agreed by the Foreign Ministers of Britain, France, and Egypt, were:

1. There should be free and open transit through the Canal without discrimination.
2. Egypt's sovereignty should be respected.
3. The operation of the Canal should not be interfered with by the politics of any one country.
4. Canal tolls and charges should be fixed by agreement between Egypt and the users.

5. A fair proportion of the dues should be allotted to the development of the Canal.

6. In cases of dispute, the matter should be settled by arbitration.

Britain and France, however, insisted on adding a second part to the resolution because they felt they had to state their position. It consisted of two recommendations which invited "the Egyptian Government to make known promptly its proposals for a system meeting the requirements set out above and providing guarantees to users not less effective than those sought by the proposals of the eighteen powers . . ." and considered that the "Canal Users Association . . . and the competent Egyptian authorities should co-operate to ensure the satisfactory operation of the Canal and free and open transit through the Canal in accordance with the 1888 Convention."

As everybody—including Britain and France—expected, the Soviet Union took the view that these recommendations amounted to the "coercion of Egypt," and Shepilov vetoed them.

However, with the acceptance by Britain and France of the six principles and the proposal by Secretary-General Dag Hammarskjöld for the Foreign Ministers of Britain, France and Egypt to meet in Geneva on October 29 for detailed discussion on their implementation, it was felt that the steam had gone out of the situation.

After the vote on the principles, Hammarskjöld said to Egypt's Foreign Minister Dr. Fawzi: "This is excellent. After the British have completed their military preparations against you, the train has passed the station."

He was wrong. The train was just pulling in.

In their efforts to persuade Egypt of the dangers of the situation and to agree to the six principles, the Americans had leaked to Ambassador Hussein the news that General Sir Charles Keightley had been chosen to command an invasion of Egypt and that he was already training his men in Cyprus.

This was one of a number of warnings about Britain and France's determination on military intervention.

Egypt's friend inside the Baghdad Pact reported that Nuri Said was convinced there was going to be an invasion.

EOKA and Egypt's supporters in the Maltese labor movement sent news of large troop, air, and shipping movements based on the two islands. EOKA sent photographs of the French Noratlas transport planes arriving at Royal Air Force bases on Cyprus.

Merchant ship captains passing through the Suez Canal told of large concentrations of warships and landing craft.

In order to meet these threats and because he still thought British collusion with the Israelis was the taboo game, President Nasser had withdrawn most of the Army units from the Sinai, leaving only two battalions at El Arish, two at Rafah, and two at Abu Agheila.

But when the six principles were accepted, President Nasser estimated that the danger of invasion had dropped to 10 per cent. He virtually ruled it out.

The proposed meeting at Geneva on the twenty-ninth had been put off, but this postponement was regarded as part of diplomatic chess, and on that day President Nasser went to a birthday party for one of his sons. There were children and cakes, games and movies. The President was enjoying himself when a messenger arrived with a slip of paper.

It carried the news that the Israelis had announced they had sent an armored column into the Sinai. So far there had been no news from the Egyptian Army because the bulk of it had been withdrawn to protect the Canal. There were not enough troops to watch the empty spaces of the desert, and so the first news the

President had came from the monitoring service that listened in to Israeli radio traffic.

The President left the party, called his colleagues to a meeting, and asked for an assessment of the situation. The first conclusion, given to the President at seven o'clock, was that it was a limited operation. But, at ten o'clock, the Israelis announced that their forces were already close to the Suez Canal. They were referring to the battalion of paratroops they had dropped just short of the Mitla Pass. That gave the whole operation a new dimension.

When the news was passed to the special assessment committee, they revised their thinking and decided that the Israelis had mounted a big operation because Egypt had been successful with the nationalization of Suez. This was their revenge for the United Nations' vote on the six principles.

Orders were given. The armored forces that had been withdrawn for the defense of the Canal were to move back into the Sinai and the Army planned to fight a decisive tank battle at the oasis of Bir Rud Selim, while an armored brigade was ordered to take the Mitla Pass and the Air Force was given the task of annihilating the Israeli paratroopers in the Pass.

These moves were taken because even at this stage nobody could conceive that there could be any collusion between the British and French and the Israelis.

Although Nasser was highly suspicious of the airdrop on the Mitla Pass—it was too far in advance of the Israeli ground forces— he still thought that a joint effort was taboo, that Eden could not possibly collaborate with the Israelis in this fashion. He and his colleagues held to this view despite tidbits of information hinting at collaboration, certainly between the French and the Israelis, if not between the British and the Israelis. There was an increased flow of arms—Dulles had sanctioned the selling of three more squadrons of Mystères to Israel. We knew about that, but there were some hints we could not bring ourselves to believe.

A Frenchman went to our Embassy in Paris and was paid £1,000 for some information about the French-Israeli collusion, but when he returned a few days later and asked for £5,000 for more information about Israeli meetings and joint military planning, his tale was not believed and on orders from Cairo he was turned away as a crook.

Nasser just could not bring himself to believe that Eden, with all the knowledge he claimed of the Middle East, would jeopardize the security of all Britain's friends and Britain's own standing in the Arab world by making war on an Arab nation alongside Israel. Nasser was completely wrong about Eden's intentions, but absolutely right about the results.

Eden had committed himself to collusion with Israel in a series of meetings at a villa in Sèvres, just outside Paris, between Selwyn Lloyd, Christian Pineau, and Ben Gurion, who was supported by Shimon Peres and Moshe Dayan. An agreement on the action to be taken against Egypt was signed by Ben Gurion for Israel and by Pineau for France. Patrick Dean, then head of the Middle East Department of the Foreign Office, was left to sign for Britain.

Five days later Israel invaded the Sinai. In his memoirs Dayan wrote: "If it were not for the Anglo-French operation, it is doubtful whether Israel would have launched her campaign; and if she had, its character, both military and political, would have been different."

But the joint operation was launched and the results in the Middle East would be just as Nasser had predicted.

It was not until dawn on the second day of hostilities that President Nasser began to suspect the true situation. Reports came in of Canberra reconnaissance jets flying over the Sinai, and as the RAF were the only people flying these aircraft in the Middle East, they had to be British.

The new American Ambassador, Raymond Hare, who had taken over in September from the ill-starred Byroade, was informed that the British were up to something suspicious and he passed this message on to Washington with a request for information. But events overtook that gambit, and before he could get a reply, Washington itself had advised all American citizens to leave Egypt.

At four o'clock the Egyptian Ambassador in London, Samy Abul-Fetouh, was called to the Foreign Office and Kamal Abdel Nabi, his colleague in Paris, was called to the Quai d'Orsay. There they were given the British and French governments' joint ultimatum to Egypt and Israel.

It was done Ribbentrop style. Neither Ambassador was offered a seat. Abdoul-Fetouh was taken by surprise and remained standing while Sir Ivone Kirkpatrick, the Permanent Under Secretary at the Foreign Office, delivered the ultimatum. But Nabi, our man in Paris, was frightened of nobody and he sat down, uninvited.

The ultimatum demanded that both Israel and Egypt should cease fire and withdraw ten miles from either side of the Canal. It further demanded that Egypt should "accept the temporary occupation by Anglo-French forces of key positions at Port Said, Ismailia and Suez." The time limit for agreement to comply with these demands was twelve hours. "If at the expiration of that time," said the ultimatum, "one or both Governments have not undertaken to comply with the above requirements, United Kingdom and French forces will intervene in whatever strength may be necessary to secure compliance."

Nasser still found it very difficult to believe that the British and French were going to intervene, but the ultimatum reeked of hypocrisy and double-dealing. What justification was there in the demand for a mutual withdrawal ten miles from the Canal when the Israelis at that stage had only one battalion of lightly armed paratroopers still forty miles from the Canal?

"This is all a lie," he said. "How can they lie? Is Eden a liar?"

He could not believe it because one of the legends of the Middle

East was that a British gentleman never lied. He was astonished. Although he disliked Eden, although he did not trust Eden and he knew that Eden wanted to destroy him, he still did not think that Eden would lie.

That night there was a meeting of the Cabinet to decide what action to take. The President took the view that to bow to the ultimatum would be catastrophic for Egypt. The ultimatum was totally rejected. The Israelis accepted it—according to plan.

Having decided on this course of action, the President set about organizing the defense of the country. He drove to Army Head-quarters at the Abbasseya Barracks and there he had a heated discussion with Abdel Hakim Amer, the commander in chief. Amer had started to push his armor into the Sinai to meet the Israeli threat. He wanted to maintain this movement to fight off the Israelis from the Canal. But Nasser insisted that the tanks be brought back to defend the Canal against the British and the French. "If they land at Port Said," he argued, "all the armor will be cut off in the desert. I prefer to evacuate the Sinai. Bring the armor back and we will defend the Canal inside the country."

The two men, old friends, spent nearly all night locked in this argument and the withdrawal of the tanks from Sinai was delayed.

The President also ordered that the Air Force should not engage in any battles because of the enemy's overwhelming superiority. Again there was a clash of opinion. Marshal Amer wanted the Air Force to fight but the President said that would be suicidal, a massacre. At that time Egypt had only thirty planes considered fit for action, but not even all of those were really ready to fight.

The day after the ultimatums were delivered a propaganda campaign of mounting fury was unleashed against Nasser. The British radio station on Cyprus was renamed the "Voice of Britain" and its programs were designed to bring about the President's overthrow by the Egyptian people. "Nasser is the enemy" was its theme. "Britain loves the Egyptian people, but Nasser is an evil man."

The broadcasts displayed a surprising ignorance of Egyptian affairs and thinking. In just one instance, when the propagandists suggested a list of eight names of Egyptians who would be acceptable to the British in a new government, two of the men they named, Hafez Ramadan and Aly Zaki el Oraby, were already dead. The broadcasts served only to increase Nasser's popularity.

The following day, October 31, President Nasser had another disagreement with the High Command. The soldiers, taking a military point of view, had decided that the best place to fight a tank battle against an invading British and French force was in the ditches of the Delta, and so they started moving units from the Suez Canal up to defensive lines in the Delta. But Nasser took a political view and he argued that the whole purpose of an invasion would be the occupation of the Canal Zone. The invaders would not want Cairo, they would want the Canal; therefore Egypt must concentrate her forces in the Zone. Otherwise, by abandoning the Canal, the Egyptian Army would be playing the invaders' game for them. So those forces that had been sent to the Delta were turned round and sent back to reinforce Port Said and Ismailia.

At five-fifty that evening the British bombed Cairo. The British planned two days of raids to finish off the Egyptian Air Force. In fact they did it in one, but nevertheless carried on with their plan.

Nasser, who was being given a message from President Sukarno by the Indonesian Ambassador when the raids started, heard the noise of the aircraft and the bombs and went up to watch the raid from his roof. After the raid he went to a meeting of the Cabinet at his headquarters to get the damage reports and to discuss what could be done. Salah Salem, the "Dancing Major," was there in a very depressed state. Salem turned to the President and said: "You have done everything you can. You have served the country to the best of your ability. But you have failed. There is just one more service you can do for the country. Sir Humphrey Trevelyan is still at the British Embassy. Go and give yourself up to him, for they only want you."

The President replied that if he thought that the British only wanted him, he would willingly sacrifice himself. "I would sacrifice myself fighting. But I am not going to surrender."

He turned to the others and asked if they agreed with Salah Salem. Not one of them did.

Salem was one of the very few Egyptians who thought that Nasser ought to surrender. Eden believed that, first, the ultimatum and, second, the bombing would be sufficient to bring him down. But Eden was wrong. There were no demonstrations—except of support. Nasser was secure. However, he realized that the Army could not hold out against the military might of Britain and France, and so he spent much of his time preparing for a popular, guerrilla war which was to be mounted after the Army had been defeated. He planned to set up his guerrilla headquarters at Tanta in the Delta. Caches of small arms were established throughout the country. Secret radio stations were set up. One radio transmitter, which was going to be used to beam propaganda against Nuri Pasha from somewhere inside Saudi Arabia, was diverted to Tanta. The Delta was chosen as the best place from which to harass British occupying troops. All that night he worked on the second phase of the struggle.

By the next day, Thursday, November 1, support had begun to come in from all over the Arab world. King Hussein of Jordan telephoned President Nasser and told him that he was going to attack Israel. But Nasser begged him not to, saying that they were facing something much bigger than an Israeli attack and that it was essential for the Jordanian Army to be kept intact.

President Shukri al Kuwatly of Syria had already telephoned President Nasser offering to put off a trip he was due to make to Moscow. But Nasser urged him to go, saying that if there were any developments he would telephone Kuwatly in Moscow.

Kuwatly told Nasser later that he received news of the bombing of Cairo as he was about to enter a meeting with Khrushchev, Bulganin, and Marshal Zhukov. He became so upset he abandoned the agenda and asked the Russians: "What is going to happen?" They asked him what he thought they could do and he replied: "You must intervene."

Zhukov then unfolded a map in front of him and said: "Mr. President, here is the map, look at it, how can we intervene?" Kuwatly told me that he leaped from his chair and cried: "Marshal Zhukov, Marshal Zhukov, Marshal Zhukov, do you want me, a poor civilian to tell you, the star of World War Two, how to intervene? You must intervene." They tried to calm Kuwatly, talking about the impossibility of military intervention and how they would have to use political means and act through the United Nations. Kuwatly replied by cursing the United Nations and the Security Council. He was near to tears with rage and frustration.

In the meantime, nationalist officers in Syria, led by Abdel Hamid al Sarraj, blew up the Iraq Petroleum Company pipeline, an action which was going to have an important effect on the West's oil supplies and on Britain's currency crisis.

It had been arranged before the invasion that the Syrians would blow up both the IPC and the Tapline pipelines when they received a coded signal from Nasser and so cut off Europe's oil supplies. Sarraj asked for permission to blow up the lines when the action started and Nasser agreed, sending the coded signal.

But after sending the message, the President remembered that it referred to both pipelines, one of which, the Tapline, was American. So, as the Americans had come out so strongly in favor of Egypt and against Britain and France, he did not want to anger the Americans and was forced to send a hurried message telling Sarraj to blow only the IPC line.

The cutting of the pipeline, along with the blocking of the

Canal and the refusal to supply oil, was part of a prearranged plan to strike back at the invaders by causing economic problems in Europe.

Every day now was invasion day. We expected a new invasion force to appear at any time. The bombing continued. The Egyptian armor, retreating from the Sinai behind a brave rearguard action, was strafed and bombed. The climax could not be long delayed. Six blockships filled with cement, beer bottles, and old iron were moored in the Great Bitter Lake, ready to be sunk in the Canal as soon as the invasion started. The British learned about these ships and bombed them heavily. But only one of them was sunk—and it blocked the Canal beautifully. The others were scuttled and formed a very effective barrier. Now nothing could get through the Suez.

President Nasser was waiting for the invasion, working in his office at the old Revolutionary Command Council (RCC) headquarters overlooking the Nile in Cairo. (It was from the courtyard of this building that, fourteen years later, his funeral procession set out, in recognition of the desperate days he had spent there, sleeping in a small, spartan bedroom next door to his equally plain office.)

Nasser had accepted sole responsibility for the nationalization of the Canal and therefore for the events that followed, but, despite everything, he remained able to sleep soundly for the two or three hours he allowed himself every night. He would go to bed saying: "Wake me if the landings start; otherwise let me sleep." But one evening during the period when we were waiting for the invasion, I called on him at the RCC headquarters and found him pacing the balcony, depressed. He had been listening to a song which had caught the public's imagination. Everyone was singing it. It was by Abdel Halim Hafiz who later became one of Egypt's most famous singers. The refrain was "We have left Egypt a trust in your hands." And Nasser told me: "I have been questioning myself; have I behaved well towards this trust or not?"

That song made an extraordinary impression on him. The next day he decided to go to the front. We tried to dissuade him. We told him the area was being strafed and bombed and that his car would be seen. "They want you and they will get you." But he refused to listen to us. He listened to the song instead and he set out for the front on November 5. He had reached Inchas where there was a great deal of strafing when he heard the news of the airborne landings at Port Said and Port Fuad.

Nasser was surprised by the extent of the airborne landings. Intelligence reports had suggested that the invasion forces did not have many paratroopers and Nasser expected a classical fleet landing with the Royal Navy steaming into Alexandria. That was one of the reasons we tried to keep two destroyers of the American Sixth Fleet there as long as possible—as insurance against a British bombardment. They had arrived to evacuate American citizens, and the Egyptian authorities delayed the evacuation by giving the evacuees long meals as their convoys rolled through Egypt towards Alexandria. But as in so many other aspects of the Suez crisis, the British did not keep to their traditional patterns of behavior.

As he turned back his car from the desert to fight the military and political battle for Suez and Egypt, Nasser tended to link the airborne landings with collusion with Israel—as another example of Eden's perfidy. Talking about this after it was all over, the President said: "If Eden had come with the British Navy and tried to invade Egypt I think the Egyptians would have forgiven and forgotten once it was all finished. Even if he had come with the French we would have said that perhaps he needed an ally. But to bring the Israelis into an adventure against the Arabs was very foolish. We were used to hating British policy but then we began to despise British policy. I hate to use the word despise. But it is the only one."

The story of Suez is largely the story of the hatred between Nasser, the Arab nationalist revolutionary, and Eden, the sophisticated embodiment of a dying empire.

Their mutual hatred was both ideological and personal. It had been brewing in each man's background for hundreds of years, seventy years of British occupation had added fire to the mixture, their one and only meeting had set the pot boiling, and now it had exploded. There were two other ingredients that complicated matters. They were John Foster Dulles and Clarissa Eden.

United States policy during this period was confusing. The Americans spoke with so many different voices. There was the voice of the Secretary of State and there was the quite different voice of his brother Allen, head of the CIA. There was the voice of the State Department and the muted voice of the White House. But there was no question about the strength of this new, rich player in the Middle East game. Nasser used to say that Eden had a velvet fist in an iron glove but that Dulles had an iron fist in a velvet glove.

There was one other factor about which there was no question. Eden and Dulles disliked each other intensely. There was some jealousy in their makeup. Dulles thought of himself as the architect of the Western alliance. Eden thought of himself as the most experienced diplomat in the West and, among other things, as an expert on the Middle East.

During the Suez affair relations between the two men became more and more strained. Right at the beginning, when Churchill was still Prime Minister, both Churchill and Eden were displeased by the pressure that Dulles put on Britain to evacuate the Canal Zone.

This was reported in a telegram from Ahmed Hussein in Washington, and later, at the time of the Security Council debate on Suez, Dr. Fawzi sent dispatches reporting that Dulles had told him that Eden was furious because Dulles, the great architect of pacts, had not given the Baghdad Pact his full support. Eden was also angry because Dulles had first committed the West to giving aid for the High Dam and then withdrew it without proper consultation with his allies. And, of course, Eden felt that Dulles had let him down throughout this Suez crisis. There was a rare bitterness between the two men.

One of the factors in Egypt's calculations during the crisis was the contempt with which Dulles spoke of Eden. He told one Arab statesman: "Anthony does not know what he is doing. He is obsessed by Nasser."

This does not mean to say that Dulles' long-term aims were any different from Eden's. He too wanted Nasser's downfall, but he had been assured by his brother that it could be arranged discreetly by a coup from within, not by an attack from outside. That way neither the Arabs nor the Russians would be provoked.

Eden's wife, Clarissa, was also determined to get rid of Nasser. We were told that she was furious about the attacks on her husband in the Tory party as "a man of straw" and that it was her dream that he should prove himself, as had her uncle Sir Winston Churchill. When the American journalist Joseph Alsop visited Nasser, he told of the day he called on her and she picked up a newspaper carrying an ugly picture of Nasser and said angrily: "How can this Egyptian challenge Anthony and get away with it?" It was our impression that Eden wanted Nasser's head if only to please his wife.

But both Dulles and Clarissa Eden were incidental to the elemental hatred that existed between Nasser and Eden. In the end, the Suez affair became a personal business, a duel between two men. It was a situation that could only end in total victory for one and total defeat for the other. Nasser won and he never felt one speck of pity for Eden. He once said to Dag Hammarskjöld: "I can deal with someone I hate but not with someone I despise."

As for the brief fighting itself, the leader of the resistance in Port Said was Kamal Riffat. Riffat was one of the Free Officers and had served as an Intelligence Officer. The 4th Armored Division had been ordered to move into the Sinai by Marshal Amer on the first day of the fighting against the Israelis but it was quickly withdrawn on Nasser's orders.

The division's transport was attacked by the RAF but the armored vehicles were unharmed and were hidden in camouflaged positions in the Sharkia area.

It was decided, however, that only militia would remain in Port Said because Port Said itself was militarily indefensible. The plan was to have the set-piece battle with the British at Ismailia and Tel el Kebir, where there was sufficient area for maneuver.

Riffat blew up the Sweet Water Canal. The governor of Port Said, Mohammed Riad, was originally a judge and he found it very difficult to carry on under the British occupation. He had no money. He could not even pay any salaries, and he was under orders not to accept any money from the occupation force. Money was smuggled to him by the wife of an important man of the old regime, a feudalist. Her name was Jinan Shawarbi, and she led an all-woman Red Crescent mission to Port Said. The leader of the Ismailia sector was trying desperately to get £50,000 to Port Said, and she heard of his problem by chance when she was in his office getting permission to cross the lines with her Red Crescent team.

She put the money in her handbag and when she reached the road blocks she was stopped by a British and a French officer. They searched everything, all the stores and medicines of the team and then they wanted to search her. And so Mrs. Shawarbi, a very good-looking woman who spoke perfect English and French, turned to the British officer and said to him scornfully: "And you call yourself a British officer?"

She then appealed to the French officer's sense of gallantry: "Do you really want to search a lady's handbag? Here you are then. Take it." He refused: "No, madame, you may pass." And so she walked through with £50,000.

The actual supply road for Riffat's resistance fighters was through Lake Manzala, with arms being ferried in on small boats.

One of the things that particularly upset President Nasser was the bombing of civilians—1,120 were killed in the bombing of Port Said; these attacks were filmed by a Swedish photographer. The President was shocked when he saw the film. However, he was so encouraged by the opposition of the Labour party in England to Eden and the invasion that he decided to get a copy of the film to London at all costs. The meeting that Aneurin Bevan held in Trafalgar Square in opposition to the invasion seemed to him to be important, so Nasser determined to get a copy of the film to Bevan for showing to members of the House of Commons. Nasser had a copy of the film flown to Emile Bustani, a friend of many British Members of Parliament, in Beirut on November 8, the second day of the cease-fire, asking him to get it to London. Bustani flew to London himself and gave the film to Lord Robens, then a Labour M.P., and Robens and Bevan showed the film for the House of Commons.

Port Said never surrendered despite Eden's announcement that it had. Even after the city had been occupied the resistance continued.

The President was torn between two things. He had to keep the resistance going so that nobody could say that the city had capitulated and at the same time he did not want to cause too much trouble so that the British would have no excuse for not withdrawing. He wanted to make it easy for them to withdraw.

False reports about the surrender of Port Said came because General Sir Hugh Stockwell, commander of the British ground forces, asked to see the governor and Riad asked Cairo for permission to do this—at that time the telephone was still working between Cairo and Port Said. Permission was given and Stockwell sent a message to London saying that he was going to see the governor in order to arrange conditions for the city. Eden took this as meaning that the governor was surrendering and, to silence the opposition, he announced in the House of Commons that the governor had surrendered and that this might be the beginning of a general surrender.

When Nasser heard this, he telephoned Riad to ask: "What's this news coming from London saying you have surrendered?" Riad, of course, denied that he had surrendered.

Nasser thought that in general the British and French invasion forces were not strong enough. His estimation was that if they continued to advance they would be vulnerable once they came out of the protected strip from Port Said to El Qantara. He was planning to attack them with the 4th Armored Division and at the same time preparing to meet an attack from the south, from the Red Sea, on Suez. He thought that the invasion force could be trapped and that the Egyptian Army could give it hell. But, in the event, international political pressures on Britain and France decided the day, and the invasion was halted.

Suez finished the Baghdad Pact. It might even be said that Eden was responsible for Nuri Said's death, for no Arab leader could be Britain's friend and Nasser's enemy after Suez. Suez cost Britain the Arab world.

After it was all over, Nasser became totally fascinated by Suez. He would spend hours with people who could tell him something about it and he read every book published about it. When Eden's own book "Full Circle" was about to be published Nasser sent orders to the Intelligence Service that an advance copy must be obtained at any price. One of our agents paid a large sum of money for a proof copy, a coup which proved a waste of money because the publishers sent a copy to the President a week later.

The book made him despise Eden even more because Eden

ignored the question of collusion and this was four years after Suez when the whole world knew the details of the meetings between Selwyn Lloyd, Christian Pineau, and Ben Gurion at Sèvres.

It was "Full Circle" that confirmed all that Nasser felt about Eden. But history had already turned its thumbs down on his fallen enemy. Eden was ill, his career destroyed. "It was," said Nasser, "the Curse of the Pharaohs."

IV

A Duel with Khrushchev

Stalin's Russia reacted to the Egyptian revolution of 1952 in strictly Marxist fashion. The Old Guard in the Kremlin saw an army take-over. They had no proper assessment of the role an army can play in a national liberation movement in an underdeveloped country. Their analysis was simple in the extreme: an army by nature is a tool of oppression; therefore, they argued, the army take-over in Egypt had to lead to an oppressive regime and could not be revolutionary.

What they did not analyze carefully at that time was the fact that the army in an underdeveloped nation fulfills a completely different function than the armies in older, more settled societies.

The Communist party in Egypt opposed the revolution from the beginning and tried to whip up more popular opposition by distributing leaflets in the streets. The Soviet Union, of course, completely supported the Communists and Moscow Radio attacked the revolution bitterly. They said that it was fascist and had been staged by the Americans to abort Egypt's revolutionary potential.

For the next three years the Russians watched President Nasser's progress with a mixture of hostility and fascination. They were still calling him a military dictator and an oppressor while he was fighting against the Baghdad Pact. They were intrigued by the role he played at the Bandung Conference in 1955 and by the reports they received from Chou En-lai about discussions with Nasser in Rangoon. And they were very interested in his various conflicts with the British.

They were slow to absorb the impact and the meaning of his policies. Even when they signed the arms deal in 1955 they felt they were dealing with a mystery. But by now Khrushchev, who was beginning to be the real power in the Kremlin, had learned enough about Nasser to think it worth while to take a gamble on the arms deal.

The events following on the arms deal which culminated in the Anglo-French-Israeli attack on Suez during 1956 brought Khrushchev and Nasser much closer together. Russia's support of Egypt's position both in the United Nations and outside played a vital part in the mobilization of world opinion against the aggression.

Khrushchev, for his part, was fascinated by the way in which the Arab nations appeared to be rallying to Egypt's help—King Hussein offered to march against Israel, President Kuwatly of Syria was in Moscow urging intervention on the Russians, a group of Syrian officers blew up the oil pipelines that feed Western Europe. This solidarity in the face of aggression made a great impression on the Soviet leader. But it was not all sweetness and light. The Soviet Union waited for thirty-six hours to make a comment on the nationalization of the Suez Canal and this delay later became a major issue in a quarrel between Nasser and Khrushchev.

Also, when arms were issued to Egyptian civilians during the Suez invasion in order to fight a guerrilla war against the British and French, a number of Egyptian Communists took advantage of the situation and tried to take control of the national militia, particularly in the Port Said area. They saw an opportunity after the Russians had issued their ultimatum threatening London with rockets and the fighting had been stopped. They judged that the Soviet Union had gained such prestige by the ultimatum that they could afford to play an aggressive role in Egypt's affairs. And so some of them were arrested.

The next year, 1957, an even more difficult situation arose between Russia and Egypt. Syria was in chaos, slipping into anarchy with the Baath party, the Communists, and rival nationalist officers (each commanding a couple of battalions or a brigade), all fighting for power. The country was torn by the influence of the Hashemite family's intrigues, by Saudi Arabia's money and Egypt's ideas of Arab nationalism.

Syria was also threatened from outside, by Turkey and a plot by the Baghdad Pact powers. In this atmosphere of confusion, with the Syrian Army hopelessly divided and the Baath party unable to provide an effective government, the Communists, led by the veteran Khaled Bagdash who had translated the *Communist Manifesto* into Arabic, were thriving.

In January 1958 the leaders of the various nationalist groups in the Army came to Cairo along with Salah el Bitar, one of the leaders of the Baath party. They went to President Nasser and told him that the only thing that could save Syria was unity with Egypt.

Among the conditions that Nasser laid down for unity was that Syria, like Egypt, would abolish all political parties. This was accepted, even by the Baath, but it was opposed by the Communist party which could no longer operate openly in Syria. Three days before the Syrian Parliament voted to join the United Arab Republic, Khaled Bagdash fled the country. The other important conditions were that the Syrian Army should be kept out of politics and that officers with political connections should resign and pursue their political convictions outside the Army.

These events did not endear Nasser to Khrushchev, and yet Khrushchev still watched Nasser's progress with fascination. The way in which he was received in Syria, the impact he was having on the Arab world, his enormous popularity, all intrigued the Soviet Union.

It was with this mixture of incipient quarrel and continual interest that Nikita Sergeevich Khrushchev and Gamal Abdel Nasser met for the first time on April 29, 1958.

Khrushchev was waiting eagerly for a chance to see Nasser. In 1957 I accompanied a delegation which went to Moscow to celebrate the fortieth anniversary of the Soviet revolution. Mao Tse-tung was there and one day when he was discussing with Khrushchev what Nasser had done at Suez, the Russian leader said to him: "You know, we are trying to get him to come and see the Soviet Union. He is arresting the Communists in his country, but we want him to see what Communism is doing."

When Nasser arrived in Moscow, he was given a tremendous reception. But at the very first official meeting in the Kremlin relations were stretched to the breaking point—because of an interpreter's mistake. Egyptian delegations always had trouble with interpretations when dealing with the Russians. Nasser could communicate quite happily with Dulles and Eden in English, but he had no Russian, we had no Russian interpreters, and the only Arabic interpreters the Russians had were trained at the

School of Oriental Studies and had never been to an Arab country. The results were appalling.

Nasser, at the head of the U.A.R. delegation—it included Syrian members—was explaining the nature of the Egyptian revolution to the Russians. He talked of being independent, anti-imperialist, non-aligned, and dedicated to Arab unity. He then went on to talk about social and economic development on a socialist and independent path. All this was interpreted with some hesitancy by a rather uncomfortable man sitting at the head of a long table with the members of both delegations sitting on either side.

He performed the same service for Khrushchev when the Russian leader spoke. At one point, President Nasser understood him to say that Khrushchev had declared that if Nasser was going to follow a socialist path he could not be anti-Communist and Nasser took this to refer to his banning of the Communist parties in Egypt and Syria.

Nasser made no reply and the meeting ended quickly. But when they met again in the Kremlin at ten o'clock the next morning he opened the proceedings by stating: "I must say frankly that I did not like our discussion of yesterday. I have spent some hours thinking about it and I felt that before proceeding with these talks I must ask for a clarification."

He went over what he had understood Khrushchev to say at their previous meeting—the interpreter now putting it back into Russian—and argued that this was an interference in the internal matters of the U.A.R.: "We are not going to allow the Communist party in the United Arab Republic. We do not think those Communist parties understand or correctly analyze the nature of the national movement in underdeveloped countries, and we are not going to allow them. I am not ready to listen to anything about those Communist parties."

Khrushchev was astonished. "I never said that," he insisted. He swore that he had mentioned nothing about the Communist parties of Egypt and Syria.

Nasser replied that nevertheless such a remark was what he had heard.

All this was being passed backward and forward across the table by the interpreter, first in Arabic then in Russian. By this time he was trembling.

Khrushchev still protested his innocence and so Nasser said that perhaps it was a misunderstanding, a mistake in translation because he understood very well what he had *heard*.

Khrushchev then began to growl: "If it was a mistake by the interpreter, then he must not go unpunished."

The poor man dutifully translated this into his poor Arabic.

Nasser took pity on him and said: "Well, never mind."

But Khrushchev was adamant: "No, no, if he makes a mistake in such an important affair, we must make him into a piece of soap."

The translator repeated every word of the threat. He was sweating with fear. The scene became too much for Nasser and he started to laugh at the incongruity of it. But Khrushchev could not understand why he was laughing.

For Khrushchev, Nasser remained a source of fascination. He was the first of the leaders of the underdeveloped nations to visit Moscow. He had blown up a storm in his own land and throughout the world. The Arab students at the university in Moscow were wild in their acclamation of him and when the wife of the Syrian chargé d'affaires was introduced to him, she collapsed. Khrushchev watched this scene and asked why the woman had fainted. He was told, "From emotion." He found it all very puzzling. He was interested in the way in which Moslems pray, and when Nasser, after lunch in Khrushchev's house, made preparations to go off to a mosque in Moscow, Khrushchev was full of questions about the prayers. When Nasser went to wash his hands ritually before praying, Khrushchev waited on him with a towel. He behaved with great delicacy.

The President then went on a tour of the Soviet Union, visiting Sverdlovsk, Leningrad, and Stalingrad before flying home on May 16 to prepare for another visit to Marshal Tito to discuss the affairs of the non-aligned nations. Khrushchev was none too happy about this visit. He was as suspicious as Dulles of non-alignment and he was particularly suspicious of Tito. "Do not trust him," he told Nasser.

But Nasser did trust Tito and on July 6 he set sail from Alexandria in the yacht *Al Hourya* (Freedom) along with the Foreign Minister Dr. Fawzi, myself, and our wives to visit the Yugoslav leader at Brioni. It was a pleasant trip and we were still in Brioni on July 14 when the BBC started to broadcast the first news of the coup in Iraq, the destruction of the royal family, and the take-over by nationalist officers headed by Brigadier General Abdul Karim Kassem.

This news burst upon an Arab world torn by dissension. Lebanon and Jordan were both on the verge of revolution.

King Saud, frightened by the union of Syria and Egypt, had paid nearly £2,000,000 to have a bomb put on Nasser's plane. However, he chose the wrong man to do the job, picking Colonel Abdel Hamid al Sarraj, Syria's chief of Military Intelligence. When Saud's agents approached Sarraj with a check for £1,000,000 drawn on the Midland Bank, he took the check and reported everything to Nasser. Nasser told him to play along with the plotters, and he collected two more checks totaling £900,000. The checks were cashed and the money allocated to industrial projects, and then the full story of the plot was made public. It was this incident that eventually led to Saud's abdication in favor of his brother Feisal.

Now the Hashemites in Iraq had been blown away. The King and the Crown Prince of Iraq had been killed. Nuri Said, disguised as a woman, was soon to be hunted down and dragged through the streets of Baghdad. The Turks were furious because on the morning they were killed these three men were due to visit Turkey for a Baghdad Pact meeting and Premier Adnan Menderes was waiting at the airport to meet the Iraqi rulers when the news arrived of their fate. (Menderes himself was hanged after a coup in 1961.)

The whole area was boiling. The Middle East seemed about to explode. Then we heard that the United States Sixth Fleet was steaming towards Beirut to land troops in Lebanon while the British were flying paratroopers to Amman. The British repeated their Suez mistake of alienating the Arab world by asking the Israelis for permission to fly over Israel. It seemed that there was once again to be collusion between the Israelis and the British in a military adventure on Arab territory.

President Nasser talked to Cairo through the special radio transmission and cypher unit carried on the *Al Hourya* and then conferred with President Tito. The Yugoslav leader was worried; he said that if the situation was not handled with care it would lead to catastrophe. World War III appeared very close that day.

Nasser asked Fawzi for his opinion and the Foreign Minister replied that he saw the officer's coup in Baghdad as a bigger gamble than Monte Carlo ever saw. It could result in a tremendous fortune or absolute bankruptcy.

The President decided to cut his visit short and so set sail for Egypt that afternoon. He went with all naval honors, flags flying, salutes, and bands playing but he also went with some apprehension. Tito was worried about his safety and sent two destroyers to join the *Al Hourya*'s own two-destroyer escort. "The Americans," said Tito, "are out of their senses and anything can happen."

Even before starting out on this visit to Yugoslavia, Egypt's Intelligence Service was worried at the prospect of trouble from the Sixth Fleet. The possibility of the President's yacht being torpedoed or shelled was discussed but Nasser dismissed these fears as groundless. He said that the Americans can only do one thing when they meet a ship flying the flag of a head of state "and that is salute it."

But to return home after the Iraqi revolution, the landings in Beirut and Amman, and the overflights of Israel was a different proposition. Tito had already suggested that the President should fly back in an Ilyushin jet instead of facing a four-day sea journey and all its possible dangers. But there had been an incident when the Israelis tried to ambush a plane carrying Marshal Amer from Syria. They shot down the wrong aircraft, the one carrying Amer's escort, and he escaped. With this in mind, the idea of flying was ruled out.

So we set sail down the Adriatic. The *Al Hourya*'s transmission room was working overtime. The first night out it handled 192 messages in cipher. Kassem had asked for a U.A.R. military mission and for arms. The military mission was ordered to be sent and convoys of arms were organized from Syria. As the situation developed, we felt that possibly the West was trying another Suez with the destruction of Arab nationalism as its object. President Nasser set out to foil them.

Then Nasser received a message from Tito relayed from one of his destroyers. It read: "Please do not proceed any further by sea. I think it is very dangerous to go on. I suggest you turn back to the nearest Yugoslav port and maybe we can arrange for a very powerful plane to take you to Cairo."

Nasser replied: "I understand your point of view. I have decided to return to Pola."

Tito had asked the Russians to send one of their new TU-104 jet airliners to take Nasser back to Cairo, the Russians had agreed, and the big jet was already on its way to Yugoslavia.

That night the President called Fawzi and me to his cabin on the yacht and he said to us: "Tito is suggesting that I should turn back to Pola and take a Soviet plane to Cairo. But I have another idea. I am thinking of going to the Soviet Union and seeing Khrushchev so that I can be sure of the Russians' position and learn what they are proposing to do, what they are ready for, and what they are not ready for. If I return to Cairo without assessing the Soviet position at first hand, then we would be in the dark.

"What do you think about this proposition?"

Dr. Fawzi said: "Mr. President, would you give us some time to think?" He was worried about the effect of such a visit on the Americans—who were behaving in a very wild fashion.

We went out and walked round and round the bridge. There were no lights because the Yugoslav captain leading the convoy had seen an American reconnaissance plane and had ordered a blackout. It was dark, quiet, and tense.

We looked at the President's proposal from all sides, the arguments for it and those against. We gnawed at it but we could not make a decision and so went back to Nasser's office. Fawzi admitted our defeat and said: "I think there is a moment in history when a leader must decide according to his inspiration and not according to any calculations, because there are times when calculations can reach a deadlock and it must be for the leader to make the decision. I am very sorry to say that we reached no decision and our advice is that you must consult with your own soul."

The President thought for thirty seconds and said: "All right, we will go."

At eight o'clock the next morning we left our families on the yacht, transferred to the destroyer *El Nasser,* and steamed at full speed for Pola where it anchored in the back bay close to Tito's residence. Nasser explained his plan to fly to Moscow to Tito over dinner that night, and Tito warned that the Americans would be furious but agreed that Nasser needed to know the Russians' position. He undertook to warn the Russians that Nasser would be arriving and to arrange permission for the aircraft to overfly Bulgaria. Then we drove to Pola airport. It was in complete darkness. We moved secretly.

We climbed into that big plane, just four of us, the President, Dr. Fawzi, myself, and the President's secretary. The captain of the jet came back, saluted and, in very good English, said to the President: "Proceed to Cairo, sir?"

The President replied: "No, to Moscow." The pilot looked at him: "To Moscow, sir?"

"Yes, to Moscow," replied the President.

"Very good, sir." The pilot saluted and walked back to his cabin.

We arrived in Moscow at dawn on the seventeenth of July. As the plane halted at the end of the runway, far away from the airport terminal, three men were waiting, shrouded in their overcoats against the morning cold. They were Deputy Premier Anastas Mikoyan, General I. A. Serov, and a translator.

Nasser, Mikoyan, and the interpreter climbed into one of two waiting cars and the rest of us were crammed into the other. The curtains of the cars were drawn as we drove off through the pine trees and sped through Moscow to a dacha at a place called Karachoa.

Mikoyan had told the President that the situation had become even more tense, that Dulles had pushed the world to the brink with his landing in Lebanon. Mikoyan said that Khrushchev would be coming to see us at ten and suggested that in the meantime we should get some rest. None of us was ready for rest.

Another man who had been disturbed early that morning was Mohammed el Kouni, Egypt's Ambassador to Moscow. The President needed him at the talks but did not want him or anybody else at the Embassy to know that we were in Russia. So it was decided that he would be called to the Ministry of Foreign Affairs. At the somewhat unusual hour of 6 A.M. a car arrived at the Embassy with an urgent call for Kouni to see the Foreign Minister. The Ambassador protested that he had no car; it was too early for his driver to start work. The Russian messenger said that was no problem: "We have a car for you." The Ambassador climbed into the car but soon noticed that it was going in the wrong direction. He tried to talk to the driver. But the driver would say nothing, just drove on at high speed. As the car flashed through the streets and out of Moscow, Kouni felt sure that he was being kidnaped.

Eventually he arrived at the dacha where he was escorted inside. Nobody offered him any explanation. He was left alone. By this time he was deeply frightened. Then he heard a voice saying: "Good morning, Mohammed," and it was a very relieved Ambassador who turned and saw his President. His relief was almost as great as his surprise at seeing Nasser in Moscow.

Khrushchev arrived promptly at ten. He was terribly excited by what was happening in the Middle East, but gave the impression that he was finding it difficult to formulate a policy because events were moving so quickly and so dangerously. The talks that day went on for eight hours. For the first two, Nasser and Khrushchev talked alone—except for the interpreter. Then Fawzi and I joined in the discussions. They were mainly concerned with assessing America's intentions.

Khrushchev was convinced that Nasser was behind the coup: "They are your men in Iraq."

Nasser denied this and told Khrushchev how the two leaders of the revolution, Kassem and Brigadier General Abdel Salam Arif, had approached Sarraj a year previously when they were serving with the Iraqi Brigade in Jordan. They met at Ramtha on the Syrian border. The Iraqis told Sarraj they wanted him to convey a message to Nasser that there was a movement of Free Officers in the Iraqi Army similar to the one he had led in Egypt. They wanted to know what help Nasser could offer them and if Egypt could assist in planning the revolution.

"When Sarraj brought this request to me, I brushed it aside," said Nasser, "and told him to give them a message from me. First, if they are really serious they must keep it a secret even from us. Second, we could not help them with a plan because a plan can only be made by those people who are going to execute it. Because it must be subject to changes at any time. It depends very much on local conditions. Third, they should not depend on our help. I did not ask for the help of anybody on the twenty-third of July. A true revolutionary should depend on his own resources and he should not try to pin his actions on help from outside."

Khrushchev said: "You told them that and then you severed relations with them?"

"Yes, I did," Nasser replied.

"Very strange," said Khrushchev, shaking his head. "But then they did it and they succeeded." Then he brightened. "But they are still your men," he insisted. "Let me drink a toast to the leader of the whole Arab world."

The toast had its irony because two months previously the Russians had been attacking the concept of Arab unity and now Khrushchev was drinking to the leader of the Arab world.

The President explained later what had transpired in the two hours of private talks he had with Khrushchev. The Russian leader had told him he thought the Americans had gone off their heads.

"Frankly," he said, "we are not ready for a confrontation. We are not ready for World War III."

Nasser had asked him for assurances, pointing out that the Americans could use the Turks to invade Syria and that a very dangerous situation would arise because if the Turks attacked, he would be obliged to fight them. Khrushchev replied that Nasser would have to lean with the storm; there was no other way because Dulles could blow the whole world to pieces. "He pretends he is a priest," Khrushchev told Nasser, "but I am sure that although I am an atheist I am nearer to God than he is because he has no heart."

The President was unhappy with this answer. He wanted to know how the Soviet Union could help him. And he told Khrushchev how he was helping the Iraqis, sending them aircraft, radar units from Syria, and British ammunition from the old British ammunition dumps seized in the Canal Zone which would fit Iraq's British weapons. But all this, he pointed out, would take time. He urged Khrushchev to prevent any Western moves against Iraq or Syria by delivering an ultimatum to the West just as he had at the time of Suez.

Khrushchev refused. He was not prepared to take any risks that could lead to war. At the end of the two hours of argument he went off to discuss Nasser's request with members of the Politburo who were waiting in a nearby dacha. When he returned he told Nasser that the most the Soviet Union could do was to declare general maneuvers on the Bulgarian-Turkish border. "But," he said, "I am telling you frankly, don't depend on anything more than that."

General Serov was given the task of planning to get the President and the rest of us safely home. He talked with the Minister of Defense, Marshal Rodion Malinovsky, and they decided that the safest way was to fly over Iran and Iraq to Damascus. The Soviet

Ambassador in Teheran was ordered to see the Shah and get his personal permission for a Soviet plane to fly over Iran. The Shah was puzzled by the request; he was not told who was going to be in the plane but he agreed and the flight was planned.

Nasser still toyed with the idea of sailing home but Serov would not hear of it. And, Khrushchev joked, Dulles would like nothing better at the moment than to make Nasser food for the fish in the Mediterranean.

Khrushchev stayed with us until midnight and came to see us off at the airport. By that time the orders had been given for twenty-four Soviet Army divisions to maneuver on the Turkish frontier. Marshal Malinovsky made a special pronouncement about them and they were played up considerably around the world. But the last thing that Khrushchev said to Nasser at the airport was: "It is only a maneuver. Please, Mr. President, keep it in your mind that it is nothing more than maneuvers."

At least, that is what he said in Russian. When the interpreter put it into his execrable Arabic, he tried to use the word "game" for "maneuver" but instead used the Arabic word for "toy." The translation Nasser got said "It is nothing more than a toy."

On the flight south we landed for refueling at a military base, and the airfield was full of fighters assembling for the maneuvers. I looked at them and said to Nasser, "My God, this is an impressive scene."

He laughed and said: "Don't forget, they are only toys."

All this time our poor bewildered families had been kept in secret at Brioni. I had been married for just two years and my wife was completely unused to this sort of business. She did not know what had happened to me or what was going to happen to her. The Chief Chamberlain, a venerable distinguished gentleman, and his assistant were convinced they had been left to die. They too had no experience of these situations, and when the Chief

Chamberlain was telephoned by the President's secretary from Damascus using a homemade code to tell him they were going home by plane and not by ship, he was completely flummoxed. "You are not coming by a duck," said the secretary. "You are coming by a sparrow."

After some minutes of incomprehensible conversation, the poor chap threw the telephone away and collapsed. Eventually they were all flown home quite safely.

Our plane passed over Iran at dawn, and when we were over Baghdad, we identified ourselves and the President sent his greetings to the revolutionary leaders. There had been a suggestion that we should land at Baghdad but the President vetoed this, arguing that it was the Iraqis' own show and he should not interfere.

After we arrived in Damascus and the news of the flight became known, Nasser went out on to the balcony of the Presidential Palace to talk to the people. They came in their thousands. He told them that the Soviet Union "is fully behind us" but nevertheless "from their position of strength we are asking for peace."

When he came in from the balcony, I said: "You know, that was very strong."

Again he laughed and said: "It would have been stronger still if the maneuvers had not been done with toys."

The crisis passed. The Americans and the British withdrew their troops and Iraq was not invaded.

However, the honeymoon between Kassem's regime and the U.A.R. did not last long. Kassem was a strange, introverted figure, suspicious of everybody, particularly of his Deputy Premier, General Arif, who had been the real power behind the revolution. Kassem saw Arif as an Iraqi Nasser, with himself cast in the role of Naguib. Arif talked about the possibility of Iraq joining the U.A.R., which made Kassem even more suspicious of his contacts with Nasser. Eventually Kassem arrested Arif and he spent many months in prison. He escaped death only because his men broke into the prison and rescued him.

The British Ambassador to Iraq, Sir Michael Wright, and the Iraq Petroleum Company's men played on Kassem's fears in their efforts to prevent Iraq from joining the U.A.R., and they supplied him with false information about Arif. There was a time when Arif represented all the nationalists in Iraq, while Kassem was representing only himself and a small group in power—and the Communist party was backing him. More and more he turned toward the Communists for support and they became more and more powerful.

They had always been strong in Iraq because the conditions in that country, with feudalism, sectarianism, repression, and exploitation, flourishing under the rule of the royal family and Nuri Said, had been conducive to the party's growth. Now, there was virtually a Communist take-over.

The nationalists became alarmed at this situation and in March 1959, just a month after Arif's arrest, Colonel Abdel Wahab Shawaf mounted a nationalist revolt in Mosul. It was not well organized and was soon crushed with much bloodshed.

The Communists then took over Kirkuk. The red flag was raised and blood ran in the streets: the Communists massacred three thousand five hundred people. They caught twenty of Shawaf's nationalists, made them dig their own graves, then shot them. It was a barbarous time.

There is something in the Iraqi nature that leads to violence. Iraq has always been a border state between civilizations and a place where empires collided and armies clashed. Violence has become ingrained in the Iraqi character and in Kirkuk it was given full rein.

Nasser had been steadily cautious in his dealings with Kassem. When Khrushchev asked him in Moscow if Iraq would join the

U.A.R., Nasser replied that he had enough difficulties already. He would wait to hear from the Iraqis first.

Later, when there was a great quarrel in Iraq over whether they should ask for "union" or for "unity" with the U.A.R., Nasser told Kassem that it was unnecessary because neither the idea of union nor of unity was under consideration. Now, with the Communist massacres at Kirkuk, the division between Communist and nationalist in the Arab world was complete. The Communists thought that they could take over Iraq completely and the nationalists fought them bitterly. The lines of the struggle were drawn.

In Damascus members of the underground Communist party distributed leaflets. They were arrested. Egypt started to attack the Communist party of Iraq and then began to attack Kassem himself. The Soviet Union, of course, backed the Communist party of Iraq and there was a great deal of displeasure with Egypt's attacks on them, as well as with the arrests of Communists in Syria and Egypt. Nevertheless, the Russians tried to heal the breach which was opening between Egypt and the Soviet Union. The agreement for the building of the first stage of the Aswan High Dam had been signed in December 1958 and the Russians were preparing to start work.

But even that agreement had some sour overtones. There were letters in *Pravda* and *Isvestia* asking why Russia was helping those who were arresting Communists. No letters of that nature would be published in the Soviet Union unless they had official approval and they reflected the Russians' disappointment that their gamble in Iraq was not coming off.

Then, during the Twenty-first Congress of the Communist Party that met in Moscow in January and February 1959, Khrushchev stood up and attacked Nasser personally.

He said that those who attacked Communists could not be true nationalists. Nasser, he said, was an impulsive young man who could not impose his will on the Arab world. He argued that the Egyptians talked about socialism but that socialism was the first step towards Communism and that Nasser did not analyze or understand the historical inevitability of the situation.

Nasser was furious. In Damascus the following day he went out on to the balcony of the Presidential Palace and replied to Khruschchev with a stinging, angry speech to the cheering thousands gathered in the square below him.

These two speeches marked the end of a period of fascination between Khrushchev and Nasser and the start of a period of conflict. The verbal warfare between the two men went on for some two weeks. Wherever Khrushchev went, at the Congress, at diplomatic cocktail parties and receptions, he sniped at Nasser. The President set out on a tour of Syria and every day in a different town he fired a fresh broadside in reply. The battle raged with no quarter asked or given. It was the culmination of a series of incidents which highlighted the differences between ourselves and the Russians.

One such incident had taken place in the Kremlin in November 1957 when an Egyptian delegation was visiting Moscow for the celebrations marking the fortieth anniversary of the Russian Revolution and to sign an agreement on industrial co-operation. Three members of the delegation, General Hafiz Ismail, General Abdel Aziz Mustapha, and General Amer Gamil Afifi met an official named Tsaisev at a reception. Tsaisev was then director of the Middle East Department of the Soviet Union's Foreign Ministry but later, during Egypt's conflict with Iraq he was the Soviet Ambassador to Baghdad. Tsaisev, whose tongue had been loosened by vodka, started to lecture the Egyptian generals. What he said seemed so important that they reported it to the leader of the delegation, Marshal Amer.

He, in turn, made a report on the incident to Nasser and in this report he quotes Tsaisev as saying: "Non-alignment is a myth. Egypt must decide to choose an international camp if it is seeking real force. She will not be able to build power unless she does so.

"Why are you afraid of Communism? Accept it and we will strengthen you and defend you. Non-alignment is walking a tight rope and it will not survive long."

When Nasser read this report he shrugged it off, saying that Tsaisev was probably drunk, and did nothing. But he remembered it and later he used it in an exchange of private letters with Khrushchev in which both men spelled out their position, their philosophies, and their grievances against one another.

These two letters are remarkable in the way in which they lay bare the attitudes and emotions of two heads of state. The exchange started when President Nasser, anxious to avoid the quarrel he saw looming with Khrushchev, sent a message to him through the Russian Ambassador, Yevgeni Kisilev, who was returning to Moscow from Cairo to attend the Twenty-first Congress.

The minutes of Nasser's meeting with Kisilev show that the President was adamant about Iraq: "We consider that the fate of Iraq affects us and we are not going to leave it under the Communists at any price.

"But we do not want this to be the cause of a quarrel with the Soviet Union. You must decide whether you want to deal with the Arab people or only a few isolated Communist parties."

He went on to explain his position: "I am not a Communist. I am a nationalist. I am a progressive—at least I think I am progressive. I consider myself a socialist. But I think there are some things in Communism which are outdated. I don't say that all Communists are bad because some of my very good friends are Communist. Tito is a Communist and he is a very good friend of mine. Khrushchev is a very good friend of mine and he is a

Communist. And because I attack Communists in the Arab world it should not be taken as criticism of the Soviet Union."

Then he reminded Kisilev that at a party at the Polish Embassy in Moscow in October 1957, Khrushchev had been asked by a foreign correspondent about Russia's support of Nasser. Khrushchev replied: "We support Gamal Abdel Nasser although we know that he is not a Communist and that he puts Communists in jail in his country. But that is an interior affair which concerns him and his people, and we back him because he is a nationalist leader who represents the hopes of his people."

Nasser quoted this back to Khrushchev through Kisilev in an attempt to contain the quarrel. He did not succeed and their battle of speeches followed. But when Kisilev returned from Moscow to Cairo in April 1959 he brought with him a long letter.

In the letter Khrushchev started cordially, with regrets "that relations between our countries have begun to be darkened, and this is no way due to any initiative of ours." But from then on, Khrushchev pulled no punches:

You will remember, Mr. President, that when the revolution occurred in Iraq and we discussed with you in Moscow questions related to the possible acts of the aggressors against the Arab peoples, I told you then that we, for our part, would take all possible measures if the aggressors were to launch an attack on the Iraqi Republic.

But at the same time I expressed to you the idea that we should make every effort to have all the questions that had arisen settled peacefully without war.

Knowing your impulsiveness, we feared that our unlimited support of your belligerent sentiments might have prompted you to take military action, which we have always regarded as undesirable, and might have been interpreted by you as our agreement to military action.

Probably, Mr. President, you will also remember well that when you approached me with the proposal that we supply you with medium-range bombers and intermediate-range rockets, I remarked that the territory of your country was so small that you would find it difficult to use these weapons.

I then asked you what in your opinion were intermediate-range rockets. You replied that you needed rockets with a range of fifty to seventy kilometers. I told you that our intermediate-range rockets were designed for a distance of 2,000 to 4,000 kilometers and that they certainly would not suit you. If the need to use these rockets should arise, said I, it would evidently be best to launch them from our territory. Therefore you have no need for such rockets, but you can count on us rendering you assistance with these rockets from our territory if the aggressors unleash war against you.

I do not want to conceal from you the fact that when we did not agree with your proposal that we supply you with bombers and intermediate-range rockets, we had in mind that in a state of excitement largely caused by the prevailing situation you might have undertaken some undesirable action leading to war.

All this was in refutation of Nasser's charges that he had stood alone against the threat of aggression when the Americans and British landed in Lebanon and Jordan.

You and everyone else [said Khrushchev] are well aware of the fact that, when we told you that we would take all the necessary steps to render you the appropriate assistance, rele-

vant action was taken on our frontiers with Turkey and Iran
to indicate our readiness to come at any time to the aid of
our Arab brothers. You will recall that similar action was
also taken on the part of Bulgaria. Therefore your assertions
that you were alone against the aggressors do not correspond
to the truth.

He returned to the theme of help against aggression later in the
letter:

I will not conceal that we were particularly surprised by
the statement you made in your speech of March 22. You
said that during the Anglo-French-Israeli aggression against
Egypt in 1956 you had only Allah and yourselves to rely on
and that up to November 6, 1956, up to the end of the fighting, you had been alone and had not even a hint of the
slightest help from the Soviet Union.

Here, Mr. President, you have taken the path of denying
absolutely obvious truths.

It is common knowledge that the Soviet Union from the
very first day of the Suez crisis resolutely and consistently
came out in defense of Egypt's legitimate rights by giving
her large scale moral support. After the armed attack on
Egypt by Britain, France, and Israel, the Soviet government
took such steps which played far from the last role in forcing
the aggressors to leave Egyptian soil.

Did anyone entertain any doubts that had the forces, which
unleashed the armed aggression against Egypt, ignored the
categorical warning by the Soviet Union and not stopped
hostilities, the Soviet Union would have used more effi-
cient means of curbing the aggressors?

Khrushchev also chided Nasser about his relations with the other Arab countries:

> You will recall that in one of our talks during your last visit to Moscow you expressed displeasure with the governments of your neighboring Arab countries and asked me what ought to be done to change the internal situation in the countries that are hostile to the United Arab Republic and what assistance the Soviet Union could render to you in this matter.
>
> As you will recall I replied that tolerance should be evinced and that the affairs of other states should not be interfered in. These countries should be influenced by means of a good example on the part of the U.A.R., by raising the level of the economy, culture, and well-being of the peoples in your Republic, by creating a regime that would enable all the national forces within the Republic to show their initiative. I advised you to seek to establish in the U.A.R. the kind of economy and regime that would appeal to the other Arab countries so as to win favor among the peoples by this positive example.
>
> You then smiled and said that I was unrealistic in my assessment of the situation in the Arab countries; you added that nothing could be changed without military interference and that more resolute measures were required.
>
> I then replied that military or any other interference in the internal affairs of other Arab states was a very dangerous thing, that it would not lead to unity but would, on the contrary, disunite the efforts of the Arab countries.
>
> But I seem to have failed to convince you, and on this point each one of us apparently retained his own views.

Much of the rest of the letter was taken up with a long lecture on the virtues of Communism and denials that the Soviet Union interferes in the internal affairs of other countries. Then, towards the end, he referred to the question of Soviet aid to Egypt:

We are told, Mr. President, that at the meetings now held in the United Arab Republic shouts of "No rubles, no dollars" can be heard, not without encouragement on the part of the authorities, and some politicians even express openly their doubts as to the unselfishness of the Soviet aid. I will not go into details about the fundamental difference between Soviet and American aid; I would like just to ask this: is it possible that Soviet rubles compromise somebody in the United Arab Republic?

It is well known that the Soviet Union has never imposed and does not impose its aid upon anybody, but renders it only if asked to do so. You know, quite well, Mr. President, that the receiving of aid from the U.S.S.R. is a strictly voluntary matter and it depends, of course, on you to receive it or not. If you are of the opinion that the aid which we agreed to give, at your request, to the United Arab Republic is a burden to you, if you want to get rid of rubles which we have given under the existing agreements, you are free to refuse them.

You may rest assured that this will in no way offend us and we shall willingly meet your wish. Indeed we have a great field where we can invest. I have in mind the vast program of economic construction in the U.S.S.R. We do not wish to be obtrusive in giving aid to countries which do not need it and vilify us instead of being grateful and set the people against the Soviet country that gives disinterested aid.

And does not the present situation, when a campaign is going on in the United Arab Republic against the Soviet Union, and consequently against the Soviet people, give rise to complications for discharging our obligations under the agreement for the construction of the Aswan Dam?

I hope you will understand that this is not a threat on our part but concern over the fact that a campaign against the Soviet Union is now going on in the U.A.R. and that it will be very difficult for us to fulfill in these circumstances our obligations under the agreement that we signed with you.

Indeed the Soviet citizens will have to stay in your country, work there, display their creative initiative so that correct technical solution can be assured in the construction of the Dam—and all this under conditions with the local population being set against them.

Even now we are getting numerous letters from Soviet citizens that express anxiety about the fate of those who will go to your country. Our people wonder how it is possible to send Soviet citizens to the U.A.R. to implement the existing agreements of economic assistance if they may be subjected to the danger of moral and perhaps physical harm. Under the present conditions there may also occur inadmissible excesses by fanatics.

We ask you to understand correctly the causes of our anxiety. And if now you do not need our assistance, refuse it; with no displeasure shall we recall our people, and we shall maintain normal relations with you as we do with all countries.

Khrushchev ended his letter in typical fashion: "Your country also may yet need, and not only once, the Soviet Union's help and its friendly and equal co-operation. Here I should like to refer to a well-known Russian proverb: 'Don't spit into the well—you may need its water to drink.'"

President Nasser's reply was just as long and just as uncompromising. "I cannot conceal from you," he wrote, "that I was so surprised by the contents of your letter that when I read some of the paragraphs I felt I was reading an article in one of the Western newspapers where the facts deviate from their origin, where the gaps between the events are filled with fancies, and where, when facts fail the writers, they resort to imagination."

He went on to answer Khrushchev's points. He said that not for one moment would he underestimate the value of the Soviet ultimatum to Britain and France at the time of Suez but added: "We were alone in the battlefield. Our soldiers were fighting alone in the land of Sinai. Our army and people at Port Said were fighting alone in the streets of Port Said. We were not expecting any help except from Allah."

He recalled that President Kuwatly, who was visiting Moscow at the time, had urged the Russians to help Egypt. Kuwatly, said Nasser, wrote to him telling him of the Russians' attitude and in this letter it was evident:

1. That the Soviet Union is not ready to enter a world war.

2. That on this basis the Soviet Union cannot interfere militarily, even by sending volunteers.

3. That the utmost that can be done to help was the dispatch of some equipment and technicians.

I emphasize to you, Mr. Chairman, that I fully understood this letter and it did not cross my mind to burden you with more than you estimated you were able to bear.

All that I did—and allow me to tell you this secret now—was that I removed this letter from the files and put it in my pocket, as I did not want it to be seen by anyone whose morale may have been affected by reading it.

This letter was not taken out of my pocket until after the battle was over, whereupon I ordered it to be returned to the files as one of the state documents.

I still believe that this document is a great honor to us, as it is the best proof that we fought and were not only alone in the field of battle; we also knew that we would remain alone.

You may be aware, Mr. Chairman, that the Soviet ultimatum—the effect of which no one can deny—was issued from Moscow quite without our knowledge after nine days had passed during which we were alone in the field of battle.

There was a possibility that we might lose our determination, and there was a possibility that we might surrender . . . after two or three days, or after a week, and it was even probable that we might on the morning of the same day your ultimatum was issued.

Of what use would the ultimatum have been that day, Mr. Chairman, if we had come to the end and fallen?

He expressed his astonishment at Khrushchev's account of his request for rockets:

I asked you for some medium-range artillery rockets and you said in your letter—and this is true—that I asked for rockets with a range of fifty–seventy kilometers, and we were surprised by your comment on this request saying that you told me that the medium-range rockets that the Soviet Union possesses are for a range between 2,000 and 4,000 kilometers.

I defined what I asked for and defined its range. Perhaps the translation and the ambiguity between the word "rockets,"

the thing which I asked for, and the word "missiles," the thing
which I did not ask for, are responsible for this mistake,
though it is difficult to believe that this is the explanation in
the light of the series of differences between the facts as they
were and your version of them.

Khrushchev's accusations that President Nasser had wanted to
interfere militarily in neighboring Arab countries met equally
vigorous denials. Nasser said he was appalled by Khrushchev's
version of their conversation, for "in both context and detail, it is
as far removed from the truth as it could be. . . . It astonishes
me that you figured that I want your help in a military adventure
against Arab countries; for how can that be relevant while we
consider any threat to any Arab country—whatever its circumstances may be—a threat to us."

The main burden of his letter, however, was his contention that
throughout the Arab world local Communist parties, with Soviet
support, were working against Arab nationalism and Arab unity
and that it was necessary for him to fight these Communists
even though it meant incurring Soviet displeasure—something that
he very much regretted.

He ended his letter, like Khrushchev, with a proverb, the Arab
one which says, "One hand does not clap."

And he added: "We want to feel that our hand outstretched
toward you in friendship will not be left hanging in the air."

It was an astonishing exchange of letters between two heads of
state, astonishing as much in the genuine misunderstanding they
showed as well as in the direct conflicts which caused them to be
written.

Inevitably, relations between the Soviet Union and the United
Arab Republic became very cool after such an exchange. The
United States saw its chance and came to Nasser with massive

offers of aid. But it was such a transparent attempt to exploit the situation that the Americans made no headway and a certain quiet developed. Nasser and Khrushchev had said virtually everything in their letters. There were no more violent speeches.

Then Bulgaria got into the act. Sofia Radio opened up a series of very rough attacks on Egypt in the last months of 1959 and the early months of 1960.

It was broadcasting all sorts of stories about the way Communists were treated in Egyptian prisons, and one particular case that they blew up into a big scandal was that of Brigadier Youssef Mansour Seddiq, an original member of the Revolutionary Command Council, who, said the Bulgarians, had been tortured to death in prison. Arab students in Sofia demonstrated against his death and there was considerable trouble.

It so happened that Seddiq, who was thought to have Communist sympathies, was alive and well and living in Cairo. When he read the accounts of his "death," he went to the Bulgarian Embassy in Cairo and demanded to see the Ambassador, whereupon he told the Bulgarian: "I have just read of my death. As you can see, I am very much alive."

He also wrote a letter to the Ambassador that read: "This is written by Brigadier Youssef Mansour Seddiq, ex-member of the Revolutionary Command Council.

"Sofia Radio in the last few days has insisted in using my name in news which is completely unfounded. It says that I have been imprisoned, that I have been tortured, and even that I am dead. . . . Such things do not benefit the people of Bulgaria and certainly not the people of the United Arab Republic. I came to your Excellency wishing to put an end to these broadcasts, which are darkening relations between two peoples which are working for peace."

He signed the letter and left. Sofia Radio did not mention him again but their campaign went on, using the names of other people.

And that was typical of the atmosphere that prevailed at that time. Egypt still attacked Communists trying to gain control of the Arab states and while Russian propagandists did not attack Egypt, those of her satellite did.

All this, then, was the background to the next meeting between Khrushchev and Nasser.

They met in the lobby of the United Nations headquarters at the renowned, riotous opening of the 1960 session in September when Khrushchev took New York by storm, giving press conferences from the balcony of the Russian Delegation Mission like some improbable Juliet and hammering with his shoe on his desk at the United Nations. Nasser suggested that they should meet and Khrushchev agreed, "because there are so many accounts which ought to be settled."

They met on September 24 in Glen Cove at the Russian Delegation's rather splendid villa, set in extensive grounds in the millionaires' area of Long Island. They talked for an hour and a half, but not very seriously because, Khrushchev warned Nasser, "This place is bugged and we have discovered the bugging." The second time they met was on September 30 but there were other people present, some members of other non-aligned countries, and they could not get down to business. Then, on October 2, they spent over three hours together at Glen Cove—in the garden, out of range of the bugs.

Nasser reaffirmed his position, telling Khrushchev that although he had banned the Communist party from Egypt, it was because the Communists had made an incorrect analysis of the way the country should develop. He was not taking part in an anti-

Communist world crusade and he was not anti-Communist. "As I told your Ambassador, you are my friend and you are a Communist. Tito is my friend and he is a Communist."

Khrushchev snorted at that: "Tito is not a Communist, he is a King."

They had a far-ranging talk and Nasser came away with the impression that some of their quarrels had been settled. But the feelings between them remained cool. They became even cooler at the end of the following May when Anwar el Sadat, who was the leader of the Egyptian Parliament at that time, headed a parliamentary delegation to Moscow for the May Day celebrations.

Sadat, at a Kremlin reception, made a traditional type of speech, thanking the Russians for their hospitality and saying that he hoped their meeting would further the cause of Soviet-Egyptian relations.

Khrushchev started his speech in a similar friendly vein, then turned yet again to his argument that Communism was the only road: "But all right, we are not going to push you to Communism, we do not believe that people can even be pushed into Paradise with a stick. You have liberated yourselves and are happy with what you call nationalism. But let me tell you, Arab nationalism is not the zenith of happiness. I don't want to force you into Communism but I believe that some members of the delegation are going to be future Communists. Because life itself will impose Communism.

"Communism is only ideas. Ideas cannot be buried in prisons. You can put a man in prison but he will still be Communist. The Tsar put Lenin in prison, but Lenin built the biggest nation in history . . ."

Sadat and the delegation were stunned. They could do nothing because they had already made their speech, but when they returned to Cairo and reported to Nasser, he was once again angry at Khrushchev's attempts to interfere in the way in which he was running Egypt's affairs. He ordered: "This must not remain unanswered." And so on June 8, Sadat wrote to Khrushchev refuting his arguments and pointing out that he knew very well that prison did not change a man's ideas because he had spent six years in prison in the fight for Egypt's freedom.

And so it remained a time of conflict between Nasser and Khrushchev until events themselves helped to heal the breach between the two men.

There was a great upsurge of Arab nationalism. In Iraq, Kassem was deposed by Arif and killed. The Communist parties in Syria and Iraq collapsed, and Khrushchev's dreams of domination collapsed with them. In 1964 Cairo became the center of many international events: the Arab Summit in January, African Summit in July, Non-alignment Summit in October. We were quarreling with the Americans over the Yemen. Events were moving quickly all over the Middle East. Nasser was riding high. Khrushchev, puzzled by this upsurge, began to move toward Nasser once again. Thus 1964 marked the end of the time of conflict and the start of the time of understanding between the two men.

This understanding centered round the opening ceremonies in May of the first stage of the Aswan High Dam. Khrushchev had often been invited to visit Egypt and now he had accepted in order to take part in the festival celebrating this huge monument to Egyptian-Soviet co-operation. It seemed a symbolic occasion.

I was asked to travel with him and his family on the ship *Armenia* bringing them to Egypt. It was a fascinating voyage. Starting off from his villa in Yalta, Khrushchev relaxed on shipboard, stealing the cakes he was forbidden to eat, talking, and watching films—he dedicated one to Foreign Minister Andrei

Gromyko; it was called *The Naked Diplomat*. It was all very pleasant and easygoing. He was keen to learn about Egypt and the Arabs and talked with me for hours, listening with fascination to the ideas of Arab nationalism that he had dismissed before. His old interest in Nasser had returned, but this time with a more intellectual curiosity. It was not now curiosity solely about one man but about an historical movement and its meaning.

One day he found me on the bridge listening to Cairo Radio and he asked about the preparations for his arrival: "Are they doing enough? Are they mobilizing the people?" I assured him that the radio was full of his visit. But some time later, as we were approaching Alexandria, I was asked to go to see him. He was very unhappy because he had been receiving radio reports that the Egyptian government was playing down his reception. I said: "This cannot be true. You are the guest of Nasser and if you are badly received the insult will be to Nasser, not to you. This is the Arab tradition, which says that the dignity of the guest is part of the dignity of the host."

Again, when we arrived at Alexandria, he said: "They are applying protocol to me. Nasser is in Cairo and only Marshal Amer will meet me because I am not a head of state."

I reassured him, saying that I knew that the President did not follow strict protocol for his friends and would be there to meet him.

Soon afterwards a boat came out to meet us and there, on it, was Marshal Amer. I went up to him, asked where the President was, and he replied that Nasser was on the dock waiting for us to arrive. When I told Khrushchev, he was delighted. He was always very concerned about these details.

He was astonished by Alexandria: "It is a *big* city." I believe he was expecting camels and the desert.

The reception he got was tremendous. He was so happy, there

were tears of gratitude and pleasure in his eyes. His visit started beautifully. He was tremendously impressed by Cairo, its museum, and its history.

But, inevitably, complications set in. Among the guests at Aswan for the operation of diverting the waters of the Nile was President Arif. In fact, along with Nasser and Khrushchev, he was to be one of the main speakers. And just two weeks before he was to meet Khrushchev two Iraqi Communists had been tried in his courts and hanged.

At Aswan, the reconciliation between Khrushchev and Nasser seemed complete. The Russian leader invested the President with the Order of Lenin and made him a Hero of the Soviet Union. Arif was a different matter. Khrushchev got an enthusiastic welcome from the crowd at Aswan, but he made a long speech and it had to be translated paragraph by paragraph. When Arif spoke, he quoted extracts from the Koran—he was a religious man—and the crowd roared with approval whenever he recited such verses. Khrushchev could not understand this wild applause, especially for someone who hanged Communists.

He was clearly upset by the reception that Arif was given and in the car going back to the Cataract Hotel he turned to Nasser and said: "My friend, President Nasser, how long are you going to impose that goat upon me?" The President said: "Which goat?" And Khrushchev cried: "Arif . . . Arif . . . Arif . . . ," and he seized a copy of a newspaper that carried a picture of Arif and asked: "Doesn't he look like a goat?"

After the actual diversion of the waters, which was tremendously impressive, it was arranged that we would have a day's rest because Khrushchev was feeling the heat. The *Al Hourya* was sailed to Berenice on the Red Sea and we took the plane there for a day of fishing because Khrushchev wanted to fish in the Red Sea.

President Ahmed Ben Bella of Algeria and Arif were with us. Boats were being prepared for those who wanted to fish, and as we waited on the yacht's deck, Arif started talking to Khrushchev, saying how much he admired the Soviet Union.

Khrushchev immediately turned on him: "We cannot be friends with those who hang Communists."

Arif was stunned. Nasser, the host, was embarrassed. Neither man said anything. But Ben Bella, who was being lionized by the Russians as the hero of the Algerian revolution, turned on Khrushchev. He defended Arab nationalism, telling Khrushchev that he understood nothing about the Arab unity or the Arabs.

He carried on, expounding this argument until Khrushchev said: "I must admit I don't understand you, for there is only one unity, the unity of the working class."

President Nasser joined in at that, saying: "Now you are bringing us back to old quarrels. As a host I did not want to take part in this discussion and I was glad to leave it to you and Ben Bella, but now I must join in.

"You say there is only one unity, the unity of the working class. How then can you explain the fact that the Soviet Union and China are quarreling—and these are the two countries where the working class rule?

"You remember, Mr. Chairman, how you used to tell me about the war. You call it the Great Patriotic War. Why? Why don't you call it the Great Ideological War? I think, judging from what you have told me, that it is because the party was defeated.

"It was nationalism that stood up to the challenge of Hitler. Do you remember what you told me three days ago? You told me that Stalin was taken by surprise when the Nazis invaded and that he locked himself in his room in the Kremlin and drank continually. He received no reports about the war and then called a meeting of the Politburo, at which he said, 'Comrades, the State which Lenin built is coming to its end.'

"I think that was a declaration of defeat from the party. But the Russian nation itself stood up and turned it into the Great Patriotic War.

"And then, when you tell us that we cannot attack Communists, how is it that you yourself attack Stalin? We attack bad Communists and Stalin is a good example of a bad Communist."

Khrushchev became absolutely furious and shouted: "I can attack Stalin, but you cannot attack Stalin. You have no right to attack him."

This heated row went on from eight o'clock in the morning until two o'clock in the afternoon. The fishing boats were standing by, but by the time the argument ended it was too late to catch any fish.

However, at the end of those long, hot hours of wrangling it did at least seem that an understanding of the Arab position was beginning to dawn on Khrushchev. The communiqué at the end of his visit took particular note of Arab unity, and from that time all communiqués in which Arab heads of state and the Soviets were involved mentioned Arab unity. The Egyptians soon felt that after all the years of misunderstanding and quarreling they were entering a period of understanding with the Russians based on real knowledge of Arab hopes and ideals.

Khrushchev sailed away from Alexandria with the cheers of an Arab people ringing round the harbor. He seemed a happy man. Nasser watched him go with optimism. He felt that now he could build a proper relationship with the Soviet Union.

But soon afterwards the word started to come in: Khrushchev was removed from power. The whole world would wait to see what the policies of the new leaders of the Soviet Union would be and no one waited more anxiously than President Nasser. He was frightened that the understanding he had reached after so many problems with Khrushchev would disappear.

"Oh my God," he said when the news first reached Cairo, "now we have got to start all over again."

V

Hammarskjöld and His Sword

Dag Hammarskjöld, Secretary-General of the United Nations, probably had more to do with Gamal Abdel Nasser than with any other world figure. They met eighteen times in four years, with Hammarskjöld visiting Cairo no less than fifteen times. These meetings charted the course of their relationship as it was determined by the pressures of world events. The first series of meetings, through the spring of 1956, reflected Hammarskjöld's concern with the Middle East. He sensed the storm that was coming and did his best to calm the whirlwind.

After it had passed he became deeply involved with clearing the debris—the problems that followed the British, French, and Israeli invasions of Egypt. The Lebanese crisis started brewing in June 1958. And then, in 1960, Nasser went to New York for

"Khrushchev's session" at which the Russians tried to force the Secretary-General to resign. Finally, there was the tragedy of the Belgian Congo, which ended with Hammarskjöld's own death.

The two men, the intellectual Swede and the Arab man of action, had little in common. But they liked and trusted each other. And the one factor that they did have in common was big enough to overshadow most of their differences. They both put their faith in the United Nations.

For Hammarskjöld this faith was almost mystical. In his speech of acceptance of the post of Secretary-General on April 10, 1953, he said: "Ours is a work of reconciliation and realistic construction. This work must be based on respect for the laws by which human civilization has been built. It likewise requires a strict observance of the rules and principles laid down in the Charter of the Organization. My work shall be guided by this knowledge."

And he went on to talk about the "truth once expressed by a Swedish poet when he said that the greatest prayer of man does not ask for victory but for peace."

Nasser's faith in the United Nations stemmed from the realization he shared with Tito, Nehru, Sukarno, and the leaders of the other non-aligned nations that the United Nations was the place where small countries could exercise their world role. They were frightened by the Cold War and by Dulles' pacts. They did not want to get involved as a third bloc battered between the hammer of the Soviet Union and the anvil of the United States. They reasoned that the world would gather at the United Nations and that its Charter would be the world's law.

Nasser accordingly based his hopes for a solution to the Middle East problem on the United Nations Resolution of 1947 for the partition of Palestine and that of 1949 concerning the treatment of the refugees from Palestine. Israel refused to have anything to do with these resolutions, but Nasser built his political and moral position on them and the United Nations.

This was the position he persuaded all the Arab states to adopt at the Bandung Conference in 1955. Egypt had succeeded in having Israel banned from Bandung, but Israel had friends at the conference and the question of the banning was bound to be raised.

It was therefore essential that all the Arab states should adopt a unified policy, based on the morality of the United Nations resolutions, in order to explain the exclusion of Israel. The various Arab states held widely differing views on the way to solve the Middle East situation, but Nasser persuaded them all that the United Nations answer was the correct one. And they spoke with one voice at Bandung.

So the whole concept of the United Nations had become of great practical importance to Egypt and, consequently, so had the man who was Secretary-General.

Egypt had not enjoyed a happy relationship with Hammarskjöld's predecessor, Trygve Lie. He was accused by the Egyptian government of being pro-Israeli and he was thought to be too sympathetic to the United States. He was one of the people who still believed in the ideal America. But Hammarskjöld was different. He and Mahmoud Fawzi, Egypt's delegation chief, became friends immediately. They had many things in common. They had both had long civil service careers, they were both believers in quiet diplomacy, they loved art and music, and eventually they developed such a rapport that they could sit listening to music without speaking for two or three hours and yet communicate with each other.

Fawzi made a report to Premier Nasser on Hammarskjöld dated July 12, 1953, in which he said that: "He is replacing Trygve Lie but nobody could be more different, both in appearance and in substance.

"Trygve Lie is swollen in everything, in body and in mind. Perhaps his way of dealing with others is the behavior of a man with education but without culture. He has some qualities that he acquired by living with decent people, but he, himself, is not decent.

"Hammarskjöld is different. Not because his father was a Prime Minister and Trygve Lie's father was a worker. No. The difference comes from the moral formation of the two of them.

"Hammarskjöld is a refined man, sharp, decisive, and he has in his vision the totality of every world problem, political, economical, human and he is completely dedicated to the idea of international life."

That was the first estimate of Hammarskjöld's character that Nasser received. Later, after news of the arms deal in September 1955 had burst upon a surprised General Assembly, Fawzi went to Hammarskjöld and explained why Egypt needed the weapons. The Secretary-General saw Egypt's point of view. He told Fawzi: "I understand completely the need for small nations to defend themselves."

These reports from Fawzi helped to prepare Nasser for his first meeting with Hammarskjöld on January 22, 1956. They met at the Premier's office in Cairo and Nasser explained to the Secretary-General the feelings of the non-aligned nations about the United Nations. He said that the United Nations was the only place in which the small countries could carry out their role and that there could be no arbitration except through the Charter.

Hammarskjöld replied: "I believe that the existence of the United Nations depends on the small powers. The big powers only need the United Nations as a rubber stamp to authenticate their decisions. When they are in the wrong they prefer to ignore the UN completely. So the people who have the real interest in the

UN are the small powers and the medium powers and this is the only way in which international participation can be fulfilled."

And, referring to the two super powers, he said: "Our world cannot live in the shadow of a holy alliance between the two or a holy war between the two."

In discussing what could be done to strengthen the United Nations, he referred to a speech that Fawzi had made in which he had said that the League of Nations had a book but not a sword and that the United Nations must have a sword as well as a book: "But how can we have a sword? That is the problem. I want the United Nations to have a sword but I don't want it to be an isolated weapon. It must be independent but not isolated. And that can only come through the backing of the small powers and through an active secretariat general."

Hammarskjöld expounded his theory of internationalism to the Premier, maintaining that it was the only hope for peace. But Nasser was still involved with nationalism. For him, it was a long way to internationalism. He argued that internationalism could not be achieved without first establishing a social equality between the poor and the rich. He anticipated an international class struggle.

Hammarskjöld said that such a struggle would be really bloody and that the way to avoid it would be through internationalism.

They then talked about specific problems involving Egypt. The Swede was fascinated by Egypt and its history and he had visited the Egyptian Museum in Cairo where he had stood in front of the statue of Thot, the Egyptian god of writing, learning, and wisdom.

"I stood there, looking at his smile," he told the Premier, "thinking that that smile had remained on his face for five thousand years, never affected by anything. Through all the history of those years that smile went on."

Nasser enjoyed this philosophical talk, but he was not Fawzi

and he brought the conversation back to the realities. Hammarskjöld was still new to the problems of the Middle East and said:
"Mr. Premier, I always try to draw a map in my mind for every
problem I tackle, and then I try to find a way through the map.
But in this case it is very difficult territory. It is explosive. I have
not yet been able to draw a map, but I feel it is very dangerous and
that is why I am so cautious in trying to find a way."

But he did not find the way. Events in the Middle East became
bloodier. The Israelis mounted a series of murderous punitive raids
because of infiltrators crossing the 1948 cease-fire line. These infiltrators were mainly men going back to their own homes to take
something that they needed but that did not matter to the Israelis.
The Israelis struck out, killing twenty people here, thirty there.
In return, Egypt organized the Fedayeen (men of sacrifice) fighters. The Israelis, in turn, murdered the two colonels who commanded the Fedayeen by sending them explosive parcels. The
French were arming the Israelis. Propaganda resounding through
the area from all sides added to the tension.

And that was the situation when Hammarskjöld paid his second
visit to the Middle East. He came to try to cool the overheated state
of affairs. He and Lieutenant General Eedson M. L. Burns, the
United Nations Canadian truce supervisor, dined with Nasser at
the Premier's house on the eleventh of April, 1956. They met
again three days later and then Hammarskjöld went to Gaza to see
for himself what was happening. He commuted between Israel,
Europe, and Egypt for the next three weeks, talking with Ben
Gurion and Nasser and other leaders in an attempt to "draw his
map."

There were four immediate problems that occupied his attention:

1. The fact that Israelis had started to divert the waters of the
River Jordan.

2. The El Auja incident. El Auja is an important crossroads in the Negev desert. It was supposed to be demilitarized and was occupied by United Nations truce officials. But the Israeli Army moved in, arrested the United Nations men, and tied them up, then took possession of the crossroads.

3. The murder of the two Egyptian colonels by parcel bomb.

4. The adoption by both sides of practical methods to lessen the tension, including one made by President Nasser that the patrols of both sides should stay one kilometer back from the cease-fire line and so decrease the chances of the accidental meetings between patrols which were the main cause of shooting incidents at that time.

Hammarskjöld's visit to Gaza was revealing. It opened his eyes to the human problems of the refugees. He was furious at the manhandling of his men at El Auja. He was harshly treated by Ben Gurion. According to Fawzi's minutes of the meeting Hammarskjöld had with the Premier after he returned from Israel, he said that he "had heard too much banging on the table." The Israelis had explained the El Auja incident by saying that it was a strategic crossroads and, after the Soviet bloc arms deal, they feared that Egypt would use it for an assault on Israel.

Nasser certainly got the impression that night that the diplomat was really upset about the treatment he had received in Israel. He would not talk in detail about it, but when Nasser started explaining to him all the things Egypt had done to lessen tension—the cutting of the Army budget immediately after the revolution, for instance—Hammarskjöld simply said: "After visiting Israel I understand your problem better."

It was not that he was taking the Egyptian side, but at that time he was nearer to the Egyptian point of view because Nasser was basing his position on that of the United Nations while the Israelis were ignoring the organization.

Nevertheless he was not deterred from his mission of trying to cool things down, and when Nasser drew his attention to the report by General Burns about the French arms shipments to Israel the previous year, he said that he had read it but urged the President to look forward—not back at things that had passed because "God did not create us with eyes in the back of our heads."

He had a fund of maxims, and when at the end of that meeting Nasser asked him if he was going to talk to the press, he said he would rather not because he "did not want to join a nudist camp."

Hammarskjöld and Nasser met again on July 22, just four days before Nasser nationalized the Suez Canal. Neither man wanted a meeting although Hammarskjöld was in Cairo. He did not want to see Nasser because he felt that something was in the wind after Dulles' insulting withdrawal of aid for the Aswan High Dam. And Nasser did not want to see the Secretary-General because he was frightened that he might reveal too much of what he was planning.

However, Fawzi arranged for them to meet on condition that it was as friends and that they would not discuss current affairs.

With the nationalization Hammarskjöld was plunged into the heart of the negotiations at the United Nations. He tried to exercise his cool diplomacy in seeking a peaceful solution and he played a major part in the discussions between Selwyn Lloyd, Pineau, and Fawzi that led to acceptance of the six principles.

These were serious negotiations and Hammarskjöld wanted them to be held as quietly as possible. That was why he was furious with Krishna Menon's behavior. Menon considered himself the star of the first London conference. The Indian minister was, in fact, brilliant in defending Egypt's position in London, and when the crisis moved to the UN, he wanted to continue his starring role. He thought out his own solution to the Suez problem.

His method of operations was flamboyant, quite different from the civil-service methods of Hammarskjöld and Fawzi. He used to say of them: "Hammarskjöld is only a Swedish Fawzi and Fawzi is only an Egyptian Hammarskjöld." They used to groan when they heard he was on his way to the United Nations.

Fawzi kept up a constant stream of dispatches to President Nasser about the negotiations. One such dispatch, dated October 4, 1956, reported a conversation he had with Hammarskjöld in which the Secretary-General urged the Egyptian government to compromise in reaching an agreement. Fawzi quoted Hammarskjöld as saying: "I know Selwyn Lloyd and I feel that he wants to reach an agreement despite all appearances to the contrary."

Fawzi added: "Hammarskjöld rules out completely the use of force by the British, but he is not sure about the French because they have their internal troubles."

On October 9 Fawzi reported another conversation with the Secretary-General: "Hammarskjöld was worried about the arrival of Krishna Menon. He thought this would create confusion and he added that with Menon's arrival 'I am neither an optimist nor a pessimist.'

"I felt that everybody was fed up with Menon, and Hammarskjöld told me he had heard the same thing from Lloyd and Pineau and Shepilov."

Eventually Hammarskjöld dismissed Menon's proposals for solving the crisis because, he told Fawzi, "I found them confused and confusing and they opened the door for different and conflicting interpretations. . . ."

A number of the meetings of Fawzi, Pineau, and Selwyn Lloyd took place in Hammarskjöld's New York apartment where they held detailed talks about tolls, canal pilots, the rights of the Suez Canal Users Association, and whether the Israelis would be allowed to pass through the Canal. Hammarskjöld always pressed reconciliation and at one of the meetings he asked them not to take notes because after the previous meeting at which they had taken notes, they all had a different version of what had been said. He would take the minutes, he said. "But," Fawzi reported, "not all the delegates were happy with his minutes. And he said that if we did not like them, we could all take our own notes, read into them what we wanted, but we should only compare notes when it came to the drafting of an agreement."

One of the themes of Fawzi's dispatches was Hammarskjöld's conviction that Selwyn Lloyd genuinely wanted an agreement but that Pineau did not. In a message to the President dated October 13 Fawzi said Hammarskjöld was beginning to get worried. He was now sure that Pineau came with orders from the French government not to reach an agreement.

"With the Security Council resolution," he said, "Pineau feels that he is in a trap and he wants to get out of it by any way possible, and Hammarskjöld says that we should not give him that way out."

Hammarskjöld told Fawzi: "I am sorry Pineau is behaving this way. I think it is arrogant and dishonest."

He was no less forthright about Selwyn Lloyd. Fawzi reported to Nasser that Hammarskjöld thought the British Foreign Minister was "nice, sentimental, easily agitated, and without influence." Hammarskjöld was reassured by Lloyd's conciliatory attitude and he thought that once the six principles had been accepted, there could no longer be any question of the British using force although he thought at one time that the French would go it alone. He believed the acceptance of the six principles made it morally impossible for Britain to open fire on Egypt, and in the end he came to the conclusion that France would not be able to act without Britain.

It was Hammarskjöld who fixed the date of October 29 for the

Geneva meeting of Lloyd, Pineau, and Fawzi and that night he asked Fawzi to send a telegram to Nasser saying that he felt it was all over.

When the British and French launched their invasion attack, he was very bitter; he felt that he had been deceived. He was particularly hurt by the British deception because he had been reassured by Selwyn Lloyd's conciliatory attitude—although he did not believe that Lloyd knew what was going on behind his back while he was in New York.

And when a British delegate attempted to explain the invasion by using the Soviet Union's veto of the second part of the six principles resolution as a justification, he became even more bitter because the Soviet veto had been practically an arranged procedure. Everyone knew about it.

The end of the Suez invasion in early November brought the beginning of a series of disagreements between Nasser and Hammarskjöld. The invasion actually gave the Secretary-General the sword he wanted—the United Nations Emergency Force (UNEF). The problem from Nasser's point of view was that the sword was in Egypt, and while Hammarskjöld was trying to strengthen the United Nations' international role in Egypt, Nasser was striving to safeguard Egypt's sovereignty.

The first problem was the issue of the use of Canadian troops in the UNEF. Nasser did not want Canadians in the force because Canada was a member of the British Commonwealth. Prime Minister Eden had made a statement in which he referred to the Canadians, saying that although the British forces were going to be withdrawn, Her Majesty's troops would still be in Egypt.

Nasser said to Hammarskjöld: "I want neither Her Majesty nor her forces from anywhere . . . the Canadians wear exactly the same uniforms as the British and perhaps our soldiers will mistake them for British soldiers and they will shoot at them and that will create problems . . . Are they your forces or Her Majesty's?"

The second problem was the clearing of the Canal. General Raymond Wheeler, the United States Army engineer who had been appointed by Hammarskjöld to organize the clearing, wanted to use the salvage fleet the British and French had assembled at Port Said. Nasser objected violently to this, maintaining that these ships were part of the invasion fleet and their use would enable the invaders to retain some influence in Egypt.

The third problem was the status and the stationing of UNEF in Egypt. Hammarskjöld wanted a special status for the UN soldiers who, he said, were representing "all human society." But as far as Nasser was concerned, they were foreign soldiers stationed on Egyptian soil. He used to grumble at Fawzi: "Well, you talked about getting a sword—now we have got it."

The fourth problem was the return of Egyptian administration to Gaza. The Israelis delayed their withdrawal from the territory they had occupied for as long as possible, then hampered the Egyptian return by planting mines and plowing up the asphalt roads. They also wrecked Egyptian installations and blew up the oil wells.

Israel's right to use the Suez Canal always caused a certain amount of friction between the two men, and during one discussion the President said: "You are going to tell me all about your legal arguments concerning the passage of Israeli ships through the Canal. I am not going to let the Israelis pass whatever the cost."

Hammarskjöld was suggesting that a treaty should be signed concerning the freedom of navigation, with all the countries of the world participating under the United Nations. But the President said: "I am not going to agree. You want this so that Israel would sign, and I am not willing to agree to that."

Hammarskjöld at this time was obsessed with the safety of the precious documents and manuscripts in the ancient monastery of St. Catherine in the heart of the Sinai Desert. These documents include an original letter from the Prophet Mohammed to the Christian ruler of Egypt and Hammarskjöld was determined that they would not be harmed or looted by the withdrawing Israelis. He ordered a UNEF detachment to dash to the monastery to protect it. That seemed to be his prime concern in the Sinai.

But President Nasser was more concerned with the roads and the mines and the oil wells and the return of Egyptian administration to Egypt's territory. The Israelis took a long time to pull out of Gaza and General Burns delayed giving the green light to the Egyptian authorities to return. So Nasser ordered the military governor and the civil administration to move back without the permission of the United Nations.

During this period Hammarskjöld used to telephone Cairo at all hours of the day and night. He forgot the difference in time between New York and Cairo and he was waking people at three o'clock in the morning in his efforts to solve the problems that arose.

Eventually they were solved. British equipment was used in clearing the Canal but only on the understanding that no British, French, or Israeli personnel were to be involved, and Egypt insisted that the names of all subcontractors should be submitted to the Secretary-General himself because Nasser trusted only Hammarskjöld. Hammarskjöld sent a cablegram to Nasser asking him to facilitate the use of the British equipment and Nasser again agreed, on the understanding "that no individual or ship would enter Egypt without Egypt's permission." Canadian troops were eventually allowed to take part in the UNEF, but members of the Baghdad Pact were barred.

The status of the UNEF was defined in an agreement with Hammarskjöld's legal adviser Constantin Stavropoulos. It is important in the light of later events to note that Nasser stipulated that since the UNEF was coming to Egypt with the consent of Egypt, then it followed that the UNEF could not remain or operate except with the continuation of Egypt's consent.

In the aftermath of Suez, Nasser and Hammarskjöld met three times in Cairo. Then in June 1958 Hammarskjöld came back on a different mission.

Lebanon had complained to the UN Security Council alleging "massive, illegal, and unprovoked intervention" by the United Arab Republic in order to "undermine the independence" of Lebanon.

Egypt replied that what was happening in Lebanon was a purely internal affair caused by President Camille Chamoun's attempts to hang on to power unconstitutionally.

The United Nations sent an observation group to Lebanon to check on the accusations of infiltrators coming over the Syrian border, and Hammarskjöld submitted a report to the Security Council based on the observers' reports. In this report he said there was "no concrete evidence" of infiltration.

When the Secretary-General arrived in Cairo, he spent five hours with Nasser discussing the Middle East in general and Lebanon in particular. "I hope you noticed what was in my report," he said. "I feel that the situation is becoming very difficult again. Tension is high. But I do not want to complicate things." And he pleaded with Nasser with one of his favorite maxims: "Let us have less hot and more cold."

Hammarskjöld returned to this theme of calm and quiet in a novel way when he next visited Cairo. It was the fourth of September. In July American ground forces had landed at Beirut and British paratroopers in Amman and now they wanted to withdraw. But they wanted certain assurances before they withdrew, and

Dulles had asked Hammarskjöld to use his influence with Nasser to curb the propaganda war being waged by Cairo Radio. "Can we disarm the radio?" he asked Nasser.

Nasser refused point blank "because disarming the radio for me would mean complete disarmament. In this business I am facing the United States and they have a great number of weapons. They can give aid. They have got their secret activities. They have got friends among the Arab rulers. But who are my friends? Where does my strength lie? I want you to look at my problem.

"How can I reach my power base? My power lies with the Arab masses. I can only reach them through my position and my principles. Egyptian newspapers are banned from entering Lebanon and Jordan. Our embassies are besieged. The only way I can reach my people is by radio. If you ask me for radio disarmament, it means that you are asking me for complete disarmament."

(Nasser believed in reaching the people directly. He believed this to be the age of the transistor. Afterwards he proved his point in the Yemen. Following several setbacks there, he ordered the distribution of 100,000 transistor radios to the tribes. That connected them to the Voice of the Arabs and it had more effect than a whole division.)

The other proposition that Hammarskjöld brought with him from Dulles to ensure the British and American withdrawal was that there should be a resident United Nations Ambassador in Damascus. He started off this ploy by suggesting to Nasser that he would like "a presence" in Damascus. The President understood immediately what he was hinting at because the scheme had been rumored in the American press. There then followed what Fawzi described as "five minutes of conversation between the deaf."

Hammarskjöld was trying to reach his point without touching it directly—and Nasser knew exactly what he was about . . . Hammarskjöld suggesting his "presence" and Nasser affecting bewilderment: "But we have a permanent representative at the United Nations and you have an office here."

Hammarskjöld replied: "Yes, but we must strengthen that presence."

And so the deaf talked for five minutes before Hammarskjöld came out with his full proposition. Nasser refused on the grounds that to accept an United Nations Ambassador would set a very dangerous precedent. It would mean that he would have to accept a United Nations Ambassador to solve any problems he might have with other countries in the future. "I am not going to have a High Commissioner in the United Arab Republic," he said, "even from the UN."

Hammarskjöld tried to persuade him, saying that such a representative would not represent a power but would represent law.

Nasser replied: "I am not accused. I don't want a judge. If there is a question of law in my country concerning my behavior, then I shall comply with the law."

Not all of the two men's conversation was devoted to politics. Nasser discovered some replicas of Thot, with his ancient smile, and he sent one to the Secretary-General, through Fawzi, with a note saying, "I want that five-thousand-year-old smile to be with you in your home."

Hammarskjöld wrote a typical letter of thanks:

17.11.1960

Dear Mahmoud,

I have daily wished to get hold of you again in order to thank you for your lovely and generous gift: the ageless smiling little Thot will preside over my reactions to our present experiences in the mild light of your lamps.

It would be good to have another talk with you soon because this morning's dual bill gives rise to some serious questions—far surpassing the visible aims of the speeches. Do
you think we could fit a time together?

Dag

The statue was nice but Hammarskjöld was scandalized by Nasser's views on modern art. Nasser used to say: "I don't understand
it; anyone can scratch that stuff on a canvas." Their ideas on
Egyptian history and the Egyptian Museum were much more in
accord and the President enjoyed hearing Hammarskjöld talk about
the things he had seen in the museum. They kept their regard for
each other through all the crises and Hammarskjöld once wrote
a letter to Nasser in which he said: "I appreciate that you never
deceived me, and that you were sincere in everything you
undertook."

That mutual regard was, however, severely shaken during the
Congo crisis of 1960 by a sequence of events that left Nasser feeling betrayed and Hammarskjöld the target of violent attacks from
the non-aligned nations. Hammarskjöld had to face two dangerous
crises at the same time: the Congo and Khrushchev's personal
attack on him at the United Nations where the Russian leader
demanded that the Secretary-General must resign and be replaced
by a "troika."

The non-aligned nations were against him over the newly independent Congo because they felt he had sold out the Congolese
Premier, Patrice Lumumba. But they supported him in the face
of the Khrushchevian onslaught, because they felt that his resignation would destroy the United Nations as the center of power for
the small nations.

When Hammarskjöld was forming his African UNEF to try
to keep peace in the Congo, he asked President Nasser for a con-

tingent of Egyptian troops. Nasser was not keen. But Hammarskjöld sent several messages asking for his help and so, under
this pressure, the President agreed. He and some other leaders
contacted Lumumba and urged him not to ask any other nation
for help—the Americans were accusing the Soviets of interference
—as he was going to get a United Nations force to protect him and
his government, he must rely entirely on the United Nations.

But when the Americans staged the coup by Colonel Joseph
Mobutu against Lumumba, the UNEF was used in such a way
that the leaders of the African nations participating in the force
felt that they had been betrayed into taking part in the destruction
of the man to whom they had given their word. The UNEF command issued a series of orders that seemed to be directed against
Lumumba. Ghanian troops were ordered to seal off the broadcasting station and one of the men prevented from entering was
Lumumba himself.

At the same time, the Egyptian contingent was ordered to
close down the Leopoldville airport, an order that would have cut
off the capital from the rest of the country. But the Egyptian commander refused to obey, saying that he could not close the airport
against the wishes of the legitimate government.

When Nasser heard of these orders he decided to withdraw the
Egyptian contingent from the Congo. Hammarskjöld, learning of
his decision, sent a cable asking him to postpone the withdrawal
until they had discussed the situation when they met in New
York for the opening of the UN General Assembly.

The President agreed to this and Hammarskjöld persuaded him
not to withdraw the Egyptian force at that time. However, Nasser
warned the Secretary-General that he was going too far in the
Congo and that he should listen to the voices of the African
nations.

The trouble was that Hammarskjöld was being forced to listen

A PORTFOLIO OF PHOTOGRAPHS OF THE MAN
WHO LED EGYPT AND THE UNITED ARAB WORLD
—AND OF THE MEN AND EVENTS WITH WHOM
HE MADE HISTORY.

1. Gamal Abdel Nasser, described by the author as an activist, impatient with protocol, quick to anger, quicker to laugh, and possessed of the dream: a new high civilization for Egypt and the unity of Arab countries.

2. (*Authenticated News International*)

3. Nasser views the building of the High Dam at Aswan . . . the construction project that became the symbol of the struggle for Egypt and an important part of its current reality. Over the question of Aswan, the Egyptian President broke with John Foster Dulles and thus, to a considerable extent, with the United States, and demonstrated that Egypt would not bankrupt itself, as Secretary of State Dulles had predicted.

4. Sir Anthony Eden, then British Foreign Secretary, greets Colonel Nasser, then Egypt's Premier in an early and perhaps the warmest moment in their relationship (February 20, 1955). Nasser later said of Eden: "I can deal with someone I hate but not with someone I despise." (*Wide World Photos*)

5. *Suez* . . . the vitally important Canal, lifeline to nations, became the center of a crucial episode as Nasser broke it away from the hold of foreign powers. Israeli, British, and French troops fought to retake the waterway after Nasser nationalized it, the United States broke with its old allies, and the lives of politicians, diplomats, and the Egyptians themselves were never the same again. . . . Here, British soldiers and a tank move through the rubble of Port Said, November 8, 1956. (*Wide World Photos*)

6. Khrushchev, Nasser, and Tito. In one meeting with Khrushchev a misunderstanding occurred between the Egyptian and the Russian—an angry exchange occasioned by a mistranslation. Khrushchev insisted that if an interpreter "makes such a mistake in an important affair we must make him into a piece of soap."

7. UN Secretary-General Dag Hammarskjöld increasingly made Cairo a port of call, as he flew around the world in his efforts for peace. His missions into the turbulent Congolese and other situations and his "almost mystical" faith in the United Nations brought him into more frequent contact with Nasser than almost any other world figure.

8.   When Presidents Eisenhower and Nasser met for the first time and
began to talk, Eisenhower said that he had been drafted into politics;
Nasser said that he had volunteered. The Egyptian then asked who
Eisenhower thought would succeed him as President of the United
States. "Eisenhower said that he would rather not discuss it but he felt
that his choice could be deduced . . ."

9. Fidel Castro and Nasser met, although not often, and there was considerable respect on the Cuban's part for the Egyptian soldier who had helped to lead his countrymen into a revolution and a chance for a better future. *The Cairo Documents* and its conversations reveal the more frequent meetings between Nasser and Che Guevara, the death-haunted figure who was caught up in the success of Nasser's revolution and, temporarily, turned toward the independence movements in Africa.

10. Chou En-lai revealed to Nasser the reasons why he hoped the
Americans would not leave Vietnam and of what sort of "help" he
planned to provide the U. S. Army—in hard drugs—for their "welfare."

The relationship between the two men was at first interested, then
warm, and eventually troubled by such matters as the Chinese military
moves against India on India's northern border.

11. The long and stormy contest between East and West for the affections or at least allegiance and co-operation of Egypt seems to have been resolved happily here, as Nasser relaxes in a shirt-sleeve atmosphere with Kosygin, Brezhnev, and Mikoyan. (They are dressed for hunting at a dacha outside Moscow in 1965.) But neither the Soviet Union nor the United States would ever be content with the fierce independence, statesmanship, or bargaining powers of Nasser.

12. Richard Nixon, on a visit to Egypt when "out of power," viewed the Aswan High Dam (an opportunity for friendship lost in part by John Foster Dulles, Eisenhower's Secretary of State) and said, the author reports: "Today I have seen America's greatest mistake."

13. Nehru, the intellectual and visionary, philosophizing, hesitating, and Nasser, the man of action, had a father-son relationship, says the author. Increasingly, the "father figure" came to admire the younger, bolder man . . . at times alarmed by his capacity for decision and action, at other times deeply in need of it.

14. In a gesture symbolic of the warmth and depth of their relationship, Mohamed Hassanein Heikal (left), the author, takes the hand of
Gamal Abdel Nasser, the man who is the principal figure of his book
and to whom he was aide, confidant, and friend.

15. Nasser, who preferred mufti to military attire, strides across the soil of the Middle East, here in the village of Salamiya, Syria, in 1960. His photograph flaps on the rough wall of the dwelling.

16. Nasser (at Mansura for a festival celebrating the capture of Louis IX during the Crusades) with his people, standing out among them.

to too many African voices for his own comfort. The new nations were filling the United Nations. Many of their spokesmen were arriving in New York with the idea of building their own domestic political prestige by wild speeches rather than working for the international good. They were using violent language from the lectern of the General Assembly against the big powers and Hammarskjöld was fearful that if this continued, the big powers would prefer to deal with their problems outside the United Nations and this would deprive the small nations of their right to play their proper role at the UN.

Nasser tried to explain to him the problems of the newly independent states, how they were facing the threat of neocolonialism and the danger of corruption among the new leaders. Nasser was worried about the behavior of some of these men and he wrote to Lumumba warning him that the private behavior of these men could not be isolated from their public behavior.

So both men in their own ways were urging restraint on the new members of the United Nations.

However, that co-operation did not, in the long run, stop Nasser from pulling Egypt's soldiers out of the Congo. He finally gave the orders for withdrawal after a number of incidents which convinced him that they were being misused. He was particularly angry when Hammarskjöld sent a cablegram to Mobutu after Lumumba had been arrested, in which the Secretary-General said that he expected Lumumba would be treated according to international law.

Nasser learned of this cablegram and sent one of his own to Hammarskjöld, in which he complained "If I have not forgotten the situation, the United Nations troops went to the Congo while Lumumba was Prime Minister and they are still there now while he is under arrest—and yet they are doing nothing to protect him except ask for mercy for him."

Nasser finally decided to withdraw the Egyptian soldiers in February 1961. His point of view was that "We are not only the witnesses of treason. We are the tools of treason."

Hammarskjöld made no reply to the President, but he wrote to Fawzi saying: "The withdrawal of your troops from the Congo is a let-down for the UN and you are leaving the UN in the swamps of the Congo surrounded by crocodiles."

What made Nasser especially angry about the overthrow of Lumumba was the fact that he had urged Lumumba to accept the United Nations completely. There had been a situation where Lumumba wanted only African soldiers in the UNEF and was demanding the right to deal directly with each of the governments taking part. Hammarskjöld wrote to Nasser saying that the "United Nations belonged to all nations and making its work depend on one race or one continent or one colour, makes its task very difficult." Nasser backed Hammarskjöld in this matter and he sent a special messenger, Mourad Ghaleb, who afterwards became Ambassador in Moscow, to explain to Lumumba Egypt's own experience with the UN and Hammarskjöld. And Lumumba had been convinced.

At that time there were elements in Egypt who felt that Nasser was paying too much attention to the Congo crisis. Nasser defended his point of view in the Cabinet and to the other Arab leaders, saying there were three reasons why he had to play a part in Africa. In the first place, he had advised Lumumba to accept the UN. Secondly, he had advised him to have faith in Hammarskjöld. Thirdly, Egypt had soldiers in the Congo. So, he said, "I cannot stand aloof."

When the African leaders went to New York they held a meeting about the Congo and Hammarskjöld came under heavy attack. He was accused of betraying Lumumba and being part of the conspiracy against him. They accused the Secretary-General of being the tool of imperialism. Nasser defended Hammarskjöld, saying: "I have dealt with Hammarskjöld over Suez and I think the man is honest. The problem is that he is pursuing an ideal but that ideal is beyond the power of the UN. The trouble with Hammarskjöld is that he is driven by a dream that he does not have the means to realize." He told them the story of Hammarskjöld's sword and said that the trouble now was that the Secretary-General had the mandate to use the sword but that the sword itself was bending.

Despite the President's support for Hammarskjöld in private, both he and Fawzi were obliged to attack him publicly in the General Assembly. But even this did not shake the intimate friendship that had grown between Fawzi and Hammarskjöld. A typical example of the way they wrote to one another is this exchange of letters labeled "Personal and Confidential." Fawzi in Cairo wrote to Hammarskjöld in New York on October 27, 1960:

27th October 1960

Personal and Confidential

Dear Dag,

Although I left New York a week ago, Forty-Second Street and the East River [the location of the UN] is often present in my thoughts. Some of these are linked naturally with the Congo. We have also considered here in Cairo, where I arrived two days ago, an aspect of which you and I spoke together; and I wish to mention that Ghaleb would be available. He would eventually be succeeded by one who is familiar with the Congo and its current affairs and able to work in the same spirit as Ghaleb's. This arrangement would leave us with all the parallel advantage of [Ambassador Omar] Loutfi's wise co-operation at and around his present post.

As I write this, I smile remembering certain things, including Belgium's spite, according to the news, at "not being treated by the UN with the consideration due to an independent state."

One should be ready to do something about that, provided Belgium really pulls out of the Congo and stops playing there the kind of game she had earned some stern scolding for. This would be a short cut to the objective of unity and real independence for the Congo, and one headache less for all of us.

There is a lot more I am tempted to write to you about, but for the moment, I choose only the pleasant duty of thanking you again for your kind welcome, and send you with a batch of Cairo's sunshine many warm greetings from all.

Sincerely,

Mahmoud

His Excellency
Mr. Dag Hammarskjöld,
Secretary-General of the U.N.,
New York

The Secretary-General replied on December 3, 1960:

Personal And Confidential

3 December 1960

Dear Mahmoud,

It is more than a month now that you have had to wait for a line from me, in reply to your kind and helpful letter of late October. You may guess the reason: over and above the usual hectic conditions which make it difficult to switch over to the personal tone and line on which I would like to reply to you, I have wanted to wait until I saw a bit more clearly regarding the issue I discussed with you and on which you make some comments in your letter.

You will appreciate that quite a few important changes have taken place in the situation with which we were dealing when we met, none, alas, to the better. Leaving aside all sorts of specific events, like the seating of Kasavubu [President of the Congo] and its prelude and aftermath, I think in particular of the clear split regarding the Congo policy of the UN which has developed within the African world over the last few weeks. The choice of assistance which seemed to me obvious when we talked over matters has increasingly become a matter which we may wish to reconsider, not because I have in any way changed my own views regarding the man concerned, but because his name may have developed overtones which might reduce his usefulness and maybe even be a source of some embarrassment. In the circumstances, I have now reluctantly reached the conclusion that I have to look for another way to take care of my headaches here; if I still were a bit hesitant a week or a couple of weeks ago, the most recent step of President Kasavubu has naturally made things rather difficult.

Anyway, my need remains because we are too few in the present operation; however, that may be better than to introduce prematurely a new element in a delicate game which even a saint (in Mr. Khrushchev's terminology) would not find it possible to pursue with impartiality in a way which would not lay him open to suspicions.

If at all possible, I have to stick to the plan to go to the Union of S. Africa early in January. During the few weeks of my absence I intend to borrow Mekki Abbas from ECA as a short-term reinforcement but, of course, that merely is an emergency measure and does not present a solution to my lasting problem. I asked both him, [Andrew] Cordier, [Ralph] Bunche, and Wieschhoff to look for possible African candidates for recruitment to the Secretariat in general, but so far the results have been meager. I would very much appreciate any suggestions that you might make.

As time passes and madness flourishes, quickly and continuously changing the assumptions on which we first undertook our responsibilities in the Congo, our work is becoming increasingly complicated. On our assembly line of quarrels we have now passed the initial clash with Lumumba and consecutive quarrels with the Russians, the Belgians and Mobutu, seeming for the present to come back to a quarrel with Russians (which, of course, in no way means that things have been straightened out with the Belgians). There is very little understanding and response from the delegations to the problem in general, and my difficulties in particular, and I often regret not to have the possibility to get your wise counsel. But, at least, we do not give up and maybe we will last longer than this perpetuum mobile of circuses and quarrels.

Anyway Thot remains smiling and joins me in the warmest greetings to Mrs. Fawzi and yourself to which I would like to add my regards to the President whose visit here is still well remembered and appreciated.

Sincerely,

Dag

H.E. Mr. Mahmoud Fawzi,
Foreign Minister,
Cairo, UAR

At the time the African and non-aligned leaders were so critical of Hammarskjöld's conduct of affairs in the Congo, he needed their help to withstand the concentrated effort by Khrushchev to drive him out of office. Khrushchev virtually ordered him to resign and said that the Soviet Union would no longer deal officially with him. Khrushchev wanted that troika, one more malleable to the Soviet desire to run the UN.

Hammarskjöld, although saddened by Nasser's public attack on him, was pleased by his private defense and he thanked the President. He said that he was upset by everything the African leaders were saying about him. But now, he noted, "the United Nations is really in the balance. If I resign now as the Russians want, there will be no Secretary-General and the United Nations will be paralyzed. The United Nations, as we agreed in our first meeting, belongs to the small nations, its success depends on the small nations, and now even its existence depends on the small nations.

"If you and the non-aligned leaders tell me to resign, then I shall resign. I submitted my resignation during Suez in opposition to a big power but that was for a principle and not as a maneuver. But this time no big power is going to push me out."

When Nasser was in New York in September of 1960, he organized a meeting between Hammarskjöld and all the non-aligned leaders. The meeting was held at Hammarskjöld's apartment and he told them the same thing he had told Nasser: he was ready to resign but he would not be pushed out by a big power.

He was facing a hostile audience. The African leaders felt that he had backed down in face of President Moise Tshombe of Katanga. They felt that he had turned UNEF into something resembling the French Foreign Legion. Some of his commanders had been accused of attending secret meetings at which Kasavubu plotted to get rid of Lumumba. Fawzi had attacked Hammarskjöld for taking energetic measures over the killing of nineteen whites. Fawzi wanted to know if Hammarskjöld would have taken the same measures for nineteen blacks.

After that speech, the Secretary-General went to the delegates' lounge to find Fawzi to tell him: "This went to my heart. Why did you say what you did? It is unfair." Several days later a newspaper arrived in his office from Cairo with an article about the Congo that said that his hands were covered with blood. He showed Fawzi this article and asked him: "Do you believe that? Can you believe that?"

Despite all this, the African leaders decided to back the Secretary-General because they felt that a troika would divide the effectiveness of the UN into three parts and it would be paralyzed.

However, there was a sharp exchange between Nasser and Hammarskjöld in which the President said: "You are facing us with a very difficult problem. We don't want the UN will to be divided, but what is the UN will? You have told me that various things happened without your knowledge. You are not able to control what is going on. That is why we have to criticize you. We know you. We trust you, yet we cannot approve of what you are doing. You are asking for a mandate from us, and we are going to back you against the troika idea, nevertheless we feel that you are undertaking something you cannot control and we can blame nobody but you."

Hammarskjöld was delighted with the support of the non-aligned nations against Khrushchev. He needed their help because he had no intention of getting into the position where he could only survive by means of a United States veto of a Soviet resolution condemning him. His position would have been impossible. But with the non-aligned countries backing him, he was able to ride out the Khrushchev storm without appearing to become unacceptably indebted to the Americans.

However, he was dejected and hurt by the attacks of those same nations on him over the downfall of Lumumba and his apparent connivance with the Americans and the Belgians in the return of imperialism to the Congo.

These attacks grew fiercer when Lumumba was killed under the flag of the United Nations. Nasser accused Hammarskjöld of being guilty of the killing.

He was terribly affected by this accusation, and Nasser was convinced that when the Secretary-General flew to the Congo in September 1961 Hammarskjöld was going not only to mediate but also to clear his accounts with the non-aligned nations. And when, on his way to Ndola in Northern Rhodesia for cease-fire negotiations with Tshombe, Hammarskjöld's aircraft crashed into the jungle, Nasser felt that the Secretary-General had lost his life in proving to the non-aligned leaders that he was not what they thought.

When he heard the news of the crash, Nasser, who had accused Hammarskjöld of killing Lumumba, took an unprecedented step. He issued a declaration from the Presidency telling of his grief at the Secretary-General's death, and he caused a stamp to be issued bearing Hammarskjöld's picture, with the legend: "The Martyr of Freedom."

VI

Kennedy and Containment

On September 26, 1960, President Nasser had a busy day in New York. It was a time of grand affairs. The "Khrushchev session" was roaring away at the United Nations. The Congo and the "troika" crises were in full spate and the American presidential election was running strong.

At eleven that morning Nasser met Hammarskjöld. The Secretary-General was waiting for him at the door of the General Assembly and took him off to the little office he had behind the main hall of the Assembly. They talked about Hammarskjöld's problems for an hour and they missed nearly all of the Czech Premier President Antonin Novotny's speech.

Previously the British Foreign Minister Lord Home had seen the Egyptian Foreign Minister Dr. Mahmoud Fawzi and the two had arranged that somehow they should bring President Nasser

and Prime Minister Harold Macmillan together. Fawzi had stipulated that Macmillan would have to go to the Egyptian Delegation to meet the President because, after Suez, the President could
not take the first step and call on the British. Home agreed but said
that the two men ought to be introduced before Macmillan could
call on Nasser. It so happened that as the General Assembly delegations were arranged alphabetically, the United Arab Republic
and the United Kingdom representatives were sitting side by side
with only a narrow passage separating them. So Fawzi and Home
agreed that their leaders would be introduced as soon as Novotny
finished speaking.

Hammarskjöld and Nasser entered together. The Secretary-
General went to his desk and the President went to his empty
seat, which the British had been eying somewhat anxiously. Home
then went across and whispered in Fawzi's ear. Fawzi nodded.
Novotny, the last speaker of the morning, finished and everybody
rose.

Macmillan and Nasser came face to face. Macmillan stepped
toward the President and said: "Good morning, I'm Harold Macmillan." Nasser replied that he was delighted to meet him. And
that was how the leaders of Egypt and Britain started talking
again for the first time since Suez.

At four o'clock Nasser called on President Eisenhower at the
Waldorf-Astoria. It was their first and last meeting. Nasser was a
student of military history and he had always admired Eisenhower
as a military manager. He admired Field Marshal Lord Alan-
brooke as a strategist, Field Marshal Lord Montgomery as a traditional commander, and Generals Erwin Rommel and George
Patton as two imaginative commanders in their own theaters of
war.

The talk started with Nasser pointing out that both he and the
American President had military backgrounds but had moved into
politics. Eisenhower said that he had been drafted into politics

and Nasser replied that he had volunteered. They discussed the special session at the UN itself and Nasser stressed the importance of the UN to the small nations. Nasser brought up the Congo crisis current that autumn, including the harm he thought it would do to the United Nations. Eisenhower proved to be a very good listener. Then Nasser brought up the problems of Egyptian-American relations. "What we want most from America is understanding—which is more important to us than aid," Nasser said. He emphasized his gratitude for the position taken by President Eisenhower during the Suez crisis of 1956, despite the personal and political risks to Eisenhower himself. "By taking that position you put your principles before your friends."

They went on to talk about the presidential elections. Nasser spent most evenings watching the progress of the election campaigns on television at the house he had taken on Long Island. This seclusion had been forced upon him by the demonstrations mounted in New York against himself, Premier Fidel Castro of Cuba, and Khrushchev.

Nasser asked Eisenhower who he thought would succeed him as President of the United States. Eisenhower said he would rather not discuss it but he felt that his choice could be deduced. Nasser said he would find it difficult to decide if he were asked to vote. He felt that the Democratic nominee, John F. Kennedy, was the more youthful, more liberal candidate, but still, he told Eisenhower, he would vote for Richard Nixon because Nixon had been Eisenhower's Vice-President during the Suez crisis and Egypt could feel nothing but gratitude toward both men for the position they took in 1956.

Later, in fact, when Nixon, out of power, visited Egypt in 1963 —carrying a letter of introduction from his conqueror, President Kennedy—he was treated with all the honors and dignity of a Vice-President of the United States, although he was in the wilderness in America, virtually out of politics. He visited the High

Dam on that trip, and when he saw President Nasser afterward, he said: "Today I have seen America's greatest mistake. It broke my heart when I saw the Russian flag flying over the High Dam, and if it had not been for Dulles it could have been the American flag flying there."

Nasser left the Waldorf and returned to the Egyptian Delegation's headquarters. Nehru called on him at six o'clock to discuss the crises in the United Nations. Nehru was followed at eight o'clock by Tito on a similar mission.

And then Nasser rushed back to his house on Long Island to meet John F. Kennedy—on the television screen. It was the night of the first great debate on television between Nixon and Kennedy, when the two presidential candidates argued their cases before millions of people.

Khrushchev, incidentally, was convinced that Nixon would win, and with his memories of his own "kitchen debate" with Nixon in a display house at the American exhibition in Moscow the year before, at which Nixon had proved just as unyielding as himself, he was certain that the world would be involved in a long period of Cold War.

But Khrushchev was wrong. Nixon, badly made-up for television, did not do well in the debate, while Kennedy used the screen to great effect and "sold" himself to the people. Despite what President Nasser had told Eisenhower earlier in the day, he was convinced by the debate that Kennedy was the better man.

He was not alone, and it is probable that this first debate tipped the balance of the election against Nixon. Kennedy won by a very small margin, but it was sufficient and he then became the man that Egypt had to deal with.

John F. Kennedy came on the scene during the third of the four stages into which America's relations with the Egyptian revolution can be divided.

The first of these stages lasted from the night of our revolution in July 1952 until the day that Dulles learned about the arms deal with the Soviet bloc in September 1955. That was the time of Seduction. During these three years the United States tried to woo Nasser. But it was not a wholehearted seduction. Dulles told Hammarskjöld in 1956 that he thought Nasser had many sensible things to say when they met in 1953 but "he did not like the man himself." Hammarskjöld told Fawzi this and Fawzi reported it back to Nasser.

After Seduction came Punishment, a period that lasted from the arms deal until Nasser's quarrel with Khrushchev in 1958. Despite Eisenhower's support over Suez, Nasser felt that the Eisenhower Doctrine for the Middle East was aimed at isolating Egypt and so accomplishing the aims of the Suez aggression by peaceful means.

Dulles told King Saud in 1957 that "the Middle East situation is very explosive and the detonator in the middle of the bomb is Nasser, so the most important thing is to move quickly and quietly and lift him out of position."

Nasser knew all about Dulles' conversations with Saud because once again copies of them were brought to him by a believer in Arab nationalism.

One of Dulles' methods of punishment was particularly mean and unfitting for a great nation. In January 1957 Egypt was in need of medicines and antibiotics to treat the Suez wounded. All the country's sterling balances in the United States were blocked following the nationalization of the Suez Canal. So Egypt asked the American government to release sufficient funds to buy the essential medicines. But Dulles refused. And Nasser never forgave him for this piece of vindictiveness.

Containment followed Punishment. When Nasser and Khrushchev quarreled over Arab unity and the role of the Communists in the Arab nations, the Americans saw their opportunity to regain the ground they had lost. They had withdrawn from Lebanon and the British from Jordan in the autumn of 1958 just before Egypt's problems with the Soviet Union came to the boil over the attempts by the Communists to seize power in Iraq. This meant that there were no major problems outstanding between America and Egypt.

The Americans watched and listened but did nothing for some months. But then they asked the Egyptian government if there was anything they could do to help Egypt. They passed Public Law 480, which enabled them to send wheat to Egypt. And they helped quietly in various other ways.

This went on throughout 1959 and 1960. The United States was giving aid to Egypt but in an unobtrusive fashion. It was as if there was a breathing space in affairs between the two countries.

Such was the situation when the young, virile Kennedy took over the world's most powerful nation from the aging Eisenhower.

Nasser liked Kennedy's inauguration speech. The new President's reference to the generation that was born in the twentieth century and which understood the twentieth century caught his imagination and so did the phrase: "Ask not what your country can do for you; ask what you can do for your country." Nasser also admired Kennedy for the way in which he used university professors in his government. Walt Rostow made a special impact on the President, in a book which I gave him called *The Stages of Economic Growth*. Nasser ordered this book to be translated and distributed to every member of the Cabinet.

However, Nasser began to get reports that the Israelis were extremely happy about Kennedy's election and that Kennedy had given them secret pledges to supply them with arms.

In the last years of Eisenhower's administration the Americans had been very cautious, they watched Egypt's quarrel with the

Soviet Union, and they helped with the wheat and other forms of aid. They saw the force of Arab nationalism. And because of all this, the Israelis were not getting much military help from the Americans. One felt that Eisenhower was not swallowing all their arguments.

At the same time President Charles de Gaulle, anxious for Egyptian help in extricating France from Algeria had passed a message to Nasser saying that he wanted to build a new relationship with the Arab world. Before De Gaulle there had always been a special representative for Israel in the French Ministry of Defense. De Gaulle stopped that, saying that France was an independent country and would not allow special missions to be stationed at the French Ministry of Defense.

So, faced with reluctance from Eisenhower and a swing to friendship with the Arabs by De Gaulle, the Israelis became increasingly desperate in the search for weapons.

It was in this atmosphere that Nasser began to receive reports that Kennedy had promised to send the Israelis the weapons they wanted. So despite Nasser's admiration of Kennedy and his wish to explore the new Administration of the United States, there was some hesitation, some doubt in his initial dealings with Kennedy.

Nasser learned the truth about Kennedy's promises to the Israelis four years later from the West Germans. In 1961, when Adenauer paid an official visit to the United States, Kennedy put pressure on him to sell arms to Israel. It took a lot of pressure. But it was done. At Kennedy's insistence West Germany fulfilled his promise to Israel for him. And that was one of the things that ruined relations between West Germany and the Arab nations. Nevertheless, despite these reports, Nasser felt the need to open a relationship with Kennedy. And on February 20, 1961, just a month after Kennedy's inauguration, Nasser wrote to him the first letter in what was to become a continuing dialogue between the two men.

The occasion of the first letter was the murder of Premier Patrice Lumumba of the Congo. Nasser was terribly grieved and desperately angry over this brutal murder and the part played in it by the United States. His letter was diplomatic but it left the young American President in no doubt about his feelings:

". . . the United States bears a special responsibility in the works of the UN . . . the support of the United States for the UN is in many cases the decisive factor between failure and success.

". . . the UN failed in Palestine in 1948 because the United States did not give it any help, but on the other hand the UN scored a great success during the Suez crisis in 1956 because the United States stood by its responsibilities to the world organization regardless of the state of relations between the Egyptian government and the American government.

"It is a pity that we cannot describe the role of the United States played in the Congo in the same way as we can describe the role it played at Suez. At that time the United States stood by its principles regardless of its friendships. . . ."

Nasser was convinced of the United States' responsibility for the existence of the United Nations. He once made Hammarskjöld furious by asking him: "Show me the line where the United States ends and the United Nations begins."

Kennedy replied on March 2, 1961, in a letter forwarded by the American Embassy in Cairo. He was equally courteous and equally firm, pointing out that a new resolution sponsored by Egypt and supported by the United States had been passed by the United Nations since Nasser's letter was prepared and that the situation had been somewhat improved by its passage.

He defined the areas of general agreement between the two countries over the Congo which he said were:

(A) The United Nations must play a larger, rather than a smaller, role in restoring domestic tranquillity.

(B) The Cold War should be kept out of the Congo.

(C) Political assassination whether of Mr. Lumumba and his supporters, or, as more recently occurred, of his opponents at the hands of the Stanleyville group, should be equally and vigorously investigated and condemned.

(D) All assistance outside the United Nations framework to any faction in the Congo, whether of men, material or money, should be viewed with the utmost gravity and strictly interdicted. . . .

I would be less than frank were I not to note that, in our view, any recognition of Congolese factions instead of the legitimate government, which has been officially recognized by the United Nations, serves only to undermine the prestige and authority of the United Nations and bring closer the likelihood of civil war and accompanying outside intervention.

Your Excellency has stressed the "special responsibilities" which you feel rest on my government with respect to the United Nations. . . . We indeed accept in full our responsibilities under the United Nations Charter. I would suggest, however, that other powers, particularly influential uncommitted states, both singly and collectively have weighty responsibilities—and special opportunities.

The United States can take care of itself, but the United Nations system exists so that every nation can have the assurance of security. Those powers who must rely to a greater extent on this system as a means of preserving their integrity and independence should take the lead in making clear their unswerving support for the continuance of the United Nations operation in the Congo under its new corporated mandate.

Only by so doing can the immediate problems of the Congo
be resolved and the United Nations itself preserved as a major
constructive force for peace and orderly development in world
affairs. I welcome the indications of your personal support
for this pressing task.

I appreciate and reciprocate your expression of personal
good wishes.

Sincerely,

John F. Kennedy

This exchange of letters exemplified the way in which Nasser
and Kennedy were to go about the business of their countries'
relations with each other. Each crisis, every problem, all the agreements brought an exchange of letters between the two men which,
just like the meetings between Nasser and Hammarskjöld,
plotted a graph of the progress of their relationship. Sometimes
the graph was up, but it was often down.

It was up on April 17, 1961, when Kennedy wrote a letter of
introduction to Nasser for Henry Cabot Lodge. Egypt, because of
its quarrel with the Communists, had had trouble with its students in Russia. They were harassed and generally given an uncomfortable time. So when the Americans asked President Nasser
if there was anything they could do for him, he asked them if
the United States would take all the 240 Egyptian students then
studying in the Soviet Union into American universities.

The Americans were surprised and hesitant about taking such
a large number, but the transfer was arranged and the students
went from Russia to America. Lodge was traveling through Africa
as a representative of the Institute of International Education,
and as Kennedy pointed out in his letter: "The Institute was
particularly helpful in connection with arrangements for the students from the United Arab Republic who came to this country

in the fall of 1959 at the special request of the United Arab Republic Government."

So Lodge was welcome.

Kennedy went on to say: "Mrs. Kennedy deeply appreciated the invitation she recently received from your Minister of Culture and National Guidance to be present at the Pyramids for the inaugural performance of 'Son et Lumière.' It is a source of regret to both of us that prior commitments have denied Mrs. Kennedy the privilege of witnessing this beautiful performance in its lovely and historic setting. . . ."

But the graph was already going down while that letter was being written, for it was the time of the Bay of Pigs and Nasser, along with Tito, had come out full-blooded in support of Castro.

In reply, Kennedy wrote him a long letter dated May 3, 1961, in which he put his case:

There has, of course, been no question of intervention in the Cuban situation by the armed forces of the United States. Had this been the case, I believe you will agree there could be no doubt as to the outcome.

The tragic events which have taken place there are but another instance, of which history has many examples, of freedom-loving citizens taking up arms to rid their homeland of tyranny and oppression. Small groups of Cuban patriots, determined at all costs to restore the political independence of their motherland, did risk their lives against overwhelming odds. They were either killed, captured or escaped to join the resistance movement in the hills which is carrying on the struggle.

The United States Government will continue to do everything it can to assure that no Americans are involved in any actions inside Cuba. As freedom-loving people, however, Americans cannot remain unmoved by the plight to which their freedom-loving Cuban neighbors have been reduced, nor fail to sympathize with those who have resorted to force to rid their homeland of this tyranny.

As a revolutionary leader, Your Excellency is well aware of the forces which can move men and alter the face of nations. There have been allegations that those free men who sought through their own efforts to overthrow the Castro regime were hired mercenaries. It had been reported, however, that the final message relayed from the rebel commander when asked if he wished to be evacuated, was "I will never leave this country." This is not the answer of a mercenary but a patriot.

The ultimate decision in Cuba will be made by the Cubans themselves. I am confident with other Americans that with such spirit, the Cuban people will win the struggle for freedom.

The stated aims of the Cuban Revolution which brought Mr. Castro to power, and with which the majority of Americans could easily sympathize, have been betrayed. Cuba's prisons have never been so full of political prisoners. Without regard for due process of law, over 600 prisoners have so far been summarily executed and the toll is mounting daily. The violation of human rights in Cuba since Mr. Castro came to power has forced at least 100,000 Cubans to flee their homeland.

Genuine nationalist revolutions, such as your own, have prompted no similar distress. For example, of Mr. Castro's original cabinet, nearly twenty-three are today in prison, in exile or in opposition, one has been executed. The American people can never conceal their sympathy for those Cubans who are struggling against this ruthless oppression.

There has, indeed been intervention in the internal affairs of Cuba. An extra-continental power, hostile to the free world, has sought through use of the Castro regime to exploit the aspirations of the Cuban people and to achieve its own imperialistic objectives in the cold war. You may recall I said to the American people on April 20th that we do not intend to be lectured on "intervention" by those whose character was stamped for all time on the bloody streets of Budapest. . . .

Nasser replied to this letter with a long one of his own dated Cairo, May 18, 1961. After the opening courtesies he wrote:

Permit me to speak to you with an inspiration from a saying by the Prophet Mohammed, "Your friend is he who is true to you, not he who only believes you." In other words I believe that in the present circumstances, it is imperative that those concerned over the future of our universe should exchange views clearly and in all sincerity. I start off with this statement to release myself from the bonds of traditional diplomatic language. . . .

I had the opportunity of meeting Dr. Fidel Castro, Prime Minister of Cuba, twice. We had lengthy discussions, and I felt his sincerity in expressing the wish of establishing cordial relations between his country and yours which is their strong, advanced neighbour.

I felt, at any rate, that the difficulty in the relations between your two countries lay in the need for a more profound study of the problems of the peoples looking forward to the development of their independent life, when, in their history, comes the moment of revolutionary outburst, and in their attitude, the residue of the past is mingled with the hopes of the future in an atmosphere affected by the elements of resistance to the revolutionary change on the one hand and by the circumstances of the cold war and resulting world tension, on the other.

In such circumstances any attempt from outside adds to the complexity of matters; the best that can be done is to allow those peoples—with no intervention in their affairs— to organise themselves and trace the path before their own true will, and this they can do.

I had hoped that, having assumed responsibility, your government would have made a new attempt towards Cuba, un- affected by the psychological circumstances that had governed relations between the two countries in the period that pre- ceded your coming into power, particularly that we saw readiness on the part of the Cuban Government to respond to such an attempt. . . .

I find it my duty here to inform you that what I felt in the United Arab Republic and what many felt all over the world was that the United States was not far from the unfortunate events in Cuba.

We hardly had to strain ourselves to reach that conclusion; a mere glance at the American press or listening to official declarations by some senior officials of the United States Gov- ernment was enough to trace before us the extent of American intervention in Cuban events, and reveal the minutest details of that intervention.

You are no doubt aware that all this came as a tremendous shock to world public opinion; but, we feel—in all sincerity— that curing that shock does not lie in denying what had hap- pened; rather, the cure lies in facing it frankly with a view to avoiding its recurrence.

We greatly admired your moral courage in declaring that you bear the responsibility of the position adopted by the United States Government towards Cuba. Following that we saw a turning point that stemmed from what had once ap-

peared to us to be a rush of American policy towards an un-
avoidable open clash with the Cuban Government. Here we
also record with appreciation the non-intervention of the
United States Armed Forces in the Cuban events, and your
insistence in all your declarations on their non-intervention.
This attitude we believe has saved the situation in Cuba from
far-reaching deterioration and has saved world peace from a
tragedy which at first sight, seemed impossible to evade. . . .

But Kennedy had already left the Bay of Pigs behind him and
moved on. He was trying to get United States foreign policy moving again after the stagnation of the end of the Eisenhower era.
Like so many other American statesmen, he was attracted to the
Middle East. Its strategic situation, its oil, the Holy Land, all
combine to make the area important. It attracts statesmen like a
magnet.

Kennedy, looking for a foreign diplomatic success after the
Cuban disaster, came with new men and new ideas. He appointed
a new Ambassador to Cairo. He was Dr. John S. Badeau, head of
the Near East Foundation, who had been president of the American University in Cairo from 1945 to 1953. This choice was welcomed by President Nasser—despite his suspicion of Arabists—
because he thought that Badeau would know about the hopes and
the problems of the youth of Egypt.

Badeau arrived full of enthusiasm, and at his first official talk
with Nasser he insisted on talking in Arabic. The problem was
that he spoke classical Arabic with an American accent and the
conversation became somewhat confused until the President asked
him to change to English. Poor Badeau. He was rather hurt.
Nevertheless, he seemed to symbolize the new, dynamic Administration which had taken over in Washington, and President
Kennedy soon made his first move in the deadlocked Middle
Eastern game.

He wrote to President Nasser on May 11, 1961. It was a long, expansive letter expressing friendship and support for the Arab nations. He also took care to mention the various items of aid that the United States were giving Egypt. But the main burden of the letter was "the unresolved Arab-Israel controversy."

"I know deep emotions are involved," he wrote. "No easy solution presents itself. The American Government and people believe that an honorable and humane settlement can be found and are willing to share in the labors and burdens which so difficult an achievement must entail, if the parties concerned genuinely desire such participation.

"We are willing to help resolve the tragic Palestine Refugee Problem on the basis of the principle of repatriation or compensation for properties, to assist in finding an equitable answer to the question of Jordan River Water resources development and to be helpful in making progress on other aspects of this complex problem. . . ." And there was much more in a similar vein.

Nasser did not reply to that gambit until August 18, 1961. He apologized for the delay, saying that Kennedy's letter required too much attention and too much care for a reply to be rushed. In fact, the reply was delayed because there had been too much trouble in the Arab world that summer.

It was a very long letter, setting out the Arab position on Palestine and although it was couched in diplomatic language, it could have left Kennedy in no doubt about Nasser's views—particularly on American policy.

The true picture of the Balfour Declaration[1] promising the Jews a national home in Palestine was, said Nasser, "a fraud which any tribunal would condemn." It was a question of "he who did not own giving to him who did not deserve."

"It is too bad, Mr. President," continued Nasser, "that the United

[1] In November 1917 Foreign Secretary A. J. Balfour promised Zionist leaders British support for a Jewish home in Palestine.

States has put all its weight against law and justice in this case. And the cause of that was American internal factors . . . the effort to get the votes of American Jews in the Presidential elections was what affected most Presidents of the United States in their Middle East policies. I have read that your predecessor, Mr. Harry S Truman, when he put all his weight, and the weight of all his position and, *par consequence,* the weight of the American nation against Arab right, had no argument for those who tried to put a different point of view to him except to ask them simply, 'Do the Arabs have votes in the American elections?' "

He went on to talk about the way the Israelis had occupied large areas of Palestine under the United Nations truce of 1949, of the dangers of Israeli expansion and the way in which the imperialists were using Israel as a tool to work against Arab unity.

He was talking frankly, he said, and apologized if he had stepped over the bounds of diplomatic niceties: "We have tried and we are still trying to stretch out our hands to the American people. It is too bad that sometimes I find my hand hanging in the air. . . ."

As a result of the Communist arms deal, "relations between our two countries became stormy and there was an attempt to distort our nationalist policy and we were subjected to psychological warfare with radio stations directed against us, trying to break the people's will and weaken their support for the revolutionary government. The peak of that campaign was the withdrawal of the promise of aid for the High Dam, a promise which the American Government decided of its own free will to offer. The method of its withdrawal was something which the Egyptian people could not accept without reacting."

He traced the progress of United States-Egyptian relations, telling how much Egypt appreciated America's support during the Suez aggression and how he was puzzled by the failure of the Americans to re-examine their Middle East policies after the collapse of the Baghdad Pact in 1959.

"Let me appeal to your youth and your courage, Mr. President. The time has come for the United States to open its eyes to the events in our area . . . relations between the United States and the Middle East are far more important than any local election. . . ."

This letter could have been used by Kennedy as a textbook for dealing with Egypt. It spelled out all Nasser's basic principles: the illegality of the Jewish state; opposition to Israeli expansion and aggression; the maintenance of Egyptian independence; the cementing of Arab unity; and Egypt's wish to make friends with the United States—but not by giving in to pressure or relinquishing one iota of freedom.

Certainly Nasser was hopeful after the exchange of letters that there would be a new American initiative toward Egypt, that the new leader and his young men in the White House would adopt a more even-handed policy in the Middle East. But it was not to be. Kennedy's Palestine gambit was lost, like so many others, in the realities of events.

A month after Nasser wrote to Kennedy the union of Egypt and Syria was broken up after a coup d'état in Syria engineered by the "syndicate of kings." Damascus was the key to the Fertile Crescent and so King Saud of Saudi Arabia and King Hussein of Jordan, acting together despite their families' traditional hatred for each other, combined to subvert Syria. They concentrated on the desert troops and some politicians. Saud paid out huge sums of money and some of the men who were bribed then have become millionaires and are living in South America.

At that time it was said that Saud financed the coup d'état with £7,000,000 sterling. But that was not quite true. When he came to Egypt as a political refugee after his brother Crown Prince Feisal had forced him to abdicate, Nasser taxed him with this, saying: "How could you pay seven million pounds to those people?" And

Saud said: "I am ashamed to tell you. It wasn't seven, it was twelve million."

The government that Saud's money had put into power in Syria collapsed early in 1962 and some of the leaders were put on trial in what became known as the "Dandeshi case."[2] At this trial it was revealed that CIA agents had played a part in the kings' plot.

Nasser was tormented by the breakup of the U.A.R. It had been the first international expression of his dream of Arab unity and it was not revived in his lifetime. Therefore, when he heard of the CIA's involvement he was both hurt and puzzled. If Kennedy was making new approaches to him, then why was the CIA working against him?

Here, once again, we find the strange contradiction of interests that runs through American policy.

There are the oil companies and their private intelligence services. They have the CIA working in close co-operation with them. Then there is official United States policy represented by the State Department. There is White House policy. And, finally, the Pentagon with its own secret apparatus. The confusion is sometimes overwhelming.

Nasser hoped that Kennedy would bring order out of this chaotic situation, but there were times when he thought that the chaos was deliberate, that one arm of United States government would pursue a friendly policy calculated to act as a cover while another arm worked against Egypt's interests. He began to be suspicious of Kennedy's true intentions.

So, by the end of 1961, there was again a period of hesitation in relations between the two countries.

[2] Dandeshi was a Syrian politician who was tried for treason. During his trial, documents came to light proving that he and a number of other Syrian politicians were in contact with CIA agents who were preparing for a coup d'état in Syria, in collaboration with and under the direction of the Special Security Committee of the Baghdad Pact.

This hesitation coincided with the renegotiations of the three-year agreement under which the United States gave Egypt surplus wheat. This aid had been agreed through Public Law 480 when the United States, seeking to take advantage of the quarrel between Nasser and Khrushchev, had asked Egypt what aid she wanted. But now the agreement was running out and there were some senators in Washington who wanted to use its renewal as a means of exerting pressure on Nasser. He was particularly allergic to senators. He was constantly being asked by the American Ambassador to receive them, and when he did, they often revealed a complete ignorance of the Middle East and then went back to Washington and made speeches demanding, in effect: "Let us starve Nasser to death."

It was therefore unfortunate when Ambassador Badeau delivered a verbal message from Kennedy in November that Nasser considered a threat of blackmail. Kennedy pointed out that there was an arms race going on in the area and that he was under pressure from some senators who said that the United States was helping Nasser to buy arms. They argued that America's giving Egypt wheat enabled Nasser to use the foreign currency he should have used for buying wheat to buy arms instead.

This implied threat to cut off shipments of wheat combined with the CIA involvement in Syria increased Nasser's suspicions about Kennedy's intentions. He also felt that for Kennedy to send a threatening message at a time when he knew that President Nasser was facing a host of troubles was also lacking in ordinary decent behavior.

And so Kennedy's initiative seeped away, lost in the continual problems of the Middle East.

Throughout the next spring and autumn there were a number of polite exchanges between the two men. Nasser, for instance, congratulated Kennedy on Lieutenant Colonel John Glenn's orbital space flight. Kennedy wrote to Nasser, introducing Ambassador-at-Large Chester Bowles: "I hope that you would speak as frankly to him as you would to me about the questions which affect relations between our two nations, the Middle East in general, and the whole range of international affairs. He would be able to convey to you my views on all these questions. . . ." There was a letter from Nasser reiterating his theme: "All we seek and desire is understanding." And there was an exchange of good wishes over the anniversary of America's Declaration of Independence.

However, much was happening behind the diplomatic courtesies. Israel was always hinting at the sophisticated weapons she was producing, and so Egypt, feeling the need to depend more on weapons she had produced herself, hired a team of German scientists, headed by Professor Wolfgang Pilz, to develop rockets and aircraft.

These scientists were first contacted in Europe by Egypt's Intelligence Service and brought to Cairo. Their presence was only too well known. The Israelis sent parcel bombs to them. Professor Pilz's secretary was badly injured by one such bomb posted in Zurich. Their families were harassed. The daughter of one of them was kidnaped. And the Israelis raised a great international fuss about the "Nazi scientists" and "Nasser, the new fascist dictator."

Nasser could not understand the outcry. He told the American Ambassador: "The Russians have German scientists working for them. You have them working for you. So why shouldn't they work for Egypt?"

So, despite the parcel bombs and the propaganda, Egypt produced and fired its first test missile on July 21, 1962—a year after the Israelis had fired an adaptation of the French Gabriel rocket, which they claimed was used for research into the upper atmosphere.

In September Badeau went to see Nasser with another verbal message from Kennedy. He had three points to make:

1. Egypt had fired a long-range rocket missile and this was bound to accelerate the arms race.

2. A rocket is only a vehicle, and the normal load for a long-range rocket was an atomic weapon. So Kennedy wanted a pledge from Nasser that he would not try to acquire atomic weapons and, to ensure that pledge, America wanted the right to inspect Egypt's Russian-built nuclear reactor.

3. The arms race in traditional arms was becoming too dangerous and there should be an agreed limit on the offensive forces of both Egypt and Israel, which the United States would supervise.

But this move by Kennedy was also destroyed by the onslaught of fast-moving events. One month after this message was delivered to Nasser the Cuban missile crisis burst upon a frightened world. The Middle East was forgotten while Khrushchev and Kennedy fought their "eyeball-to-eyeball" duel and the rest of us wondered if the world was coming to an end.

Kennedy was anxious, however, that everybody should know what action he was taking and why he was taking it, and on October 22 he wrote to Nasser. His letter was short and very much to the point:

> The evidence that offensive nuclear missile bases have secretly been installed in Cuba by the Soviet Government is accurate beyond question. Moreover, extensive work is in progress for additional bases. Your Ambassador here will be briefed on the details. This Soviet action is being taken in direct contradiction of Mr. Khrushchev's statements, confirmed to me personally even a few days ago by Foreign Minister Gromyko, that only defensive weapons were being supplied to Cuba.
>
> You will recall that I stated publicly a month ago that "if at any time the Communist buildup in Cuba were to . . . become an offensive military base of significant capacity for

the Soviet Union, then this country would do whatever must be done to protect its own security and that of its allies."

An immediate nuclear quarantine, therefore, is necessary to prevent further offensive missile installations by the Soviet Government in Cuba. I trust also that this action will lead to the elimination of the offensive missiles already in place.

I have told Mr. Khrushchev that I hope we can resume the path of peaceful negotiation.

I am also requesting an urgent meeting of the United Nations Security Council. I have asked Ambassador [Adlai] Stevenson to present on behalf of the United States a resolution calling for the withdrawal of missile bases and other offensive weapons in Cuba under the supervision of United Nations observers.

This would make it possible for the United States to lift its quarantine. I hope that you will instruct your representative in New York to work actively with us and speak forthrightly in support of the above program in the United Nations.

The Department of State will keep your Ambassador informed of all developments.

John F. Kennedy

President Nasser replied to this letter on October 31. But events had moved so quickly that the danger was past and the world had begun to breathe again. The letter expressed Nasser's reservations about the American blockade and again left Kennedy in no doubt about Nasser's views on the gigantic responsibility that the United States bore for the whole of mankind:

It is with much concern that I received your letter dated 22nd October attached to your official statement to the American nation on the situation in Cuba. Indeed I do appreciate your effort to clarify the trend of American policy before those concerned about world development and preoccupied with peace issues.

I believe that now there is no longer scope for discussing the different views on the nature of the bases which existed in Cuba and roused your suspicion.

At the same time there is no longer scope to discuss the American measures based thereon.

There is no longer scope for such discussion which no longer has any bearing, for, fortunately enough, the concern of the peoples of the world for peace, their determined resolution to safeguard it, their efforts within and outside the United Nations as well as the wisdom, sound assessments and sense of responsibility which characterized the attitude of all parties to the dispute—all those factors make it better and more profitable to look forward to the future than to stick to the past.

Here I have to record a few observations:

FIRST. We appreciate your response to Acting United Nations Secretary-General Mr. U Thant's call, as well as the cooperation extended to him by the United States delegation to the United Nations. We still believe, and many peace-loving peoples share our belief, that sincere cooperation within the framework of the United Nations is the best guarantee of a sound solution to problems.

SECOND. We deeply appreciate the fact that the American measures—irrespective of our opinion of them—were carried out in a way devoid of aggressive incitement.

THIRD. We appreciate your promise not to invade Cuba militarily and we feel that this pledge was a genuine contribution to easing tension.

Here we would confidently declare our belief that the United States with her might and prestige can, more than any other, consolidate peace. In this respect she bears a historic responsibility before mankind as a whole, since peace based on justice is a human demand that precedes all others; for not only does it preserve but it also honours life.

Please accept, dear President, my best wishes,

Gamal Abdel Nasser

This was a crisis that Khrushchev never forgot. When he came to Egypt in 1965 he kept going back to it, talking about it, harping on it. It had left a mark on his soul.

Kennedy was dead by this time and Khrushchev, discussing him with Nasser, said that he had had much to offer while he still had much to learn. At the beginning, said Khrushchev, he had much hope for Kennedy, although, discussing their first confrontation in Vienna, he maintained that "Kennedy came into that meeting like a peacock and he left like a drowned sparrow."

Khrushchev was always bitter because people thought that Kennedy had made him back down over the Cuban missiles. "It's not true," he told Nasser. "We wanted to bring danger close to the United States so that we could extract from them a pledge not to invade Cuba. We did not plan to keep missiles there. We had an aim and that aim was fulfilled. The Americans promised not to invade. So all that American propaganda about the missiles is untrue."

Nevertheless, the way in which he kept going back to Kennedy and Cuba gave one the impression that the mark on his soul was very deep.

Despite the Cuban business Khrushchev retained his respect for Kennedy and one of the aspects of the Kennedy administration which pleased him was the way in which the young men surrounding Kennedy had brought the realities of nuclear power into the White House.

Khrushchev felt that President Eisenhower never really understood the realities of the Bomb, that to the old general nuclear weapons were just bigger and better cannons giving more and more fire power. Khrushchev was sure that if Eisenhower had understood the meaning of nuclear power he would not have allowed Dulles to go to the brink so often with his threats of massive retaliation.

While the world's attention had been riveted on Cuba, another crisis had sprung, full-grown and armed, from the stony desert of the Yemen.

The old Imam Ahmed of Yemen died on September 18 of natural causes, after having survived four assassination attempts. He was an extraordinary man, a fairy-tale character from the Middle Ages. He crushed Nasser's hand when they first met, treating the Egyptian President like one of the tribal chieftains he used to dominate by the strength of his grip. His rule in the Yemen was autocratic and repressive. There was no freedom of the press. But he used to read the Egyptian gossip magazines and the very first question he asked Nasser was: "Did that actress marry Omar Sharif?"

He really was a fantastic man, hung round with beads and bandoliers and daggers. There was kohl round his eyes and his face used to twitch, each muscle moving independently because of the qat[3] that he chewed.

He told Nasser about a coup that he had foiled. He had been imprisoned in his Palace when he saw a guard searching one of his maids.

"By God," he shouted, "women will not be searched as long as Ahmed is alive!" He jumped on a horse, galloped at the guards, seized a machine gun, and then started firing it into the air from

[3] A dangerous narcotic that induces stupor. It is used in Southern Arabia and East Africa.

the Palace tower. People saw him and started to shout: "The Imam has won, the Imam has won." And the coup failed.

He beheaded the leaders of the coup and, he said, hung their heads in a tree "like ripe fruits."

He and Yemen were anachronisms. Nasser used to tell the story of God coming down from Heaven with the Archangel Gabriel to see how the world had developed since he had created it. They roved round the world on a cloud and God looked down and said: "I don't know this place." "But that is England," said Gabriel. "How changed it is," said God. "I did not recognize it." Then they went to the Americas and God said, "Where's this?" "Have you forgotten?" said Gabriel. "Those are the two big islands you created at the very end." "But it has changed so much," said God. "Look what they have built." The same thing happened over Egypt when he saw the Pyramids. But then they came to a country that he recognized immediately. "This is the Yemen," he said. "It has remained exactly the same as the day I created it."

When Ralph Bunche was sent to the Yemen by the UN, he returned via Cairo and said to me, "My God, seeing the Congo, I saw the crime of imperialism. But when I arrived in the Yemen I thought that it was too bad there wasn't a little bit of imperialism there."

The old Imam was succeeded by his son, Prince Mohammed al-Badr, who was always used by the Imam on missions to Egypt. President Nasser wondered about him. He wondered if Badr would be able to lift the Yemen into the modern world—until one day Badr asked to see the Cairo zoo. He went with an official delegation and all went well until he discovered a qat tree that nobody else had recognized and climbed into the tree, sat on a branch, and chewed qat. When this incident was reported to Nasser, he wondered no more about Badr's capabilities.

Badr ruled for one week until he was overthrown by Colonel Abdullah al Salal, commander of the Royal Guard. He had this appointment despite the fact that he had been imprisoned for five years by the old Imam. Those five years he spent pinioned to a chain; food was thrown to him and his sanitary arrangements were limited to the length of ground he could cover on his chain.

Some of Salal's people came to Egypt to ask for the President's support in establishing a republican regime. They saw Anwar el Sadat, who was then Chairman of Parliament. Sadat wrote a memorandum about his meetings with the Yemenites, and it was decided to recognize them, send them advisers and give them some small arms.

Badr had escaped in a farcical fashion. Salal ordered his troops to surround the Palace, but when lunchtime came they all left their posts to eat and to chew qat. Badr rode out of a back door on a donkey and disappeared before the soldiers came back to take up their positions again.

There was considerable confusion. It was not known what had happened to him, if he was alive or dead and if he was alive, where he was. At that time his uncle Prince Saif al Hassan was at the United Nations where he was the chief Yemeni representative. Hassan flew to Saudi Arabia and asked King Saud for help, despite the long-standing enmity between their two families.

Saud was a frustrated man at that time. The men he had put into power in Syria had fallen and there was a republican revolution at his back door, so he readily gave help to the Yemeni royal family.

The Saudis set up arms dumps. Hassan raised the tribes, while Saud bought their loyalty with his oil money. Then Badr appeared from hiding to fight against the republican government. However, not all the Saudis wanted the royalists restored; three Saudi Air Force pilots flew their Fairchild transport aircraft to Egypt and asked for political asylum. These aircraft were loaded with arms and ammunition in boxes stamped with the clasped hands of the American aid program.

Nasser protested to the American Ambassador, saying that this was no way to give aid—that this was giving death, not friendship.

Saud grounded his Air Force after the defection of his three pilots and hired King Hussein's Air Force to supply the royalists. But exactly the same thing happened with the Jordanians. In one week the three Hawker Hunters of the Royal Jordanian Air Force stationed at Jidda were flown to Egypt by their pilots, led by the commander of the Air Force.

So many Saudi and Jordanian officers flew their aircraft to Cairo and asked for asylum that Ambassador Badeau began to ask Nasser: "What's the pigeon count today?"

However, the royalists gathered strength and captured Sada and worried the republicans in the capital of Sana by giving the tribes permission by radio to loot the city—a traditional way of paying off the tribes.

Nasser sent troops to the Yemen to sustain the republican government and was forced to send more and more as they were swallowed up in the wilderness of the country. He used to joke ruefully: "I sent a battalion to raise the siege of Sana and then I reinforce the battalion with a division."

Many different influences then came to bear on the situation. There was discontent in Saudi Arabia over the vast amount of money the King was spending on the war. The oil companies became afraid that the Egyptian Army was going to march on the Saudi oil wells. The British were worried about their colony of Aden. However, Saud still sustained the royalists, so Nasser decided to scare him. An Ilyushin bomber of the Egyptian Air Force was sent over his capital and bombarded his Palace—with flares. The Palace, ironically, was a new one where Nasser had been the first guest and it was named, after him, the Nasseriya Palace. When Saud came to Egypt as a refugee two years later he told Nasser how frightened he had been and how much he hated the Egyptians.

Because of this raid, Prince Feisal, who was now the real power in Saudi Arabia, went to Washington and asked the Americans to provide him with air cover to protect the country against the Egyptian Air Force.

Soon afterwards, on November 17, Kennedy wrote the first of a long series of letters to Nasser about the war in the Yemen. In it he set out his plans for ending the war and he sent identical letters to King Hussein of Jordan, Prince Feisal of Saudi Arabia, and President Salal of Yemen.

Kennedy wrote:

The key elements of the plan are (1) phased but expeditious withdrawal of external forces from Yemen, (2) termination of external support to the Royalists, (3) phased but expeditious withdrawal of forces introduced after the revolt in Yemen into the vicinity of the Saudi-Yemeni borders. In effecting the withdrawal I would envisage direct contact between the parties concerned, the good offices of a third party, or possibly observation or supervision of the disengagement process by the United Nations. My representatives will be prepared to discuss the modalities further.

I propose the following initial steps to be taken promptly:

(1) Issuance by the United Arab Republic of a statement signifying its willingness to undertake a reciprocal disengagement and expeditious and phased removal of troops as: (a) Saudi and Jordanian forces are removed from the frontier and (b) Saudi and Jordanian support of Yemeni Royalists is stopped.

(2) Reaffirmation publicly by the Yemen Arab Republic of its intention to honor international obligations, to seek normalization of and friendly relations with its neighbors, and to concentrate on domestic affairs; an appeal by the Yemen Arab

Republic to Yemenis in neighboring areas to be law-abiding citizens.

(3) Upon issuance of suitable statements as envisioned above and establishment of normal operating conditions for the United States Aid Mission in Yemen, the United States will immediately extend recognition to the Yemen Arab Republic.

While the disengagement envisioned is being undertaken, we would of course hope that none of the parties would engage in activities contrary to the spirit of this understanding.

I invite your urgent and immediate cooperation in this important task before the conflict over Yemen enters a more dangerous phase.

May God grant us all the strength and wisdom to pursue these important endeavors to their successful conclusion.

Sincerely,

John F. Kennedy

Nasser replied in a letter that he described as the first time he had allowed himself to discuss the problems of the Arab world outside its boundaries. However, he said,

I wish to assure you—immediately—that I have accepted without the least hesitation your constructive proposal to avoid clashes on the Yemeni border. This in fact was the basic aim behind the despatch of the United Arab Republic forces to Yemen.

We tried to avoid clashes peacefully through the several communiqués released by the United Arab Republic defining her policy towards the national revolution in Yemen. Foremost among these communiqués was that released in Cairo in the early hours of September 27th, stressing the necessity of avoiding foreign intervention in the Yemen's affairs and urging that the Arab people of Yemen be left free to shape their own will the way they chose.

Unfortunately, His Majesty King Saud misinterpreted the situation; he imagined the Revolution in Yemen to be a battle between the monarchical and republican regimes. With that erroneous impression, he launched himself with all his power and potentialities in an attempt to invade Yemen from the outside. . . .

It was, therefore, imperative to accede to the request formulated by the Arab Republic of Yemen for placing some of our forces at its disposal to help it face the fierce assaults. . . .

The Americans then recognized the Yemen Arab Republic in December and thus enraged King Saud and King Hussein. They felt that they were monarchs who had been sold out to republicans. However, the United Kingdom did not recognize the Yemen on the grounds that it had not proved its viability.

Kennedy formed a task force in the White House under Robert Komer, a former intelligence officer, to handle the Yemeni situation, a situation that rapidly became known as "Komer's war." It was Komer who secured the American fighter squadron as protection for Saudi Arabia.

Kennedy also sent former Ambassador Ellsworth Bunker to Cairo the following spring to talk to Nasser, and Nasser told him to tell the American President that the rumors that he was going to march on the Saudi oil fields were nonsense. "Tell the President," he said, "that I am not Hitler and I don't have a Rommel in the Yemen.

"It is a great compliment. But it is beyond our means. We went to Yemen for a certain purpose and we are ready to disengage. If the Saudi Arabians will stop their aid to the Royalists we will withdraw immediately. I don't want to keep any troops in the Yemen."

In February 1963 Dr. Ralph Bunche also came to the Middle East seeking peace in the Yemen as UN Secretary-General U Thant's representative.

The correspondence between Kennedy and Nasser over the Yemen went on for more than a year. The substance of it was that Kennedy was urging Nasser to withdraw from Yemen and Nasser was refusing to do so on the grounds that the Saudi Arabians were continuing their aid to the royalists.

On January 19, 1963, Kennedy wrote about Egyptian suspicions of American behavior over the Yemen and denied that the United States was pursuing a double policy. He went on:

> Perhaps more serious is a possible United Arab Republic feeling that we ought to be able to force the Saudis to disengage in Yemen. Once again let me say that we have been urging Feisal in his own interest to do just this. You are well aware, however, that it is not the United States method to bring forcible pressure on any Arab leader who is our friend. Nor would Feisal respond. At this moment he considers his policy toward Yemen as essential to maintaining the very integrity of Saudi Arabia. I am afraid that it is United Arab Republic and Yemen Arab Republic words and actions that have helped persuade him to this effect. Indeed each time we have felt we were making some progress toward disengagement, such actions as the Najran bombings have set us back . . .
>
> Similarly the United Kingdom hesitations about recognizing the Yemen Arab Republic spring clearly from their concern over Aden. Recurrent threats uttered by President Salal do nothing but heighten these fears. . . . I earnestly desire United Kingdom recognition but I am not in a posi-

tion to press the United Kingdom to recognize in face of unwise statements from Sana. . . .

I hope that this letter will help clear the air between us. Many people in both of our countries question whether good relations between us are really possible. I think they are wrong, but it is up to us to prove them wrong.

On March 3 Nasser replied to this letter, once again setting out the Egyptian point of view, and he added that he was sure of Kennedy's honesty over the Yemen: ". . . there were doubts as to the United States endeavors in the Yemeni problem. . . . My view—which I have personally explained to many of my companions—was based on the feeling that the emanation of the American endeavor from you personally should fully clear from our minds any doubts that the attempt was a mere political manoeuvre.

"My opinion was, and still is, that even if the United States sought a political manoeuvre, she hardly needed to involve the President of the United States personally in such an attempt."

The fact was that doubt was growing in President Nasser's mind about America's motives. Once again United States policy seemed to be divided. Ellsworth Bunker was in Cairo talking peace while "Komer's war" was being waged by mercenaries brought up from the Congo.

The following day Badeau called on Nasser. During this long meeting, according to his "Memorandum of Conversation," he drew Nasser's attention to the increasing Egyptian military involvement in Yemen and he suggested that this could lead to unfavorable Congressional action toward the American aid program.

"President Nasser," said the memorandum, "listened attentively and patiently to this long exposition." The President went on to explain that the U.A.R. had waited patiently for five months for the American-inspired disengagement to succeed and he argued that the military action he was taking was solely "to stop or make ineffective Feisal's support of dissident tribesmen." He insisted that "the purpose of the campaign was not a prelude to an attack on Saudi Arabia or a campaign to overthrow Feisal's government."

Badeau then urged Nasser to stop the attacks on Saudi soil particularly during the period of the Ellsworth Bunker-Ralph Bunche missions:

"After a thoughtful pause, President Gamal Abdel Nasser stated that he would agree to ceasing the attacks for the immediate future while the Bunker-Bunche missions were operating and that he would so instruct Marshal Amer. To obviate any misunderstanding, the American Ambassador replied, 'Then I may inform my Government that you will order the cessation of activities over the Saudi border such as the ones we have been discussing while the Bunche and Bunker missions are under way?'

"President Abdel Nasser confirmed this, but pointed out that that did not mean that the United Arab Republic would not consider remounting attacks when and if current disengagement efforts failed."

At the end of March, Ellsworth Bunker, having visited Feisal, presented the basis of a disengagement plan to Nasser. It included the use of United Nations observers and it seemed to have a fair chance of success. Nasser and Feisal agreed to it. But it failed because of continued Saudi support for the royalists which made it necessary for the U.A.R. forces to stay in the field.

Disillusion set in during the summer and autumn of 1963. Nasser began to feel that he was being double-crossed by Kennedy. He even began to feel that part of the American design was to get him more and more involved in the Yemen, with the Egyptian Army tied up in the desert wilderness. This involvement pleased the Israelis because so many Egyptian soldiers were facing the Saudis and not themselves. This advantage to the Israelis, the use of mercenaries, the failure of the Americans to make their Saudi friends stop arming the royalists all combined to make Nasser suspicious of Kennedy.

These suspicions went right back to the early days of Kennedy's presidency when Nasser had begun to hear the reports of Kennedy's promises to supply arms to Israel. They had been confirmed by an incident in September 1962, when Badeau went to see Nasser with a verbal message from Kennedy who wanted him to know about the Hawk missiles agreement with Israel.

The United States government announced the Hawk deal officially on September 27 and there were stories in various American newspapers that President Nasser had been consulted and therefore had no grounds for complaining.

Nasser felt then that he had only been told about the Hawk missiles in order to tie his hands. He felt it was a deceitful maneuver by Kennedy.

This background of suspicion did little to help the Yemeni problem. It also did little to help curb the arms race. Kennedy had suggested the inspection of Egypt's nuclear reactor, but Nasser refused, saying that the reactor could not produce atom bombs.

He felt that although Kennedy had come with new ideas, the young American President was trying to impose them by ruthless means and sometimes without any sense of direction.

By the time of Kennedy's assassination, relations between Egypt and the United States had begun to slip out of the period of containment into the period of violence.

Kennedy's last letter to Nasser in October 1963 demonstrated his irritation with Nasser's refusal to bow to his wishes:

> I must tell you of my own personal concern over the United Arab Republic's failure to date to carry out its part of the Yemen disengagement agreement.
>
> I think it fair to say that the Saudis are carrying out their

end of the bargain. Indeed, I gather the United Arab Republic shares the view of our own intelligence that arms supply over the border has been almost if not entirely cut off.

We are confident that the United Kingdom Government and the Saudi Arabian Government are honoring their assurances to us that they are not aiding the royalists.

I therefore have no leverage with Feisal when, having carried out his end of the bargain, he continues to see Egyptian troops in Yemen and hear expressions of United Arab Republic Government hostility from Cairo.

On the other hand, the United Arab Republic has not made phased withdrawals to a scale consistent with our understanding of the spirit of the agreement. While we think we understand some of the reasons, we cannot blink at the fact, which is becoming public knowledge, that the United Arab Republic is not carrying out a compact made with the United Nations, and in effect, underwritten by the United States as a friend of both parties.

Because of my own personal role in the matter, I think you will understand why I feel involved when the United States is criticized both at home and abroad . . .

And those were Kennedy's last words to Nasser, the end of a correspondence that lasted virtually from his inauguration until his death. It displayed the growing distrust between the two men. Kennedy did not believe in Nasser's genuine wish to leave the Yemen and Nasser had begun to distrust the whole of Kennedy's Middle East policies.

On Friday, November 22, 1963, President Nasser went to bed early saying that he was going to read. The first news of the shooting of Kennedy came in a news flash at 9:30 P.M. Cairo time. I telephoned the President. He was stunned. He kept telephoning for more reports and when eventually the news came through that Kennedy was dead, he was heartbroken.

He got up and dressed and went down to his office. But then when he got there, there was nothing he could do. "My God," he said, "why have I dressed, why have I come here? There is nothing any of us can do about it."

The Egyptian people were genuinely grieved. The whole film of the funeral was played four times over on Cairo television. It was a time of sorrow, for a young man who had promised much. But his relations with Egypt had long since lost their first promise. It is difficult to say what would have happened if he had lived. With America ruled by his successor, Lyndon Johnson, events marched inexorably to the time of violence.

VII

Johnson and Violence

President Nasser had an instinctive dislike for President Lyndon Baines Johnson. He did not like what he had heard about this Texas politician, the party man, the wheeler-dealer. This sort of politician was not to Nasser's taste. Also, like so many other people, he made Johnson pay for succeeding the murdered Kennedy. In the end this instinctive dislike, this allergy was proved correct.

When Nasser was dealing with any man, he used to gather a collection of photographs of him and study them, trying to assess his character. He would get as many as twenty-five photographs in different poses, maintaining that he could learn more about a man from those photographs than he could from a long report. He started to make a collection of Johnson's pictures. And two of them shocked him. The first showed Johnson with his feet up on his desk; the second was the famous picture of the American President showing off his operation scar. Nasser felt that these photographs displayed a rudeness and a lack of sensitivity. "How can the leader of the United States do that?" None of the reports or photographs reassured him. He felt that Johnson lacked experience in international affairs and was by nature a purely local politician.

Johnson came to power while three important problems still soured relations between the United States and Egypt: the Congo, Yemen, and the wheat deals. And over all there was the question of Israel and the supplying of arms. In 1964 President Nasser was involved with a number of important events. On January 13 there was the Arab Summit, convened to heal the differences in the Arab world. Out of this came the first real preliminary agreement to solve the Yemen problem and the setting up of a United Arab Command. There was Khrushchev's visit to Cairo in May—which did not please Johnson very much. There was the African Summit in July. There was another Arab Summit in Alexandria also in July. And there was the Non-aligned Nations Summit in October.

Nasser was busy throughout the whole year, and while all this was going on, he got the impression that Johnson was terribly unhappy that such events were happening without him. He wanted to be involved, he felt jealous that he was being left out. Two years later when Nasser was going to a non-aligned summit meeting with Prime Minister Indira Gandhi of India and President Tito of Yugoslavia at Delhi, Johnson was due to meet Southeast Asian leaders in Manila on the same day. Lyndon Johnson hated this because he felt that even a sideshow would detract from the impact of his big show, and so the Indians and the Egyptians were subjected to some pressure to postpone their summit. But the pressure did not succeed. Both events took place as scheduled. And Johnson was furious.

This conduct was typical of the man and when all those events took place in 1964—obviously with impact on American policy— he was frustrated because he could not influence them. The non-aligned conference discussed Southeast Asia and he did not like that. The United States was condemned because of its power politics and its part in the Cold War. He did not like that. During the African conference there was a violent condemnation of American policy over the Congo. He did not like that. Throughout 1964 he was either under attack or receiving unwelcome news coming from the general direction of Cairo. Three specific incidents occurred while he was conducting a campaign to be elected President in his own right.

In November, when the Americans mounted a big rescue operation for white hostages in eastern Congo, there were protests by Africans in several countries. In Cairo Congolese student demonstrators burned down the United States Information Service library—on Thanksgiving Day. The students, who had asked for permission to demonstrate against the landing of Belgian paratroopers from American planes in Stanleyville, were given permission, but they took the police by surprise. One of the students went into the library quite normally before the demonstrators arrived. He took with him three delayed-action incendiary devices. They began to burn just as the demonstrators rushed the building and the police were diverted between the fire behind and the crowd in front.

The building was destroyed. President Nasser was put in a very difficult position. He took the Minister of the Interior to task, saying that he had been proud that demonstrations could not get out of control in Egypt. There were a great many unpopular foreign visitors, but nobody harmed them. So how could this happen?

He said to the Minister: "How can I tell other people that this demonstration got out of control?" To disguise the fact that the police had lost control he was prepared to accept responsibility and even to be truculent about it.

When the American Ambassador, who was now Lucius Battle, went to him and demanded compensation and an apology, Nasser would give neither.

Johnson saw the Egyptian Ambassador, Dr. Mostafa Kamel, in Washington. He was angry. "How can I ask Congress for wheat for you when you burn our library?" he said. The thing that angered him most of all was a picture of the Stars-and-Stripes being burned.

The second incident was equally unfortunate. A private aircraft, owned by John Micham, a Texas oilman whom the President knew, was flying from Libya to Jordan. The plane had not received proper clearance to fly over Egyptian territory and so an Egyptian Air Force MIG fighter was sent up to intercept it and order it to land. But the radio in the oilman's plane was out of action; it seemed to ignore the fighter and flew on. The MIG was ordered to shoot it down and it fell into a swamp outside Alexandria. The Swedish pilot and an American representative of Micham's company were killed. That was just a month after the burning of the library.

The situation became very tense. The American Ambassador told Nasser that Johnson was personally upset because "First you burn his libraries, then you kill his friends." Johnson demanded that an American committee investigate the shooting, but he was told that he could only have an observer on the Egyptian committee investigating the incident.

The third episode came during negotiations for the extension of the supply of American wheat. The Minister of Supply was getting anxious about the grain and he asked the American Ambassador to call and talk about it. The timing of the meeting was unfortunate. It took place on the afternoon of the day that Battle had been to see the wreckage of the plane owned by President Johnson's friend. Battle was deeply distressed, and when the Minister offered him a glass of orange juice, the American refused, apologizing politely, saying that he was sorry but he had no appetite for it.

He also said that he thought it was an inappropriate time to press President Johnson about a supply of wheat. The meeting only lasted five minutes.

The following day, the twenty-third of November, President Nasser was traveling by train with all his Ministers to celebrate the anniversary of the Suez victory at Port Said. The Minister of Supply sat with Premier Ali Sabry and told him the story of his meeting with the American Ambassador. Sabry immediately went to Nasser and told him the story as if the Americans had completely refused to supply any more wheat. And the story that Nasser heard and repeated in his speech that day was that Ambassador Battle had said: "By God, I cannot discuss this at all because we do not like your behavior."

Nasser, of course, was enraged by the alleged remark and in his speech he attacked the Americans: "The American Ambassador says that our behavior is not acceptable. Well, let us tell them that those who do not accept our behavior can go and drink—" and he asked the audience, "From where?" And they shouted, "From the sea!"

"And if the Mediterranean is not enough to slake their thirsts," he added, "they can carry on with the Red Sea.

"What I want to say to President Johnson is that I am not prepared to sell Egyptian independence for thirty million pounds or forty million pounds or fifty million pounds. We are not ready to discuss our behavior with anybody. We will cut the tongues of anybody who talks badly about us. This is clear and this is frank.

"If we are now drinking tea seven days a week, we can make do with it on only five days. If we are drinking coffee five days, we can make do with four. If we are eating for four days, we can make do with three. We can tighten our belts.

"I want to say that we have troubles. We don't mind troubles. But we are not going to accept pressure.

"We are not going to accept gangsterism by cowboys."

It was a catastrophe. The President of the United States had been personally insulted in a public speech. The American Ambassador was shocked and when he saw President Nasser eventually and told him what had actually happened, it became clear that the story of his meeting with the Minister of Supply had become distorted. But the damage had been done.

Nasser felt that he could not trust Johnson and Johnson was bitter about a chain of incidents that seemed to be aimed at him personally.

The wheat deal was eventually renegotiated, but only for six months at a time—the Americans would send grain for six months and then leave off shipments for six months. Nasser said that it was as if they were writing a line, then omitting a line. However, Premier Aleksei Kosygin, at a time of shortage, diverted to Alexandria grain ships that were heading for the Soviet Union from Canada and Australia.

Nineteen sixty-five began badly. Relations between the two countries and the two Presidents were very tense. And they grew worse as the year went on. Nasser had a group of American and European friends and all told him the same thing: that Lyndon Johnson was frustrated and angry with Nasser. Robert B. Anderson, a former Secretary of the Treasury who came from Texas and was a friend of Johnson's, tried to explain to Nasser the mentality of a young man from Texas going out into the world to make his career in politics—but he only succeeded in making Nasser even more suspicious of Johnson.

These suspicions were increased still more when a British Army sergeant, Percy Allen, working in the War Office in London, sold Britain's contingency plans for the Middle East to an Arab diplomat.

The plans dealt with intervention in Egypt and every other country in the area, all based on the assumption of joint action with the United States. The American Sixth Fleet would work with the Royal Navy. American fighter and bomber squadrons would work with the Royal Air Force, etc.

On top of that, Premier Levi Eshkol, pressed in the Knesset about the defense of Israel, said that the American Sixth Fleet was Israel's strategic reserve.

None of these events helped to ease the situation.

However, Johnson, like Kennedy, had maintained a correspondence with Nasser. The Egyptian leader wrote to the American expressing his grief at Kennedy's death and Johnson wrote back, thanking him, on black-edged mourning paper.

Then, on February 17, 1964, Johnson wrote: "I have carefully read your extensive correspondence with President Kennedy and am struck by the degree of mutual respect and understanding it revealed. I sensed also a genuine will to move forward in areas where we could, while setting aside and working to limit the impact of those issues where we necessarily disagreed. For my part I would like this sense of growing confidence on both sides to continue, and to forestall the misconstruing of each other's policies which has marred our relations in the past . . .

"I would like to continue the frank and friendly dialogue that has already contributed to understanding between our governments. The next few years will be a strain on both of us, but the

United States and the United Arab Republic have so much to gain through good relations that we must both strive to maintain and expand them rather than letting our two nations drift apart."

This was written, of course, before those incidents of 1964 which so upset the American President.

Nasser replied to this letter on April 26. He welcomed Johnson's wish to maintain the correspondence and discussed some of the current events, pointing out that the Middle East was engaged in a social struggle, that the "freedom of the election ticket is tied to the freedom of the loaf of bread."

These were the opening shots in the Nasser-Johnson dialogue. The correspondence went on throughout the year. It covered the nuclear test ban agreement and space exploration, and there was an exchange of congratulations as each man was re-elected President of his nation. Johnson also sent a message to Nasser for the opening of the non-aligned nations conference on October 3 that revealed his antipathy toward the conference. And he sent Ambassador Battle with a verbal message about the Congo situation that virtually accused Egypt of helping the Russians and the Chinese to move into the Congo. This message said: "I believe African support of the rebel movement is based on an incorrect analysis of the nature and purposes of the rebellion, and is contributing to the reversal of the forward movement of African nationalism. Such support will inevitably serve the cause of the Soviet Union and Communist China by providing new opportunities to extend their influence in the continent. In the African nations' drive toward full independence, an objective with which we sympathize, we hope they will guard against alien influences whose ultimate aim is to subvert the independence of the whole African continent."

The letters reflected the growing estrangement between the two countries. Behind the façade of diplomatic courtesies, the time of containment was running out. The time of violence started on

March 18, 1965, when Johnson presented what Nasser understood to be an ultimatum.

Ambassador Battle sought an interview with Nasser at which he presented two documents. The first was a personal letter marked "SECRET" from Johnson to Nasser. LBJ wrote in his usual style:

> The best way to deal with difficulties . . . is to discuss them man to man, with full respect for each other's rights and responsibilities . . .
>
> The problem which needs this kind of discussion today is that of the best way of dealing temperately and responsibly with the growing arms race in the Middle East . . .

Then he got to the heart of his letter:

> Our position has been established within the framework of our traditional policy of restraint with regard to arms sales. The principles of that policy are two:
>
> First, we shall to the greatest extent possible, continue to avoid selling arms to the principal parties to the Arab-Israel dispute.
>
> Second, in no case will we sell arms that will give one side a military advantage over the other. This is the policy we have followed and will continue to follow . . .

However, the second long document, which was from the Department of State, told a very different story. It said that:

> The Israelis have been reacting strongly to what appears to them to be spiteful aspects of the Arab Jordan water diversion schemes, to the inflammable and belligerent tone of Arab

statements, to the United Arab Command buildup, and then to the cancellation of the German arms shipments.

As part of a continuing United States effort to reduce tensions, President Johnson sent the Honorable Averell Harriman and Mr. Robert Komer [of "Komer's war"] to Israel to calm down the Israelis . . .

These talks have eased the situation but basic problems remain and are still a potential cause of war. The Arabs appear concerned that Israel will make a military strike outside its borders. But Israel in turn is disturbed by statements attributed to some Arab leaders expressing an intention to wipe out Israel some day . . . because of such pressures we also feel that the Israelis may some day consider that they are forced to shift from a peaceful nuclear program to weaponry . . .

We reassured the Israelis that to the extent we agreed on the existence of a dangerous imbalance that cannot be corrected by arms from other sources, the United States would make a direct but limited sale of arms as an exception to existing policy . . .

The United States has been most reluctant to become a direct supplier of military equipment to any of the principal parties to the Arab-Israel dispute . . .

But our restraint has not been matched by the Soviet Union. While making massive supplies of arms to states in the area the U.S.S.R. has pretended that it is working for peace. At the same time the Soviets apparently believe that it is to their interest to use the Arab-Israel dispute to foment discord.

We regard arms rivalry as self-defeating since each side ultimately can match armaments obtained by the other, but always at the risk of provoking pre-emptive attack . . . Thus there is danger that one side will get a military advantage substantial enough to tempt it to launch a pre-emptive attack —particularly if that advantage appears to be declining.

The key to the shaky peace in the Near East, therefore, may lie only in preventing imbalances to categories of arms that might lead to pre-emptive strike . . . It means . . . that it may be in the overall international interest to accede to some arms requests in order to prevent conflicts . . .

In observance of this principle, the United States Government sold Hawks to alleviate Israeli apprehensions of U.A.R. bombers. For the same reason the United States Government now would be prepared to sell Israel limited types and quantities of arms required for their defense if assured of Israeli restraint . . .

The need of the United States to sell arms to Israel will, of course, be governed by what the Arabs do. It should be realized that if the Arab countries make a major issue of a limited arms sale by the United States to Israel this might provoke a public reaction in the United States that would jeopardize the United States Government's restraint and even-handed approach to the Arab-Israel problem. The Government of the United States has always resisted going as far as Israel keeps pressing it to go. If the Arabs exacerbate the issue they would undercut United States incentive to limit arms sales to Israel and would force the very polarization of the Near Eastern situation that the United States Government seeks to avoid . . .

It is important to understand that impartiality and restraint remain the basis of the United States' arms policy. Any United States sales of weapons to Arab states or to Israel will be the minimum dictated by the circumstances.

In this connection President Johnson wishes you to know

that we have agreed to sell certain arms to Jordan. We considered the Jordanian request carefully over a period of several months. Although the Arabs may not appreciate the danger, the alternative of Soviet arms in Jordan would mean a Soviet presence and influence in the area from which they have previously been excluded. Resultant dangers to stability of the entire Near East would threaten Arab as well as outside interests. The United States, therefore, decided it would sell arms to Jordan to prevent Soviet exploitation of the situation . . .

This communication appalled President Nasser. In the first place, there was the letter from Johnson appearing to say that the United States was not going to sell arms. But then attached to it was a document that first hinted that Israel was going to develop nuclear weapons, that America was going to supply arms to Israel, and then that if Nasser made a fuss about it, America would send even more arms to Israel.

He felt that he had been double-crossed and was then being blackmailed into keeping his mouth shut about the double-cross.

What made him even more furious was the way in which Johnson used Jordan in the blackmail. Because Johnson was giving an Arab country arms as well as the Israelis, Nasser was being forced into a position where he could not protest. The Americans could claim that they were being evenhanded, that they were giving weapons to both sides. But there was no parity between the arms they sent to Israel and those they sent to Jordan.

Nasser said that the Jordanians were being used as the "mohallel." Under Moslem law, if a man divorced his wife and then wished to remarry her, she must first marry another man. So they hire a Mohallel—a legalizer—to go through the ceremony with her.

In this instance, King Hussein was to play the legalizer in the American-Israeli marriage.

Events moved from bad to worse all that year. The wheat shipments were cut from six-month to three-month agreements and ill feeling grew. However, there were still many people trying to work out an understanding between Egypt and the United States. Kennedy had planned to make a big political push in Africa and the non-aligned countries, had he lived to enjoy a second term of office. One of the items that Johnson found on his desk when he took over the Presidency was a plan to invite Nasser to Washington in 1965.

This plan was revived in 1966 and Nasser was asked if he would like to visit Johnson. He said: "I cannot go now because the relations between Johnson and myself are tense, and if I went to Washington it would do more harm than good. I will be picketed and the Zionists groups will demonstrate against me and it will only make matters worse."

Eventually he agreed that Anwar el Sadat should go to Washington in February to meet Johnson in an effort to ease the arduous path of United States-Egyptian relations. It was arranged that Sadat's visit would be returned either by Secretary of State Dean Rusk or Vice-President Hubert Humphrey, to pave the way for Nasser to visit Washington in 1967. Sadat arrived in Washington with his wife, and Johnson and his wife, Lady Bird, went out of their way to charm their visitors. When Johnson met Sadat in the Oval Room at the White House, he pointed out a number of signed photographs of heads of state. Johnson was effusive: "I like you. I admire your country . . . I like President Nasser . . . Now look, I have a space here waiting for a picture of President Nasser. Why doesn't he send me one? Why do we make enemies of each other? We should be friends . . ."

Sadat then delivered a message from Nasser to Johnson. It was simple and short: "President Nasser has asked me to tell you that we want one thing. It's not that we want wheat or that we want aid. What we want, and we think it is the key to everything, is understanding. We don't want anything more than understanding. I have no other message. When I asked President Nasser what I should tell you, he said 'Tell him that all we want is understanding.'"

Johnson replied by saying that: "What we need is quiet diplomacy. Why does President Nasser stand up and openly attack me and the policy of the United States? I have always had quarrels with Lady Bird although we love each other. But we normally try to solve our problems in whispers and nobody knows about the quarrel. What I want to do with President Nasser is to solve our problems in a whisper." And all the time he was leaning toward Sadat and talking in a whisper. When Sadat reported this back to Nasser, the President called the American Ambassador and sent a verbal message through him to President Johnson. The note, addressed to the Ambassador, said: "I want you to understand two things. You know that we have a plan for development. We have big hopes but we have big problems and that is what makes us sensitive to any pressure because if we submitted to any pressure then we would be losing whatever we had gained. We cannot adhere to anything except our principles. That is why we are not going to allow anybody to put us in a situation where there is a contradiction between means and ends. We want to develop but we must do it with dignity. Otherwise we will find ourselves opportunists and opportunism either in individual relations or international relations does not help anybody achieve anything.

"Secondly, please tell President Johnson that I am not convinced by what he said to Sadat about quiet diplomacy and its uses. You have got money and atom bombs, riches and power without limit. These are your means. What have I got? The main weapon of the Revolution is its masses, the conviction of the masses and the mobilization of those masses. I have always been able to move those masses to defend themselves against any danger. The weapon of the Arab Revolution is the masses. So perhaps quiet diplomacy would suit the United States. But quiet diplomacy would not suit us because I would be cut off from the support of my masses. If I am to be ready with my weapon I must always be ready to talk to the Arab people. I must always explain to the Arab people. I must put all our secrets in front of them. Otherwise I would be facing battle without my weapon."

So Sadat's visit to Washington did not really make the path any smoother although Johnson still exerted all his charm to ease personal relations between himself and Nasser. When the Egyptian Ambassador to Washington returned to Cairo shortly after the Sadat visit he asked Nasser: "Can you give me a picture of yourself for President Johnson?" Johnson still wanted to fill the gap in the Oval Room.

But Nasser, who was not in the habit of giving pictures of himself, refused, complaining that Johnson was trying to confuse them with nice words which had no bearing on his policies. So the Egyptian Ambassador returned to Washington empty-handed. Two weeks later he sent a secret telegram asking for permission to return to Cairo to bring a personal message from Johnson. When he arrived, the message turned out to be a copy of Norman Rockwell's picture of Johnson, across which was written: "I hope to convince you that one day we can be friends. Lyndon Johnson."

At about the same time Nasser's daughter, Mouna, was visiting the United States with her husband. Johnson and Lady Bird entertained them at the White House and Johnson spilled over with charm: "You are a bride . . . I have a daughter who is also a bride . . . therefore I am like your father . . . come to the ranch . . . tell your father I want to be his friend . . ."

Nasser, who was a reserved man, could not understand this behavior at all. He wondered what it all meant. He felt that Johnson was giving him nice words but that American deeds were completely different from those nice words. So 1966 passed badly.

The fighting in Yemen still went on. The Americans were backing the mercenaries and the British ordered the RAF to attack Harib.

Then, early in 1967 there was shooting in Taiz in Yemen and the direction finders showed that two bazooka shots had come from the direction of the headquarters of the United States Point Four Aid Program—which was the CIA's cover organization.

Yemeni government forces attacked the building, seized it, and arrested the four people inside it. They opened all the safes and found an enormous number of documents, which were photographed by Egyptian intelligence experts. The Americans were furious at the attack on the building and demanded their documents back. They were returned three weeks later, but by that time their secrets were known.

During March and April of 1967 the situation between Syria and Israel became very dangerous. The Israelis were complaining about infiltrators from Syria, and Major General Itzhak Rabin and Premier Eshkol both threatened that Israel could occupy Damascus if necessary. There were troop movements, clashes on the border, and dogfights in the air.

At that time Sadat was in Moscow on his way home from a visit as head of a parliamentary delegation to North Korea. He met Kosygin on April 29 and the Russian Premier told Sadat that they had information that the Israelis had massed two brigades on the Syrian border.

Eshkol again threatened to occupy Damascus. This threat, combined with Kosygin's information, led Nasser to believe that the situation was getting out of hand. Egypt had a mutual defense agreement with the Syrians, who now felt themselves in danger, and so Nasser ordered part of the Egyptian Army to move into Sinai. He thought that the presence of Egyptian forces in there would deter the Israelis from attacking Syria. It was a purely defensive move designed to draw off Israeli forces from Syria. If Israel had attacked Syria, then the Egyptian Army would have carried out operations in support of the Syrians. But no offensive operations against Israel were envisaged.

The United Nations forces were occupying positions in the Sinai, so General Mohammed Fawzi, the chief of staff, wrote to the United Nations commander, the Indian General Indar Rikyhe, on May 16, telling him:

> I have given the order for the United Arab Republic's Armed Forces to be ready to act if Israel starts any aggression against any Arab State.
>
> To implement these instructions some of our forces have been mobilized on our Eastern Front in Sinai. To secure the safety of the United Nations Security Forces which are concentrated in checkpoints, I would ask you to remove those troops from the checkpoints. I have given my instructions to the commander of the Eastern Front concerning this. I hope to be informed.

It is very important to understand what Fawzi asked. He wanted only those UN troops in the checkpoints where Egypt confronted Israel across the border between Gaza and Elath to be removed so that there would be no clash between the United Nations forces and the Egyptian Army. He did not ask for the troops stationed at other points such as Gaza or Sharm el Sheik to be removed because there was no chance of a clash between the Egyptian forces and the United Nations where there were no Israelis on the other side.

Rikyhe transmitted this letter to the UN in New York where U Thant discussed it with Bunche, the supervisor of the truce agreement. Bunche's reaction was that the peace-keeping was integral; it was one entity and could not be divided. It was either all or nothing.

U Thant agreed and passed his decision to President Nasser. And Nasser said, very well, if you want to take them all out, take them all.

The Israelis say that there was a pledge that United Nations forces would not be withdrawn from Sharm el Sheik. There was no such pledge. Hammarskjöld did not give them one. They say that they got it from President Eisenhower when he was pressing them to withdraw from the Sinai in 1956. They say they have a letter from him saying that if they withdrew, he would see that the Straits of Tiran would not be closed to Israeli navigation.

But once the United Nations forces were withdrawn from Sharm el Sheik, it was reoccupied by Egyptian forces and the Israeli ships could not pass in front of them. So the escalation continued.

At the same time a number of people were working to restrain events. Kosygin, in Moscow, told Egypt's Minister of War, Shams el Din Badran: "We are going to back you. But you have gained your point. You have won a political victory. So it is time now to compromise, to work politically."

But Badran appears to have misunderstood Kosygin. He gave Nasser the impression that the Russians were prepared to back Egypt to the hilt. However, Ahmed Hassan el Fekki, the Under Secretary of State for Foreign Affairs, took minutes of the meeting with Kosygin, and after Nasser had made a speech in which he spoke of Russian support he sent the minutes to the President with a note saying, please read them.

U Thant came to Cairo with a plan that was said to have the backing of the United States. The plan was in three parts:

1. Israel would be asked not to send any ships through the Straits of Tiran to test the Egyptian decision to close them.

2. Other nations with ships passing through the straits would be asked not to send strategic materials on them to Israel.

3. The United Arab Republic would be asked to wait before it exercised the right of inspection of ships passing through the straits.

This plan, according to U Thant, would give everybody a breathing space. Nasser accepted.

Lucius Battle had been recalled and replaced by Richard Nolte as American Ambassador in Cairo, but he had had no time to present his credentials—in fact, he never did. But events were moving so quickly that Nolte asked to see Mahmoud Riad, the Minister of Foreign Affairs as soon as he arrived in Cairo. And on May 23 he gave Riad a message from Johnson to Nasser.

This message said that the "transcendent objective" was the avoidance of hostilities. On the same day that this message was delivered, the Egyptian Ambassador in Washington was called to a meeting with Under Secretary Eugene Rostow at the State Department. The burden of that meeting was the same: the avoidance of hostilities and the immediate stopping of war if it once started. Rostow said that the United States had told Israel frankly "that they would resist any attack against any Arab state."

At that time both Abba Eban, Israel's Foreign Minister, and General Attaron Yariv, Israel's Director of Intelligence, were in the United States. Yariv was sent because the Israeli military people were suspicious of their own government. There were elements in the United States who were fed up with Egypt and Nasser—especially after the attack on the CIA headquarters in Taiz—and it is said that Yariv was asked "what are you waiting for?" Certainly the Rostow brothers, Walt and Eugene, as well as Arthur Goldberg, America's permanent representative at the United Nations, were self-confessed Zionists.

On May 26 Ambassador Kamel was again called to the State Department. Eugene Rostow was waiting for him with a message from Johnson, which he wanted sent directly to Nasser. The Israelis had told Johnson that Egypt was going to attack that night. If the Egyptians attacked and fired the first shot, said Johnson, the United States government would adopt a very severe attitude toward Egypt. The United States government was not going to allow that to happen while the Secretary-General of the United Nations was conducting his negotiations.

At the same time, in Cairo, the Soviet Ambassador went to Nasser's house without an appointment. It was three o'clock in the morning of May 26. He asked for the President to be wakened. The Ambassador explained to Nasser that he had received orders from the Soviet leadership to see him immediately. He had to tell Nasser that the Americans had contacted the Kremlin and told the Russians that the Israelis had information that the Egyptians were going to attack at first light.

He said that if that was true, the Soviet Union urged the President not to go ahead with his plans because whoever fired the first shot would be in an untenable political position. As friends, they advised Egypt not to fire that shot.

Nasser replied that he had issued no orders for an attack, that there were no plans for an attack in the morning.

The following day he received Johnson's message from Kamel, and he was surprised by the whole business. It appears that Abba Eban went to the State Department two hours before his appointment was due and asked to see Secretary Rusk at once, saying that the situation was too grave for diplomatic niceties because "Israel is going to be attacked and destroyed today." He was actually in the State Department, still talking to Rusk, when Kamel was summoned by Rostow.

Nasser was astonished. He could not understand where the Israelis got their story, because there was no truth in it. However, in order to make his position absolutely clear, he made speeches on May 27 and 29 in which he said: "We are not going to fire the first shot . . . We are not going to start an attack." He thought that this was like giving a press conference to the world. He was making a public pledge to President Johnson and the Soviet Union not to start a war. It was also his reply to President de Gaulle, who had sent a message asking for restraint and who said he would base his position on who fired the first shot—and he did.

He thought he had made his position plain and devoid of misunderstanding.

On June 1 Robert B. Anderson came to Cairo with a verbal message from Johnson. The American President was disturbed by events and felt the need for more contact between Egypt and the United States. Nasser reminded Anderson that in a previous message Johnson had suggested sending Vice-President Humphrey to Cairo and he said that if the Americans were not ready for that, he was ready to send his Vice-President, Zakareya Mohieddin, to the United States. He pointed out that he had accepted U Thant's proposals for a breathing spell and he would use that time to send Mohieddin for talks with Johnson to try to work out a settlement. Anderson contacted Washington with this proposal, and it was arranged that Mohieddin would fly to America where Johnson would be waiting to meet him on Tuesday, the sixth of June. Mohieddin prepared to leave on Monday the fifth. He did not take off that morning. The Israelis throttled and broke the breathing spell.

However, while Nasser was being bombarded with peaceful words by Johnson and had reacted to his urgings by pledging not to fire the first shot, by arranging to send Mohieddin to Washington, he was still suspicious of America's true position. He felt that once again the United States was speaking with at least two voices. On June 3, just two days before the Israelis attacked, the Americans put on what Nasser thought was an unnecessary show of force. They sent the aircraft carrier *Intrepid* through the Suez Canal with all its planes lined up on deck. This made the Egyptian people furious; they lined the bank of the Canal and threw old shoes at the carrier. At the same time the Sixth Fleet flexed its muscles and made ready for a war situation. It added up to a flagrant show of power by the Americans.

At the same time Abba Eban reached an agreement in Washington that the United States would always keep the balance of power between Israel and the Arab countries, which meant that America would ensure that Israel was always as strong as all the Arab countries combined.

The agreement also said that in the event of hostilities the United States would not force the Israelis to withdraw from occupied territory as they had in March 1957 and would not permit Israel to be blamed in the United Nations. We know this is so from conversations with eminent American officials; it was also referred to, or at least strongly hinted at, by Israeli Foreign Minister Abba Eban in several of his public statements and by United States Ambassador to the UN Arthur Goldberg in some of his speeches. These extraordinary commitments by the United States to Israel seemingly bind America permanently to Israel's side whatever the merits or wrongs of all Israeli actions in the future.

Nobody knows what Yariv got from the Americans.

When the Israeli attack started, the Egyptian High Command was taken by surprise, and it fell apart under the impact of the Israeli air strikes. Marshal Amer was in the air, flying to Sinai to visit the troops there, when the waves of Israeli planes swept over

Egypt. He turned back and landed at Cairo International Airport to find that it had been bombed and nobody was there. He took a taxi and drove to the High Command's headquarters. There he started to receive the damage reports which showed that Egypt's Air Force had been practically destroyed.

When Nasser arrived at the headquarters the facts were hidden from him. He was not told the full extent of the damage, and the numbers of Israeli aircraft shot down were exaggerated. That night, when the full volume of the tragedy was eventually reported to Nasser, he was told that the Israelis could not have done it all on their own. The Americans must have helped them.

Nasser refused to believe this. He became angry and left the High Command saying: "I will only believe the United States took part if I am shown the wreckage of an American plane. Unless you can do that I will not accept it . . ."

On the third day of the fighting he was assured by men he trusted that two American fighters had been identified over Egyptian positions. The American insignia had been clearly seen.

He still could not believe that the Americans were taking part in the attacks on Egypt. But one hour after the American planes had been reported, the Soviet Ambassador went to see the President—again without an appointment. He was carrying a message from Johnson to Nasser sent via Kosygin.

The message said that two American fighters had been obliged to pass over Egyptian positions on their way to help the American communications ship *Liberty*, which had been attacked on June 8 by the Israelis. Johnson wanted Kosygin to convey this to Nasser as evidence of its truth.

But Nasser smelled a double-cross in all this. First of all, there were the American planes over Egyptian positions. Secondly, the message was passed through Kosygin so it was not directed at Egypt—it was directed at the Russians in an effort to neutralize

the Soviet Union, blinding them against an operation being conducted against Egypt. Third, he learned that the *Liberty* was a spy
ship that had been listening in to Egypt's communications and
deciphering them. Who knew where those decoded messages ended,
to whom they may have been passed?

So he began to see the shape of collusion. It was reported over
the American wire services that when Walt Rostow went to the
President with the news of the Israeli attack, Johnson turned to
Lady Bird and said: "We have a war on our hands."

To Nasser it appeared that Johnson was pretending surprise. All
his previous suspicions of Johnson came to the surface, and when
he combined these with the American overflights, the Kosygin
message, and the *Liberty*, he felt that it was impossible for the
United States not to have played some part in the aggression. He
did not know exactly how they were involved, but everything
pointed toward it and he reasoned that as we had not learned
the full facts of the British and French collusion with Israel until
four or five years after Suez, so American collusion could also be
shrouded in mystery. Another incident that aroused his suspicion
took place in the United Nations on the first day of the war.
America's representative Arthur Goldberg first said that the United
States did not know who had started the fighting—but then went
on to accept the Israelis' story that Egypt had attacked first.

Nasser was disgusted with Johnson. He felt that he had been
betrayed by honeyed words and that while Johnson had been sending him messages pleading for peace, the Americans had been
preparing to involve themselves in the Israeli aggression. So he
accused Johnson of collusion, broke off diplomatic relations with
the United States, and ordered all Americans out of Egypt. Several
other Arab states did the same. Soon Johnson, already angered by
the charge of collusion, had to watch the humiliating spectacle of

twenty-four thousand American men, women, and children being thrown out of the Middle East.

Johnson never forgot and never forgave.

It remained like that through the rest of the Johnson era. There was nothing but distrust and dislike left between Johnson and Nasser.

One day in 1967 (October 4) Mr. Johnson invited six ambassadors of Arab countries[1] to lunch in the Fish Room of the White House. He wanted to demonstrate that the United States was not completely cut off from the Arab world. It was later reported that when they sat down to eat, one of his pet dogs was in the room and that he played with it and fed it scraps while the Arab ambassadors were talking about the situation in the Middle East. Suddenly he said: "Gentlemen, let us not talk politics. Let's make this a social gathering."

And so they chatted further until, at one point, Johnson is said to have called the dog and started to talk to it, asking, in approximately these words: "What can I do? One man was so nasty to his neighbor that his neighbor was not able to stand it any more . . . so his neighbor took hold of him and gave him a good beating. What can I do to him?"

President Nasser's reaction to the report of President Johnson's conversation with his dog is best left to the imagination.

[1] Ambassador Abdul-Hamid Sharaf, of Jordan; Ambassador Talat Al-Ghoussein, of Kuwait; Ambassador Ibrahim Hussein El-Ahdab, of Lebanon; Ambassador Ibrahim Al-Sowayel, of Saudi Arabia; Ambassador Rachid Driss, of Tunisia; Ambassador Fathi Abidia, of the Kingdom of Libya.

VIII

Tito: Calculations and Balances

On September 28, 1961, precisely nine years before Gamal Abdel Nasser's death, his attempts to achieve Arab unity received a severe setback when the Syrians seceded from the United Arab Republic.

His friends, Josip Broz-Tito, President of Yugoslavia, and Jawaharlal Nehru, Prime Minister of India, felt his grief deeply and at the same time they admired his conduct. He refused to interfere militarily against the Syrian secessionists because he felt that this would mean Arabs fighting Arabs, something that was abhorrent to him, and that unity could not be imposed by force of arms; it had to grow, willingly, from the people. Nehru admired this refusal to use force because the shedding of blood was against all his principles; Tito admired it because he thought force would lead to international complications.

Tito, wanting to express his support for his friend in this time of trouble, suggested to Nehru that they should visit Nasser. Nehru agreed. And so, a month later, the three men met at the Koubbah Palace in Cairo where, like any other close friends, they sat reminiscing and discussing their problems.

Nasser told the others that he had been warned by Shukri al Kuwatly, President of Syria until the U.A.R. came into being, that it would be no easy affair to be joined with the Syrians. After Kuwatly had signed the agreement in 1958 setting up the U.A.R., he had turned to Nasser and said: "Congratulations, Mr. President, you don't know what you have inherited.

"You don't know the Syrian people. You have inherited a nation half of whom are politicians, another quarter consider themselves prophets, and an eighth of the whole nation think themselves Gods. You have got people who pray to God, people who pray to the Devil, and you even have sects who pray to a certain part of a woman's anatomy because they consider it the spring of life."

Nasser told Tito and Nehru that he joined in the joke and asked Kuwatly why he had not told him this before signing the agreement. But Kuwatly did nothing but laugh.

Nasser smiled wryly at the memory of Kuwatly's laughter. Nehru said that he too had his troubles: "I have got four hundred million Indians and that means I have got four hundred million problems."

Tito was not to be outdone: "I have seven complicated problems. I have got *one* state that uses *two* alphabets, the Latin and the Slav; which speaks *three* languages, Serb, Croat, and Slovenian-Macedonian; has *four* religions, Islam, Orthodox, Catholic, and Judaism; *five* nationalities, Slovenes, Croats, Serbians, Montenegrans, and Macedonians; *six* republics; and we have got *seven* neighbours."

So there were the three of them at a time of crisis, laughing together, drawing strength from one another, enjoying their solidarity. At the end of the fifties and the beginning of the sixties these men were like the Three Musketeers on the world scene. They were all so different. Tito was an atheist, Nasser was a Moslem, Nehru a Hindu affected by Islam. One came from Europe, another from Asia, and the third from the Middle East.

Nasser was the man of convictions and actions, Tito man of calculations and balances, Nehru man of intellectual articulation and hesitation. They were an unlikely casting for Porthos, Aramis, and Athos, and yet they behaved like the Musketeers: "All for one and one for all." Defeat for one was defeat for them all, victory for one was victory for them all. They rejoiced in each other's successes and commiserated with each other in failure.

They were the prophets and the statesmen of the concept of non-alignment, a concept they believed to be vital to the peace and the development of the world. Sandwiched between the superpowers of the Soviet Union and the United States and their certain—even if accidental—victims in a nuclear war, Nasser, Tito, and Nehru did not try to form a third bloc but strove to remain independent, hoping to settle international problems on their merits without regard to the policies of the Cold War powers. In this way they felt that they could bring pressure to bear on both Russia and America without bias, using the United Nations and the international rule of law as their weapons. "We are the conscience of the world," said Tito, "not its muscles."

Nasser and Tito first met in February 1955. At this time the Egyptian leader was preparing for the Bandung Conference, he was in conflict with the British over the Baghdad Pact, and he was searching for arms because it had become obvious that the Americans were not going to keep their promises to supply the weapons that Egypt needed. Events were moving. There was the scent of trouble in the air.

Tito had been on a visit to Nehru and the Indian leader suggested that he and Nasser should meet. So when the Yugoslav's yacht *Galip*—the Seagull—reached Suez, Nasser went on board and sailed with Tito to Lake Timsah.

It was a cordial meeting, but it lacked the warmth of their future friendship. They did not quite click. They were feeling one another out. Nasser was rather put off by what he considered the excessive protocol with which Tito was surrounded. Nasser still had ideas about the austerity of Communism and he was rather taken aback by Tito's way of life. Tito wore the uniform of a field marshal, Nasser that of a colonel. One of the things that Nasser discovered on this voyage was Tito's love of animals. Tito took him below deck and showed him the lion cub and monkeys that Nehru had given him. Nehru had also given him an elephant but Tito explained that he thought it safer to keep the elephant on an escorting destroyer.

They talked about world affairs, but nothing important occurred. It was essentially a meeting of reconnaissance between two men.

It was different when Tito returned to Egypt in December of that year. Nasser had pulled off his Soviet arms deal, he was vigorously opposing the British over the Baghdad Pact, and he was demonstrating his determination to be independent. Tito admired Nasser for all this. And Nasser in his turn admired Tito for the way he had stood up to Stalin. This time they clicked immediately and the concept of non-alignment as a power in the world emerged from their meeting.

To Tito, non-alignment meant the very existence of Yugoslavia. He spoke to Nasser of the Yalta Conference in 1945 when Stalin, Churchill, and Roosevelt were carving up the world into spheres of influence. The Americans allowed the Russians to have 100 per cent influence in one country, the Russians were conceding the Americans 100 per cent in another; they all had their slices of cake, but Yugoslavia was the slice they divided. Tito was convinced that this division of influence meant that any shift in the balance of power in Yugoslavia would lead to catastrophe for his country. The Russians would not allow the Americans to penetrate Yugoslavia and the Americans would not allow the Russians to enjoy the freedom of the Mediterranean through the Yugoslav ports on the Adriatic.

Tito felt therefore that non-alignment was not only Yugoslavia's way to peace, but also the very basis of its independence and its security.

The Egyptian attitude to non-alignment had emerged in a different fashion. There had always been talk of a neutral Egypt even in the days of the Nationalist party. Some members of the Nationalist party advocated turning Egypt into a Middle Eastern Switzerland. Their reasoning was that the big powers would support such a move because it would remove the Suez Canal from the danger of being caught up in any conflict.

One of the prominent men who put this policy to President Nasser was Dr. Mahmoud Azmi, a respected writer and politician whom Nasser later appointed Egypt's Permanent Representative at the United Nations (where he died of a heart attack in 1954 while defending Egypt's right to close the Gulf of Aqaba). Azmi's idea was that by declaring the country completely neutral, Egypt would be able to get rid of the British who were then still occupying the Suez Canal Zone. But Nasser argued that Switzerland was a special and different case. All the big powers had an interest in maintaining Swiss neutrality because of investments, communications, the International Red Cross, all those services which Switzerland could offer to countries that were only too often at war with each other and because conquering Switzerland would serve no useful purpose. But Egypt could not be so easily removed from conflict. Every big power recognized Egypt's strategic importance as the crossroads of the world and they would not allow Egypt to be neutral in the Swiss sense.

Nevertheless, Nasser was searching for a way out from between the two big power blocs. What he wanted to insure was Egypt's independence and by the time of this meeting with Tito, non-alignment had emerged as the best way for Egypt to remain independent. Nasser rejected all Dulles' blandishments to join the anti-Soviet pacts and at the same time he stamped on Communist attempts to acquire power in Egypt.

So the two men came to non-alignment by different routes. Tito had it virtually forced upon him by Yalta and the Cold War; and Nasser arrived at it through a process of logical inevitability which eliminated all other courses of action.

Curiously enough, Tito was just as afraid of the end of the Cold War as he was of its existence. He was afraid of the Cold War because of the dangers of a nuclear holocaust involving the whole world, and he was afraid of a *détente* between the Soviet Union and the United States because that could mean a world settlement imposed by the two superpowers that would benefit only them—a kind of nuclear Yalta.

The third meeting between the two men was the historic one at Brioni in July 1956 when Nasser, Tito, and Nehru met together for the first time, making the Kremlin suspicious and enraging Dulles.

Nasser went to Yugoslavia before Nehru, and Tito took him on an extensive tour of the country, showing him the nation's industrial and agricultural development. When Nehru arrived, the Egyptian and Yugoslav leaders were at Brioni to meet him. Nehru greeted both warmly, but he was worried because he had met a group of foreign correspondents at the Pola airport who, he thought, were making too much of the meeting. He had told them: "This is not a conference, it is a meeting of friends." Tito laughed at him: "Why do you try to diminish the importance of our meeting? Why do you deflate us?" But Nehru was truly worried. He said: "Those foolish correspondents. They talked about us as if we were another bloc while we are against all blocs."

However, in the end the meeting turned out to be more important, or rather to have more important events stem from it, than anyone then imagined. For it was on the way back from Brioni that Nasser received the news of Dulles' contemptuous withdrawal of his offer of aid for the Aswan High Dam, and the events that followed that radio message could hardly be more historic.

Brioni also had its extraordinary moments. One of them came at the start of their talks when Tito was reading to Nehru and Nasser the letters he had received from around the world about their meeting. They were nearly all letters of congratulations and good wishes. He came to one and said: "I have received this letter from a man who wants to come here and join us in our discussions and is even ready to join with us in non-alignment. I am not going to tell you his name because I want to see President Nasser's reaction."

And he handed to Nasser a letter in which the writer asked Marshal Tito to mediate the Arab-Israeli conflict. The letter writer added that he was ready to fly to Brioni to join the non-aligned group. Nasser read it and said, "Well, this *is* a funny beginning . . ." What made the letter not only "funny" but extraordinary in retrospect was that its author was Ben Gurion who, at that moment, was actively preparing for his onslaught on the Sinai in collusion with the French and, later, the British. Even at that hour, Nasser was able to demonstrate quite easily to his friends, not that it was really necessary, the impossibility of David Ben Gurion and his country ever being non-aligned.

One of the most important aspects of the talks was an effort by the three men to judge how Khrushchev would run the Soviet Union and how his policies would affect the rest of the world. Tito had been in Moscow around the time of the Twentieth Congress of the Soviet Communist party—the de-Stalinization congress in February of that year—and he was able to tell Nehru and Nasser about Khrushchev's famous speech attacking Stalin and the start of the de-Stalinization process. In fact, although it was not announced at the time, the possible world effects of de-Stalinization, was the second most important subject, after non-alignment, discussed at Brioni.

Tito knew about virtually everything that happened in the Soviet bloc. Nasser admired the way in which the Yugoslavs gathered and analyzed information, and Tito used to send Nasser and Nehru copies of reports that were of interest to them. He would write on them "interesting reading" and sign them. Tito also maintained a very close watch on the Vatican. He considered the Vatican a most important diplomatic and political post, and he thought he could obtain more important information about the West from the Vatican than from any other place. However, the Yugoslavs did not consider that Pius XII, who was then pope, was the real pope. They thought that the effectual man of power was Francis Cardinal Spellman of New York.

In these important talks, the future of the policy of non-alignment was mapped out. The friendship between the three men was sealed. But there was one aspect of Brioni that displeased Nasser and that was the elaborate protocol which he had disliked on his first meeting with Tito and that still enmeshed the Yugoslav President. Nasser's Chief of Protocol received from his Yugoslav counterpart a list of functions and the dress to be worn at them—a dinner jacket for one, white tie for another. This was hateful to Nasser.

He wore a dinner jacket just once, and the evening he wore it he begged Tito not to allow any photographers to take his picture. "I feel ashamed," he said. "I feel like a monkey." He also had a uniform as supreme commander of Egypt's armed forces but he could only bring himself to wear that once, after which he went back to wearing either his colonel's uniform or a civilian suit.

One evening when Nasser was entertaining Tito at dinner in Yugoslavia, the Egyptian Chief of Protocol, who had survived in his post from Farouk's time, prompted Nasser: "Mr. President, you will wait under this chandelier for your guest." Nasser asked why. "Because, Mr. President this is your place." Nasser asked: "But why do you fix me in one place? I don't want to stay here." The Chief of Protocol was puzzled: "Why not, Mr. President?" Nasser laughed and said: "Because the chandelier might fall on my head." That was a bad day for the two Chiefs of Protocol. They were both highly nervous. After Tito had arrived and been greeted by Nasser at the door, the Egyptian Chief of Protocol started to leave, walking backwards. He slipped on the marble floor and fell down. The sudden fall of such a dignified man made Tito and Nasser laugh, while the Yugoslav Chief of Protocol looked on the sprawling Egyptian with astonishment. But in one second he was beside him on the floor. He too had slipped—and there were the two Chiefs of Protocol, on the floor like romping schoolboys while their two heads of states laughed at them. That moment was the great fall of protocol. Neither Nasser nor Tito were bothered by it again.

They each had more important affairs to worry about. Particularly Nasser because the events that led to the Suez crisis had started to unfold before he left Brioni. And by then he was not just trying to keep his footing—he was fighting for survival.

Another meeting that affected both men deeply took place in July 1958, just before the overthrow of Nuri Said and King Feisal of Iraq. Tito invited Nasser to attend the fifteenth anniversary of the battle of Sutjeska. This was the battle designed by the Germans to annihilate Tito's partisans. The Germans had surrounded Tito's nineteen thousand warriors with six divisions. The battle was fought without quarter being asked or given. In the end the Germans failed. Although the partisans suffered heavy casualties, they lived to fight on and free Yugoslavia from the Nazis.

The battlefield became something holy. It was not touched.

When the partisans—thousands of them from all over Yugoslavia—gathered together again in 1958, for the first time since the fight, the battlefield was lit with campfires flickering on the faces of old comrades as they sang the songs that had given them heart in the bitter battle fifteen years before.

Tito sang with them and thus Nasser saw another aspect of Tito. He saw the partisan leader among his men. Nothing did more to strengthen relations between the two leaders than the time they spent on the battlefield of Sutjeska. The mood was very sentimental. Tito told Nasser of the partisan, a girl, who came to him during the thick of the fighting with a scarf on which she had embroidered his name. "How did you get this?" he asked. And she replied: "I bought it for you with a kilo of butter."

While the campsite for the celebrations was being prepared, the grave of Tito's personal bodyguard was found. He had been killed in the fighting and buried on the battlefield. Tito was told, and he and Nasser went together to pay homage at the grave of one man who had died fighting for freedom fifteen years before. Koca Popovic, the Yugoslav Foreign Minister, apologized to President Nasser for the emotion of the occasion: "Mr. President, please don't blame us if we behave like children. But life and death was decided in this place for all of us."

Tito talked to Nasser about his partisans and his problems in leading them out of war into peace, of turning his fighters into a cadre of leaders for the new nation. He also talked of his problems with Stalin, of how Stalin could not understand that the Yugoslavs wanted their independence, wanted to be non-aligned, and wanted to follow their own road to socialism.

He told Nasser how he had ordered an assessment of the Soviet attitude towards Yugoslavia very soon after the war. The result was an evaluation that said that Soviet policy towards Yugoslavia would be either opportunistic or hostile. Vice-President Aleksandar Rankovic had protested furiously at this, turning on the man who had made the assessment and asking him: "Don't you know who makes the policy of the Soviet Union?"

"Yes, I know," said the official, "it is Stalin."

Tito was forced to break into the argument and explain that he had asked for the study of Soviet policy to be made "regardless of who makes it."

Rankovic, the Stalinist, was later imprisoned for plotting against Tito. Nasser was shocked when Tito told him about the bugging of his home, a bugging so thorough that microphones were even discovered in Tito's bedroom. A few years later Nasser's own telephone calls to friends were being bugged by plotters in his own country. However, that is another story.

Stalin's lack of understanding and suspicion of Tito became embedded in Soviet thinking. Khrushchev was always highly suspicious of Nasser's friendship with Tito. One day when Khrushchev and Nasser were together, the Russian saw a picture of Nasser and Tito kissing one another on the cheek in greeting. "I know you are friendly with Tito," said Khrushchev, "but do you believe him?" The President replied: "Yes, I do believe him. I like him very much."

Khrushchev would have none of it: "He is a hypocrite. Whenever he kisses you, he gives one cheek to you and the other to the Americans."

Nasser defended Tito, then went on to ask Khrushchev: "Why do you tolerate me as non-aligned while you will not accept Tito's non-alignment."

Khrushchev was blunt: "Don't you know why?" Nasser shook his head. "Because," said Khrushchev, "if Tito succeeds, he will affect our bloc, but if you succeed, you will affect the other bloc."

On another night at Sutjeska Tito talked angrily about the way things were going in Yugoslavia. Although he did not agree with the way Milovan Djilas made his points in *The New Class*, he did agree with many of those points. He told President Nasser:

"I have heard about a case where a public employee took an official car eight hundred kilometers to watch a football match." He was worried about the money being spent on official functions and parties, about waste and high living. He said that he had told Stalin and was constantly telling his assistants that if the results of experience contradicted Karl Marx, he would obey the lessons of experience and not Marx. "I still tell my associates that I want more fertilizers and more tractors and less socialist slogans."

The Sutjeska episode was a happy and fruitful one for relations between Egypt and Yugoslavia. It ended with Nasser's dash to Moscow because of the revolution in Iraq and the danger of American intervention there, but the drama and danger of those events served only to cement the friendship between Tito and Nasser.

One example of this friendship was the voyage that Tito undertook to Africa and Asia for two months in 1958 when, at Nasser's request, he represented Egypt as well as Yugoslavia. It was a peace mission, a voyage to spread the gospel of non-alignment. Nasser said then: "Non-alignment is not a state, it is a trend, so that anybody who is a bearer of the idea can represent it."

Tito started his visit in December, passing through Port Said on his yacht, and when he returned two months later, he went to see Nasser and the two men traveled to Syria together where Tito was enormously impressed by the reception they were given. During their visit they were driving from Damascus to Homs when a blizzard blocked the road. Only the car containing the two presidents managed to get through the snow drifts into the small village of Yarek where they sought shelter in the first house. The owner of the house was out. His surprise may be imagined when he struggled back through the snow to find bodyguards outside his home and two presidents inside it. Surprised or not, he promptly slaughtered a sheep in their honor. Despite the blizzard, his neighbors learned of his guests, the word spreading until in a quarter of an hour twelve sheep were slaughtered and Tito had to appeal to Nasser to stop the bloodshed.

Altogether Tito and Nasser met more than thirty times and spent many hours together. One of the most enjoyable places where they used to meet was on Vanga, a little island behind Tito's villa on Brioni. Tito loved this island. It was there that he released the monkeys that Nehru had given him. He had filled it with animals and birds. There were royal pheasants strutting the paths. The local farmers, when they learned of his interest, went to the island and planted orchards and fruit groves for him. He had his own wine cellars and he delighted in taking his visitors into the cellars to drink his wine. It was his own private domain, and after I paid my first visit there I made the mistake of describing him as "the first Communist King." He may be a king in the way that he lives, but he is a Communist to the tips of his fingers. He pulled my leg about that description when we met the next time.

The discussions around the wine-cellar table on Vanga were long and fascinating. Nasser did not drink at all, Tito used to drink two whiskies a day on doctor's orders, and there was wine for the rest of the company. Nasser was eager to learn about the Yugoslav experience. There were ideological discussions, talks of the past, and hopes for the future. These were relaxed meetings among friends. Such meetings, talks, plans culminated in 1961 in the first conference of the non-aligned nations in Belgrade. Both Tito and Nasser were anxious about the success of the conference. International events were moving through an unsettled phase. President Kennedy was still new in his post, nobody really knew which way he was going; there was the Cuban fiasco; the meeting between Kennedy and Khrushchev in Vienna had done more harm than good; there was an escalation of fighting in Laos; so the signs were not propitious.

Tito wrote to Nasser on August 3 expressing disappointment

that some heads of state had decided to send only "their representatives or to refrain from participating at all."

He went on to say: "Intensive preparations for the conference
are being made and everything will be ready on time. I must confess that I personally did not believe that such voluminous pre-
paratory work would be required. . . .

"As was only to be expected, some great powers have not remained idle. They are already exerting pressure upon the heads
of individual non-aligned states in order to induce them not to
attend this conference or not to send their representatives to it.
This cannot, of course, be said only for one side but for both of
them. That was at least the case at the beginning. In my opinion,
precisely this fact is now preventing some heads of state from
coming personally to the conference. I believe that you know
whom I have in mind. . . ."

Two days before the conference was due to open, the Soviet
Ambassador to Yugoslavia handed a personal letter from Khrushchev to each of the fifty or so representatives to this conference.
The letters said that the Soviet Union was going to resume the
testing of nuclear weapons.

This news threw the conference into turmoil. The resumption
of testing was against everything the non-aligned nations stood
for. Nobody could understand why Khrushchev had first of all
decided to resume testing or, second, had announced his decision
to coincide with the conference, giving the news in such a pointed,
personal fashion.

Nehru joined Nasser and Tito while they were discussing the
new situation in the light of their policy of non-alignment. The
Indian leader listened to them, extremely agitated by the dangers
he saw stemming from the resumption of testing, then burst out:
"Non-alignment or no non-alignment—this is no longer the problem. We are now facing the question of peace or war. . . . It's
peace or war."

Tito and Nasser sat down with their foreign ministers, Fawzi and Popovic, and the four men analyzed the Soviet announcement, trying to get at the logic behind it. They could not understand why the Russians should set out deliberately to affront the non-aligned nations. Nasser opposed the Soviet resumption of nuclear testing, and its timing. He said he was "shocked" by the resumption and added that a mistake was a mistake whether committed by a friendly people or by one's opponents. The mistake of a friend should not be forgiven automatically. Eventually Fawzi and Popovic pointed out to their leaders a sentence in Khrushchev's letter: "History will prove later that this decision of the Soviet Union will be in the interests of peace." They came to the conclusion that Khrushchev was trying to impress on the conference that it was now or never. They had to make their influence felt now or they would never be able to again. According to this assessment, he was deliberately bringing pressure to bear on the conference so that the non-aligned nations in their turn would bring pressure to bear on the United States to come to a settlement of world affairs before it was too late.

Nasser, acting on the assumption that he had read Khrushchev's message correctly, changed his opening speech to the conference and said: "There is now no alternative for us. It is either war or negotiations."

He told the conference: "We must try to break the ice between the two powers," and he suggested that they should try to arrange a summit meeting between Kennedy and Khrushchev.

The conference agreed and adopted Nasser's proposal to send envoys to each of the two most powerful men in the world. Sukarno of Indonesia and President Modibo Keita of Mali were sent to the White House, while Nehru of India and Nkrumah of Ghana were sent to the Kremlin. They carried messages—which Nehru insisted on drafting—to Khrushchev and Kennedy asking them to meet and negotiate for the peace of the world.

"For the first time in history," said Nehru, "the least powerful are making demands on the most powerful."

They did not succeed in their mission, and relations between the Soviet Union and the United States degenerated over the following months into the Cuban missile crisis. Nevertheless, the determined attitude of the non-aligned nations over the resumption of tests must surely have helped to bring about the subsequent partial test-ban agreement between the Soviet Union and the United States.

After the conference Nasser was immediately plunged into the Syrian crisis and the division of the United Arab Republic. Tito wrote to him in sympathy and admiration on October 8:

> May I, first of all, congratulate you on the very wise and statesmanlike decisions taken by you in the grave situation caused by the military coup d'état in the Syrian province of the United Arab Republic. All of us are very much impressed by your decision not to intervene militarily against the rebels who are, whether they are conscious of it or not, the tools of the local reactionaries as well as of the foreign enemies of Arab solidarity. We are also impressed by your statement to the effect that you will not oppose the admission of Syria to the United Nations and the Arab League.
>
> These are, indeed, extremely far-reaching decisions, as you have thereby wrenched all the weapons from the hands of Syrian reactionaries and imperialist forces, which are attempting with their propaganda to deceive not only the Syrian people and the Arab world but also world public opinion as to the true nature and intentions of the coup d'état. . . .
>
> Allow me to convey to you my sympathies and sincere wishes, as well as those of our people for the achievement of full success not only in your just struggle for a better and happier future for your people but also in your fight against

all designs of reactionaries and colonial powers directed against your country and Arab solidarity in general.

There was a constant exchange of letters between the two men. The Cuban missile crisis, Yemen, the conflict between India and China, all were discussed in long, cordial letters, and they were usually in agreement on every point. Tito, for instance, fully supported Nasser's assumption of "a great burden in helping the revolutionary government of Yemen and I am wondering what we, and other countries, could do in order to ease your burden, that is to say, to help the revolutionary government of Yemen." The Indian-Chinese conflict was particularly painful to both of them. Tito wrote to Nasser on November 22, saying:

> . . . it is most important to put an end to armed action immediately and to start negotiations. It goes without saying that India should not be humiliated and that, on the other hand, China should also accept your suggestion concerning withdrawal to the positions held prior to October.
>
> I have sent to Prime Minister Nehru a letter in which I expressed the conviction that he would succeed in finding a way to ease the situation and would not permit further entanglements, liable to lead to extremely serious consequences and to a further complication of the already tense relations prevailing in the world. Owing to the specific character of the relations we have with one of the parties to the dispute, our activity cannot manifest itself to the extent we would wish. Nevertheless, we have considered it to be our duty to communicate to the representative of the People's Republic of China in Belgrade our views on their conflict with India and on the inevitable adverse consequences of its prolongation. . . .

Nasser set out his problems with relation to the quarrel between India and China in a long letter to Tito on February 12, 1963:

This dispute has, for the first time, faced us with a new problem, namely, that the danger of war on a large scale emerged all of a sudden between two Asian countries, both members of the Bandung Conference. They were even bound by the "pancha chila" (five principles) declaration as a path to peaceful coexistence before the Bandung Conference.

Our position towards the problem was most difficult. We felt without the least doubt that China had, premeditatedly or otherwise, committed a grave error, and that important world elements and even some local elements in India herself wished to seize the opportunity to shake India's faith in the policy of non-alignment.

In such an atmosphere, and despite our clear view of China's policy in the problem, we avoided releasing a statement strongly condemning the aggression so that the situation might not get more involved and we might not block the road completely before every endeavor was made to find a way out of the crisis.

Sometimes we felt that our position was criticized in India for various reasons ranging from lack of depth in viewing matters to an obvious desire to shake the policy of non-alignment. Fortunately enough however, Pandit Nehru— with whom I exchanged several messages in those days—saw matters with a strong clarity of mind and deep faith in the soundness of the logic of positive endeavors. The mere condemnation of the aggression in those circumstances was the easiest solution; to our mind it was a negative attitude with no bearing on the problems whatsoever. Yet I did not conceal my opinion from China in numerous messages I exchanged in that period with Premier Chou En-lai.

The cause of non-alignment was continually expressed in the correspondence between Tito and Nasser. Vietnam, the United Nations, Congo, nuclear testing—this was the currency of their letters as they preached the value, the necessity, of non-alignment to the world.

The second non-aligned conference was held in Cairo in 1964. Personally it was a sad occasion for them, for it was the first time they had met since Nehru's death.

It was during this conference that Premier Tshombe of the Congo arrived as President Kasavubu's representative. Efforts had been made to persuade Kasavubu not to send Tshombe, but he persisted. Tshombe's passport was presented for a visa at the Egyptian Embassy in Leopoldville, and naturally enough the visa was granted. It would not have been possible to refuse a Prime Minister a visa. But while it was not possible to refuse Tshombe the visa, Nasser was adamant that he would not be allowed to attend the conference. He was still sick with grief over the assassination of Lumumba and considered Tshombe a murderer. So when Tshombe arrived in Cairo, he was driven to a guesthouse and detained there.

Tito asked Nasser what he had done with Tshombe, and Nasser replied that he was being held in a guesthouse and would not attend the conference. Tito's first reaction was to ask: "I wonder what Nehru would have said if he had been with us." He knew that Nehru would have questioned the legality of Tshombe's arrest.

The memory of Nehru's questioning, of his intellectual morality, stayed with them, and they were always asking one another what he would have done if he had been with them. When Mrs. Indira Gandhi took over the leadership of India after Prime Minister Lal Bahadur Shastri's death in 1966, Tito and Nasser rallied to their old friend's daughter and traveled to India to show their solidarity with her in the troubles she faced immediately after she assumed power. There were no longer Three Musketeers—but they never forgot that they had once been three.

Tito demonstrated just how close they were during President Nasser's darkest days in 1967 when Egypt had lost most of her arms in the Sinai Desert. Little remained of the Army. The Air Force had been destroyed. Tito set out to do what he could to help rebuild Egypt's forces. He called a meeting of the Communist party leaders of eight East European nations in Moscow and urged the rearmament of Egypt. When the Russians were preparing to fly to Egypt their huge Antonov transport planes filled with MIG fighters and other arms, the Russians procrastinated, saying they had no landing rights in Yugoslavia where it was essential for the planes to refuel. Egypt's Ambassador in Belgrade explained this problem to Tito and he picked up the telephone and gave the order: "Open everything to the Antonovs; no restrictions; as far as Egypt is concerned I am no longer non-aligned." And the giant aircraft poured through Yugoslavia to Egypt, three of them arriving every hour in a massive airlift of a new Army and new Air Force.

Tito tried to do everything he possibly could to help Nasser. He came to Cairo in August 1967, then went to Damascus and to Baghdad to rouse Arab resistance to the Israelis and support for Nasser.

Early in 1968 Dr. Nahum Goldmann, president of the World Jewish Congress, went to Belgrade and asked Tito to mediate with Nasser in an attempt to reach a solution of the Middle East problem. Tito wrote to Nasser about this meeting: "I met him at his request and he talked to me about the situation in Israel and about the thinking of various people and groups there and I think this information may be of use to you." Goldmann told Tito that it was essential to solve the problem by a timetable, and it was necessary therefore to know quickly what the Arab side would and would not accept. He said that it was possible that a meeting could be arranged in New York at which Heikal could represent Egypt unofficially. Nasser turned down this suggestion and wrote to Tito refusing it.

"I said," replied Tito, "that I would keep you informed of what he told me." Two people were trying to get Tito to put pressure on Nasser at this time. One was Goldmann and the other was Lyndon Johnson. But Tito was too deeply committed to his friend Nasser.

The last big affair with which Tito and Nasser were concerned before Nasser's death was the overthrow of Alexander Dubcek of Czechoslovakia. I had traveled with President Nasser to Moscow in the summer of 1968 and as he never went to Moscow without calling on and talking with Tito, I took the opportunity of interviewing the marshal, too. He was worried about the troubled events in Czechoslovakia and I asked him: "What do you think about what is happening in Czechoslovakia in the light of what happened in Yugoslavia in 1948, when you had your famous quarrel with Stalin and you decided to maintain your independence?"

Tito replied: "Events in Czechoslovakia are of a different nature and we should not exaggerate or be theatrical about them. I don't think that people exist in the Soviet Union who would be so short-sighted that they would resort to force to solve a problem that is an internal matter for Czechoslovakia. There were moves that could be construed as pressure against Czechoslovakia, but we have heard today that the forces of the Soviet Union are pulling back and I do not think that the interference of one state or a group of states in the affairs of another state would be correct behavior. Moreover, I do not think there is any danger for socialism in Czechoslovakia, and if there is any danger, then I think that the socialist system in Czechoslovakia is ready to defend itself. It has got its socialist army, its socialist party, its working class, just as we have in Yugoslavia and we don't need anybody to rescue our socialism. Everybody can solve their own problems."

That interview took place on a Sunday morning and I flew home to Cairo to prepare it for publication in my Friday morning column. But on Monday morning I received a telegram from the editor of *Tanjuk* telling me that Tito had ordered the interview to be released in Yugoslavia immediately.

I cabled directly to President Tito pointing out that I was saving the interview for my weekly column in *Al Ahram,* which has the biggest circulation in the Arab world.

Tito replied: "Can you release the question concerning Czechoslovakia?"

I therefore arranged for just that question to be published in advance of the rest of the interview. Afterward, at Aswan, Tito gave me the reason for the rush: he knew of the Russian plans to invade Czechoslovakia and he wanted the warning contained in his answer to be released immediately. He had not wanted to seek out a newspaper correspondent specifically for that purpose.

Nasser, who had not believed that the Russians would invade Czechoslovakia, reacted mildly to the invasion. He made no violent denunciation, and Tito, who had wanted Nasser to be more severe, was not happy with Nasser's attitude. At Aswan he told Nasser: "We are non-aligned, we *must* state our position on these matters."

"You must see the realities of my situation," Nasser replied. "Part of my territory is occupied. I cannot be completely non-aligned. No nation which is partly occupied can be completely independent."

He asked Tito: "What if my relations worsened with the Soviet Union? What would happen if I attacked them over Czechoslovakia? It would mean that my position in the Middle East would be lost completely because the Soviet Union is my only hope of getting the arms I need to regain the lost territory. And if that happened, who would benefit from the situation? The Americans. Do you want them to benefit in the Middle East?"

And Tito replied: "No." This was one of those occasions when they both felt that the spirit of non-alignment had their hands tied.

Later Tito wrote to Nasser about the Czech situation and told of a meeting he had with the Russian leaders on April 30, 1968:

> . . . I volunteered to draw their attention to the grave results [of intervention], hoping that this would dissuade them. This was the same thing that I tried to do in my interview with Mr. Heikal when you were visiting us.
>
> The Czech leaders had assured me while I was visiting them that they were sufficiently strong to oppose the anti-socialist groups in Czechoslovakia and that they could defend the western frontiers of their country. They showed me clearly that they wanted to remain in the Warsaw Pact[1] and in Comecon[2] . . .
>
> I think that the Czechoslovak party and its government and leadership have the confidence of their people and that there is no danger of invasion of Czechoslovakia from the West or of a counter-revolution inside the country, because the counter-revolutionary forces there are very weak compared with the forces of the party, the Army, and the main bulk of the Czechoslovak people who have chosen socialism.
>
> As a matter of fact, socialism is not in danger in Czechoslovakia, but what aroused suspicion in some quarters was that the Czechoslovak leadership started to give a democratic touch to political, social, and economic development. This came at a time when the Central Committee of the Soviet

[1] A mutual defense alliance formed in 1955 by Bulgaria, Czechoslovakia, East Germany, Hungary, Poland, Romania, and the U.S.S.R.

[2] An organization formed by the Communist countries to centralize arrangements for trade, credit, and technical assistance. Its members are U.S.S.R., Bulgaria, Czechoslovakia, Hungary, Poland, Romania, the German Democratic Republic, and the Mongolian People's Republic.

Union took a contrary position and it is quite clear now that the road taken by the Czech party after the meeting of the Central Committee last January was not accepted by the Soviet Union.

The official pretext given for the military intervention and occupation of Czechoslovakia—that it was done to prevent counter-revolutionary forces changing the balance of power in Czechoslovakia—is, to my mind, false.

Yugoslavia was not informed beforehand about the military intervention in Czechoslovakia. As a matter of fact the Soviet Union informed the United States and other governments, including the Federal German Republic, that they were intervening not because of anything that would affect them but that it was an internal affair concerning only the Warsaw Pact countries. So the Soviet Union has given itself the right to use its non-acceptance of the internal development of a Communist country as a pretext for intervention.

This is something we would never have imagined, whatever the criticism between socialist countries. This is a blow not to the worker's movement and socialists alone but also to relations between peoples and world security and peace in the world.

Tito wrote of the Brezhnev doctrine:

It is very, very dangerous, and it is strange that now we are trying to make intervention legal, because it will be military intervention whether it has an ideological basis or not.

As far as Yugoslavia is concerned we will stand up against this doctrine. . . .

The Soviet Ambassador in Yugoslavia delivered an ultimatum to us because of our position over Czechoslovakia. He went so far in his ultimatum as to compare the position of

Yugoslavia with the position of the German militarists who are seeking revenge. I refused categorically to accept this ultimatum. I asked our Ambassador in Moscow to tell Mr. Podgorny that we would not accept any dealings outside reason and dignity. But until now we have received no reply.

One of the points that Tito made in this letter was that it was strange what the experience of Czechoslovakia had proved: "Even belonging to a bloc is no protection of national integrity and sovereignty."

In Nasser's discussions with Tito, the Yugoslav always gave his assistants the chance to speak. He used to say: "I want to train them to think while I am still alive. I don't want to be imprisoned in my own ideas." And one day he said: "I feel that everybody outside Yugoslavia and many elements inside Yugoslavia are asking what comes after Tito? But I am myself working for what comes after Tito. The West is putting its hopes in the youth of Yugoslavia. The East is putting its hopes in the Army. But I am going to foil both of them while I am alive."

On another occasion he turned to President Nasser and said: "I envy you. You started young. You attained power when you were only thirty-three. Normally one sees the results of one's work after twenty-five or thirty years. Unfortunately I will not live to see the result of what I did, but you are going to live to see the results of your work."

Alas, this was a prophecy that was not to be fulfilled. Only one of the Three Musketeers is left now.

IX

Nehru: Intellectual Hesitations

When Gamal Abdel Nasser and Pandit Nehru met for the first time in 1955 they had a deep and instantaneous effect on one another. It was rather like a man looking across a crowded room and falling in love with a woman he has never seen before. The bond between Nasser and Nehru was as immediate and as strong as that.

As in so many cases, this bond was formed between two people who were totally dissimilar. Nasser was big and strong, a man of action. Nehru was slight and fragile, a man of thought.

I believe that before they met Nehru had a limited interest in Nasser—a strategic interest—because this was the time of talk about a pact encompassing the whole of the Islamic world, and such a pact would have given Nehru's enemy, Pakistan, a great depth of power throughout West Asia and would have put India in a very difficult position.

Nasser fought against such a pact. He concentrated his efforts on Arab, not Islamic, unity. He used to say: "What do we have in common with the Indonesians apart from religion? If we rely solely on the unity of Islam, we will be making a grave mistake. Arab unity depends on geography and history as well as religion."

He argued for an Arab pact and he argued that under no circumstances should it be linked to one of the big powers.

This, of course, suited Nehru perfectly in the light of his dispute with Pakistan. Under an all-embracing Islamic pact, Pakistan would have had the support of the Moslem nations from Afghanistan all the way west through the Middle East. But with Nasser concentrating so fervently on his ideal of Arab unity, this sweep of support was denied to Pakistan.

A curious aspect of the situation was the extent to which Nehru was influenced by Moslem ideas. A Hindu, he had been born in the Moslem city of Allahabad, and he was intellectually involved with Islam. He would talk at great length and with great learning about the Moslem philosophers. He was fascinated by history and he felt that the era of Moslem power, through the Ottoman empire, had preserved all that was sacred to him of ancient Greece. It was the Arabs who translated the works of Plato and Aristotle and kept them in Spain where they were eventually taken back and retranslated by Europeans. It is ironic that it was the Arabs who gave back to Europe the work of its first great philosophers.

It was perhaps this feeling for history that gave Nehru his breadth and depth of outlook. He had a sense of the unity of the world and the unity of history. When faced with any problem, he would reach back into history for its origins. Tito used to laugh at him: "With Nehru, everything starts B.C."

What Nasser saw in Nehru above all else was a man who could think, a man who could look at a problem from all its aspects and reason out its origin, its effects, and its solution. It was this rational intellect that appealed to Nasser. On his part, Nehru felt toward Nasser as he would toward a son. As with most fathers, there were things about "his son" that he admired and that at the same time frightened him. He admired Nasser's boldness but he was frightened by it. He was proud of Nasser's capacity for action and he envied it but he was scared by it—just like an intellectual father whose son goes mountain-climbing.

Their first meeting took place on February 15, 1955, when Nehru started an official three-day visit to Cairo. It went so well that Nasser decided he wanted to have a full day of talk with Nehru away from official distractions, and so he arranged for them to spend the next day on a Nile steamer sailing from the Semiramis Hotel to the Nile Barrage. It took them four hours to get there and four to get back and they talked the whole time except for a break for lunch. After the meal Nasser wanted to resume the talks immediately, but Nehru refused: "No, you must give me time to doze." He sat in his chair and looked at the banks of the Nile gliding past, then napped for about five minutes. After that he was ready to go on with the discussions.

Nasser had started the talks in the morning by saying: "Yesterday we talked officially. But today I want you to talk to me. I want to listen to you."

Nasser was convinced of the need for planning, but all he knew about it at that time was the word. He had no experience in planning the future of a nation. He thought that the Indians had acquired this experience and he asked Nehru specifically: "How do you plan?" And they spent the whole morning discussing the planning of a nation as the steamer slipped past ancient villages along the Nile where the word was unknown.

At one stage Nehru said: "I wish that I could give up politics altogether and concentrate on planning because this is the field in which one can get things done." But then, in one of his characteristic moments of intellectual hesitation, he added: ". . . yet I doubt if anyone can get things done." He continually made statements, thought about them, then canceled them out. Perhaps he thought too much.

In the afternoon the talk turned to international affairs. Nehru was anxious that Communist China should be recognized by the rest of the world. "China is like the Himalayas," he said. "You cannot say that the Himalayas do not exist in Asia. If you ignore their existence, you first of all ignore a fact and, secondly, you prevent yourself from discovering what lies beyond them."

He was deeply interested in atomic power: "It means strength in war and strength in peace, either through victory or through productivity." Small matters did not interest him. He painted a broad canvas with big subjects—science, peace, war. The talk went on through the day with the young Arab revolutionary listening intently to the experienced Hindu intellectual, the one with clear-cut ideas of where he was going and what he was going to do and the other with his path strewn with intellectual reservations.

Yet at the end of the day Nehru said to Nasser: "The more we talk the more I discover we have the same thoughts."

They met again in April at Bandung. It was a considerable occasion for Nehru. He was riding high. The Chinese were there. Nasser had refused to join an Islamic pact. Nehru's ideas were gaining ground through the newly liberated countries. He was respected throughout the world.

Dressed in his plain, high-buttoned tunic decorated with a single red rose, he was the star of the Bandung Conference. He would talk philosophically about history, culture, sense of direction, and Nasser would listen with admiration. Nehru sensed the admiration and enjoyed every moment of his success.

They flew back to Delhi in the same plane and from then on they saw each other constantly. They visited eight times between February and July in 1955. Whenever Nehru was flying to Europe or the United States, he always stopped in Cairo, and even when he had no time to come into the city, he would hold his plane for several hours at the airport while Nasser drove out to talk with him.

Then came Brioni, the withdrawal of Western aid from the Aswan High Dam, and Nasser's nationalization of the Suez Canal. Nehru was convinced that Nasser could not have planned the take-over in the short time between receiving the radio message about the withdrawal of aid while he and Nehru were flying back to Cairo from Brioni and the actual seizure six days later. He was certain that Nasser must have had his plans made before he went to Brioni, and he was hurt that Nasser had not told him, either in Yugoslavia or during the day he spent in Cairo, before cutting his visit short when it became apparent that the storm was about to break. But even this hurt was hedged about by intellectual reservations. He was hurt because Nasser had not told him, and yet he was not certain he had really wanted to know because he fought shy of such dire actions. Nehru was also, of course, directly concerned with the Suez Canal because so much of India's commerce depended upon it. The closure of the Canal would cause India to pay a heavy price.

Yet, despite his hurt feelings and concern about the Canal, he still felt a certain responsibility toward Nasser, as toward a son who has got himself into a spot of bother.

On August 3, 1956, he wrote to Nasser:

Soon after my return to Delhi from Cairo and Brioni I learned of your decision about the Suez Canal. As this had not been mentioned by you in the course of our talks at Brioni and Cairo, I thought that decision must have been taken after I left Cairo. Our Ambassador in Cairo has confirmed this after a talk he had with Minister Ali Sabry. This has helped me to understand this aspect of the matter. I have today received from your Ambassador in Delhi a copy of your statement of 31st July. Thank you for this.

I have till now made no comments on these developments beyond saying in Parliament that this matter was not discussed between us at Brioni or Cairo. I was hoping to have fuller information about the future to enable me to make a statement in our Parliament. A matter of this kind has international repercussions. I want my statement in Parliament to be as helpful as possible. Our direct interest is as users of the Canal like others but we are naturally also interested in a friendly settlement.

We are in no doubt as to the sovereign right of Egypt and note that the position adopted by you in 1954 is that the Suez Maritime Canal, which is an integral part of Egypt, is a waterway economically, commercially, and strategically of international importance and that you have expressed the determination to uphold the Convention guaranteeing freedom of navigation of the Canal signed at Constantinople on the 29th October, 1888.

Then Nehru made his suggestion:

I venture to express the hope that you will decide to take the initiative yourself to call together all those interested in the international aspects of the development and on the basis of Egypt's sovereignty. Such a step would be fully in accord with your declared intentions and help the consideration of such mutually agreeable arrangements consistent with your law as well as international usage and to clear any misconceptions.

I am sure you will appreciate that my suggestion is in no way designed as an interference in Egypt's affairs or with your decision but is actuated by the desire to see that there should be as little acrimony about this as possible and to assist in a peaceful and conciliatory approach.

The whole letter was couched in the anxious-pleased tone of a father who is delighted to discover that his son had not deceived him as he had feared and is now going to try to extricate him from his spot of bother with as little trouble as possible. The two men maintained a correspondence in this style throughout the Suez crisis. Nasser wrote to Nehru:

> I would have understood the agitation over nationalization if we had been unfair about compensation and the rights of stock or shareholders . . . in the absence of justification for any such objections and to mislead people unacquainted with the relevant documents . . . the nationalization issue is being deliberately mixed up with the question of the security of the canal and the freedom of navigation.
>
> No one asks who looked after these when the British troops evacuated. Did the Company do it? The Canal passes through Egyptian territory and is recognized by the 1954 Treaty as an integral part of Egypt, and its security and freedom of navigation are the responsibility of Egypt which had guaranteed and continues to guarantee them. The guarantee itself would be meaningless if it had to be fortified by another authority and no such authority was ever thought of before as necessary. The British say we prevented Israeli ships from passing and blockaded ships going to Israel. This was done in a state of war and since 1949 and, with 80,000 British troops present in the Canal Zone, the British did not then think of protecting the freedom of navigation.
>
> All these arguments are baseless and are used as excuses to foist a new domination on us. . . .
>
> I can see wisdom and statesmanship in all international

waterways being brought under the international regime of the United Nations and I propose, instead of rejecting the British invitation [to the London Conference of Canal users], to make a counterproposal to that effect. . . . We would also be willing to execute a fresh treaty with all concerned nations guaranteeing again the security of the Canal and freedom of navigation and that treaty can be registered with the United Nations.

I shall await your advice regarding this proposal before announcing it and would welcome any other suggestion you may have in view but I hope you will appreciate my reasons for NOT agreeing to respond to the British invitation and I do sincerely trust that, in view of those reasons, you will also oblige us by NOT accepting it. . . .

Nehru answered on August 5:

I am grateful to you for your kind reply to my message and appreciate your assurance that you are doing everything to make conciliatory approaches. I would like to express the hope that your attitude will remain firmly conciliatory in spite of provocation. It is more likely that this would lead to more satisfactory results and strengthen reasonable positions.

We are studying your proposal and will send you a reply very soon. The proposal for reference to the United Nations requires further consideration, but I welcome your readiness to execute fresh treaties with concerned nations on an international basis. This may well give an opportunity for others to find a common ground for coming to suitable arrangements.

With regard to my own position in regard to the British invitation, we have sent them no reply and are considering the matter. We shall not in any event accept the invitation without reservations regarding the arguments and grounds stated in the joint communiqué and the composition of the Conference and certain other matters. We cannot, also, subscribe to any form of settlement without full consideration ourselves and consultation with you.

Our object would not be to weaken your position but, as you yourself have been doing, to work for conciliatory approaches. . . .

Nehru followed up with a longer, more considered reply the following day in which he set out the advice he had for Nasser:

I would suggest that you express your surprise at the UK convening a Conference on the Suez Canal issue without consulting or even referring to Egypt. . . . Your reply may say that Egypt is agreeable to a Conference to be composed of an agreed list of invitees based on the Constantinople Convention. . . . Egypt would be willing either to execute a fresh treaty with all concerned nations or to agree to a Convention which will guarantee the security of the Canal, freedom of navigation, and safety of passage. . . . Egypt cannot agree to any challenge to her sovereignty. . . .

We do not think it wise for you to suggest that the present problems should be considered by the United Nations. In the present state of the world the alignment of forces there may not be favorable. Further it can also lead to the interpretation of a prior acceptance of international control. It is wiser to be cautious about bringing in the United Nations just now. . . .

I have made these suggestions in response to your kind request and in the belief that they would contribute to a helpful approach to the problem. . . .

A month later, after the failure of the Menzies mission, which attempted to mediate the dispute, Nasser wrote to Nehru about his fears of military intervention:

> Even if there is NO direct military intervention immediately, I have to be prepared for it especially as I suspect incidents may be provoked by the defection of pilots or in other ways. [Robert] Menzies [Prime Minister of Australia] also threw out hints of trouble. For that reason and before the British Parliament meets on Wednesday, I must take some initiative to show the military and economic threats and measures taken against Egypt on the one hand, and on the other, my willingness to negotiate in a proper body.
>
> I intend, therefore, as soon as Menzies leaves, to lodge an appeal with the Security Council and, at the same time, to issue a statement clarifying our position. . . .
>
> I would greatly appreciate your urgent advice regarding the move to appeal to the Security Council. Even if the British and French use the veto, the facts relating to their military preparations and economic sanctions will be made public before the world as real threats to peace, and the Security Council, being seized of the matter, may prevent possible military moves by them and also influence British and world opinion. . . .

Then, when the British and French went ahead with their landings despite world opinion, Nehru wrote on November 1:

> I need not tell you how deeply shocked we have been at recent developments. The Israeli aggression was bad enough and is to be condemned, but much worse has been the ultimatum to Egypt by the UK and France and the subsequent action they are taking. All our sympathies are with you and

I am sure that the countries of Asia and Africa and many of the countries even of Europe and America will realize that naked aggression is taking place against Egypt and that the freedom of a country which has recently been liberated from colonialism is in peril. This is a reversal of history which none of us can tolerate.

The future of the United Nations itself also is at stake. The countries that were associated at Bandung have a special responsibility in this matter.

I have conveyed my views in firm language to Eden. Also to President Eisenhower and President Tito and asked them to use their influence. I am also communicating with Moscow, Rangoon, Djarkarta, Colombo, and Karachi.

In the grave crisis and responsibility that you are facing we send you all our good wishes.

In December, when the active stage of the Suez affair was over, Nehru wrote a letter in a somewhat different vein to Nasser:

I am happy to find that the Anglo-French and Israeli troops will at long last be withdrawn by them from Egyptian territory. I feel sure that this would not have been possible had not world public opinion overwhelmingly stood by Egypt. . . . I am anxious that the revulsion of feeling caused by the aggression against Egypt should not be sidetracked by extraneous factors. As it is, developments in Hungary have to an extent come in the way of concerted action against the aggressors in Egypt. I feel therefore that it is more than ever important to prevent other things coming in the way of the world expressing itself fully in favor of Egypt.

In this context I venture to draw your attention to the reports which are circulating abroad that considerable pressure direct and indirect is being brought to bear on the large number of British and French nationals and persons of Jewish origin in Egypt.

. . . the large majority of these are innocent victims of the wrongs committed by their Governments and I would request you to show them compassion. If you do not wish British or French nationals to remain in your country, they might, I suggest, be given reasonable time to wind up their affairs and not be forced to leave immediately. Even from the short term point of view a little patience and tolerance at this stage would help in the discussion of higher issues in Egypt, in the UN and elsewhere.

I would not have made this appeal to you had I not felt sure that you would not misunderstand me.

With kind regards,

Jawaharlal Nehru

British and French property was sequestered at this time; later the problem was settled by compensation negotiated between Egypt on the one hand and the British and French Governments on the other. No Jewish property was sequestered since Jews were considered Egyptian subjects, though it is true that many did leave Egypt after the Suez war.

The relationship then was still in the proud father-admiring son stage. Nehru would advise, comfort, support, and sometimes chide Nasser, while Nasser still looked to Nehru with admiration. But Nasser was growing up and Nehru watched the progress of his growth proudly. He used to say of the Egyptian leader: "He is a youthful challenge to us all."

Nehru, however, remained the respected intellectual giant. It was Nehru who in November 1957 appealed to the world to use the atom for peaceful means: "I venture to appeal to the great leaders of the United States of America and the Soviet Union. I do so in all humility, but with great earnestness. We in India have grave problems to face. But, I am overwhelmed by the thought of the crisis in civilization which the world is facing today, the like of which it has not known ever before. I believe that it is in the power of America and Russia to solve this crisis and save humanity from the ultimate disaster which faces it.

"Our earth has become too small for the new weapons of the atomic age. While man, in the pride of his intellect and knowledge, forces his way into space and pierces the heavens, the very existence of the human race is threatened. There are enough weapons of mass destruction already to put an end to life on earth. . . .

"Millions of people believe in what is called Western capitalism; millions also believe in Communism. But, there are many millions who are not committed to either of these ideologies, and yet seek, in friendship with others, a better life and more hopeful future.

"I speak for myself, but I believe that I echo the thoughts of vast numbers of people in my country as well as in other countries of the world. I venture, therefore, to make this appeal to the great leaders, more especially of America and Russia, in whose hands fate and destiny have placed such tremendous power today to mold this world and either to raise it to undreamed heights or to hurl it to the pit of disaster. I appeal to them to stop all nuclear test explosions and thus to show to the world that they are determined to end this menace, and to proceed also to bring about effective disarmament. . . ."

He sent a copy of this plea to President Nasser with a covering letter in which he said: "Here, in India, we have great problems of our own, and you, in Egypt, face many difficulties. While my problems are my immediate concern, my mind thinks more and more of the major problem that confronts humanity. . . ."

Despite Nehru's involvement with these major world-wide problems he had an astonishing affinity with the people of India, an affinity that was demonstrated one day in the spring of 1960 when Nasser was his guest in Delhi. There was a public meeting that Nehru was to address in the Ranjilah Square in Delhi and Nasser went with him. He was astounded to see the number of people who turned up—something like four hundred thousand people, whole families, mothers with their children, people who had walked for miles, all sitting down in the square.

It was a fascinating spectacle. There was a small platform built for the speakers and from it one could see nothing but a multitude, a sea of upturned faces. Nasser thought that nobody would be able to hold the attention of that vast crowd. How could anybody do it? Then Nehru stood up and started to speak. He talked in English and it was translated into Hindi, but he had the whole of that vast audience captive, held in the palm of his hand. Nasser had expressed his doubts to Nehru before the Indian Prime Minister started to speak. When he had finished, Nehru turned to him and asked: "Well, what did you think?"

"It was an extraordinary achievement," Nasser replied. "Why?" asked Nehru. "Because," said Nasser, "you made them laugh. I think that the greatest task facing a public speaker at a big gathering is to get the audience so with you that they burst into laughter. When a man can get four hundred thousand people with him then that is a great accomplishment."

Nasser was convinced that by doing this Nehru had demonstrated the link that existed between his leadership and the mass of the Indian people.

Their friendship and mutual admiration grew all the time. It was studded with pleasant incidents. On one occasion when Nehru was passing through Egypt, his plane had a mechanical fault and he was obliged to spend one complete day in Cairo. He insisted on spending that day studying examples of Moslem architecture. And when Nasser went to India, Nehru took him to see the Taj

Mahal and other monuments of the Mogul empires. He was extremely interested in this period of Indian history and would talk for hours about the great Islamic dynasties that had ruled his country. He would have nothing to do with the quarrel between Hindu and Moslem; intellectually as well as politically he was a bridge between the two civilizations.

I remember one day when he was discussing the Moguls with Nasser and me and we were talking about the collapse of the two Moslem empires, one in Spain and the other in India, I put forward the theory that their collapse had been caused by the multimarriages of the Moslem rulers. The enmity between their numerous heirs led to civil wars and the breaking up of the empires. Nehru never let me forget this theory; whenever we discussed any problem, he would tease me: "Do you think it all started with multimarriages . . . ?"

In January 1960 the first part of the diversion of the Nile to enable the Aswan High Dam to be built was carried out with a spectacular explosion. Nehru was unable to attend the ceremony and he was extremely disappointed, so when he did visit Egypt in May of that year, he found that Nasser had saved an explosion especially for him and Nehru was able to go to the dam site and actually press the button to detonate the charge that sent the Nile waters surging into their new channel. Nasser did this for no one else, and Nehru always enjoyed the thought that something was being kept especially for him.

Nasser clearly enjoyed his company; he found pleasure in his conversation and he took comfort in the older man's advice—even though he did not always follow it, for Nehru always wanted to compromise, to conciliate, to talk about problems rather than to take action. "In the problem of peace or war," he used to tell the President, "always take the first step . . . then take the second step . . . then take the third step . . ."

The time came when their destinies changed and the father, in a time of crisis, needed the help of his son.

In October 1962 China attacked India across the Himalayas, supposedly in a dispute over the McMahon Line, the border arbitrarily drawn by the British between India and Tibet. But Nehru was absolutely convinced—and Nasser tended to accept his point of view—that the Chinese attack was rooted in something bigger than a border dispute, that it was an attack on the whole concept of non-alignment.

The Chinese had thought that non-alignment was just a passing phase. They accepted it because they thought it would not last long, but when they discovered that it was growing in strength and that the Soviet Union, with whom they were quarreling, was strongly supporting the non-aligned countries, they felt that non-alignment had become a force with which they had to reckon. So, according to Nehru's reading of the situation, the Chinese attacked India, knowing that there was a strong right-wing element in India, in the hope that Nehru's socialist and non-aligned policies would be discredited, the right wing would take over, and political feeling in India would become polarized between the right and the left.

Nehru could see a number of possible avenues of Chinese thinking. One was that they hoped India would collapse under attack and thus come under Chinese domination. But he did not think this was likely to occur because Indian nationalist feelings would be aroused and China would not be able to control another vast nation. A second possibility was that they expected the Indian right wing to take over and lead inevitably to a complete Communist uprising. A third was that they thought India would turn to the West with, once again, a Communist reaction. Through all his attempts to read the Chinese mind and the future, Nehru remained certain of one thing—that the attack was not to breach the McMahon Line and occupy territory with Chinese troops, but to destroy non-alignment and occupy the minds of the people with Chinese strength.

Speculations aside, the Chinese assault came as a shock to the Indian leader. Nehru could not believe that one great Asian nation, one participant in the Bandung Conference, would invade another. He was bitter. He was humiliated. Before Bandung the Chinese had accused him of being a "lackey of the imperialists." However, he felt that they had got over that hurdle and that all was well between them. But it was not to be.

Chou En-lai had spoken to Nasser at Bandung about the border problem with India and complained that the Indians kept putting off talks about it. But Nasser did not think it was an urgent problem and it never occurred to him that the Chinese would attack India. When the attack was launched, it was more than a shock to Jawaharlal Nehru—it was a shattering blow from which he never recovered.

The right wing in India immediately turned on him, so that he was under military fire at the front and political fire in Delhi. He desperately needed help. Where could he turn? He thought at one stage that he would be obliged to appeal to the United States. But that would have brought him under immediate suspicion of truly being a "lackey of the imperialists." The Soviet Union could not help because at that time the Russians still could not put themselves in the position of openly helping a nation at war with Communist China. Nehru had to rely on the non-aligned nations—not for military help but in order to bring about a peaceful settlement of the conflict. But even with those nations there was a problem: Tito was persona non grata with the Chinese.

The only man left to whom Nehru could turn was Nasser, in all his capacities as non-aligned, Afro-Asian, and the friend of Chou En-lai. And, in the end, it was Nasser who played the most important role in bringing about peace.

But Nasser had to play his part with much subtlety. When

Nehru first wrote to him giving his assessment of the situation, Nasser replied that he would not be able to give wholehearted support to India's position in public or attack Communist China for their aggression. For, he said, "if I want to keep the ability to mediate, then I must keep my channels open with both of you."

Nehru understood and agreed willingly to Nasser's quiet approach. But the Indian right wing used it as another stick with which to beat Nehru. They sneered at him: "What have the non-aligned countries done for you?" And they attacked Egypt for not condemning the Chinese: "What about your friendship with Nasser and the Arabs? Where are they now when you need them?" Nehru did his best to defend Nasser. At the same time he was trying to prevent the Americans from interfering and trying to encourage the Russians to bring pressure to bear on the Chinese. He was a man in a mess.

Nasser got in touch with Nehru and asked him: "What do you want me to do?" Nehru replied: "You can do more than anybody else." He explained the situation with regard to the Americans and the Russians, the problems of the Indian left wing and right wing, and said he thought that Nasser was the only world leader capable of helping. But the attacks on Nasser continued in the Indian Parliament, and when Nehru said that "our friend Nasser is helping us," one of the members of Parliament stood up and said, "Yes, helping us by keeping silent."

After that, Nehru said to the Egyptian Ambassador: "Tell President Nasser not to worry about the attacks on him. I can control them . . ." But then, typically Nehru, he added, "for a week." And Nasser thought that a week was too short in which to bring about peace.

Nasser decided that his best policy was not to attack China for its aggression and not to defend the McMahon border but to defend the concept of Indian non-alignment from attacks by the Chinese and by the left wing and right wing in India.

There were jibes at Nasser in the Indian press and Nehru wrote to him, explaining that the Indian newspapers were all owned by big business and the right wing, telling him not to worry about them, and saying: "I wish I could close them all."

Many of the Indian members of Parliament were on the payroll of the millionaires like J. D. R. Tata, and these millionaires used to send to them, in their government-provided guesthouses, meals from the best restaurants. Nehru told the Egyptian Ambassador to disregard the attacks on Nasser from these men because "they are only waiting for a good lunch from Tata."

Throughout the conflict, a stream of letters and messages passed between the two leaders. Nasser wrote to Nehru on October 23, 1962, urging conciliation—Nehru style. The Indian Prime Minister replied with a long exposition of the situation, which ended: "I am sincerely grateful for your message in the context of conditions that exist today. However, it is our clear duty to continue our resistance unless the Chinese heed the advice of disinterested friends like you and others and correct the situation created by them . . .

"If the Chinese aggression continues, we will continue to resist and we hope we will have your sympathy and support and the sympathy and support of all right-minded countries in this sacred task of maintaining the honor and integrity of our Motherland."

Later Nehru wrote Nasser:

China has challenged the whole concept of peaceful coexistence on which Soviet policy is based. While Soviet policy aims at the avoidance, or elimination, of war and lays greater stress on peaceful competition, China has proclaimed its adherence to a policy based on revolutionary violence and what are described as "just wars." China's main purpose seems to be to disrupt the policy of non-alignment which has gained widespread support, not only among the Afro-Asian countries, but also from the Great Powers.

I think our own conflict with China should be seen against this background. I have written to you about this in the past and I will only repeat that while we shall resist aggression and take all necessary measures for the defense of our country, there will be no change in our policy of peace and non-alignment. Our objective will always be to have a peaceful settlement which preserves the honor and dignity of our country. For this reason, we welcomed the initiative of the Colombo Conference and we also accepted the proposals as clarified to us. As you are perhaps aware, China has not yet done so. Its so-called acceptance is subject to reservations which are completely at variance with the proposals.

. . . I will only add that both our Government and people have greatly appreciated your own approach to this problem. . . .

I look forward to the further strengthening of friendly co-operation and understanding between us in the interest of peace.

With my warm personal regards,
Jawaharlal Nehru

Yet, despite these expressions of cordiality and thanks for support, there was one aspect of the conflict with China that Nasser found objectionable: while Nehru was relying on Nasser, other elements in India had turned to the Israelis.

Nehru had first been introduced to the facts of the Arab quarrel with the Zionists at the Bandung Conference, which the Israelis were making desperate attempts to attend. They had the Burmese leader U Nu on their side and had asked Nehru for his support. Nehru, taking his usual philosophical and historical view of the situation, was inclined to agree to the Israeli application. He was not aware of the truths of the Palestine problem and talked about the joint contributions of Jewish and Arab philosophers and the way in which Jew and Arab lived together without racial discrimination under Islam. To tell him that there were a million refugees from Palestine meant little to him. As he explained, he had sixteen million refugees after the partition of India in 1947. And the fact that a country was divided meant little to him because that, too, had happened to his own country. What he did resent about Israel was the fact that it was a state based on religion —and that reminded him of Pakistan.

He had to be taught the real facts of the situation from the start. But once he had learned, he understood it very well, and when he stood up in the political committee at Bandung and put forth the Arab point of view on the admittance of Israel, he did it with a clarity, grasp, and brilliance that few Arabs could have.

Israel was not admitted and Nehru remained a supporter of the Arab cause from that day on. But when the trouble with China started, the Israelis approached the Indian Intelligence Service and convinced the Indians that the best way of defending the high mountain regions against Chinese incursions was to set up paramilitary settlements of the Zionist type. To do this the Indians would of course need Israeli experts to show them how to do it, it was claimed.

This project was going on while at the same time Nasser was working on India's behalf, and he was obliged to draw Nehru's attention to it. Nehru ended the talks with Israel immediately. But there was a new incident when the Israelis offered the Indians their Uzzi sub-machine gun. Some of the Indian military people thought that it was a good, light weapon that would give their soldiers greater mobility in the mountains. Once again Nasser was forced to draw Nehru's attention to his officer's links with the Israelis. Nehru cut the links and wrote to Nasser: "Those foolish people wanted to examine the case on its merits. But in this case there are no merits. It is a matter which must be decided by me."

Poor Nehru. He had enormous problems. The Americans were also trying to interfere. They wanted to set up antennae on Indian territory to beam the government-controlled Voice of America to China; some of Nehru's senior ministers agreed to this plan, and once again Nehru was forced to step in and stop the project. Meanwhile, the Chinese were attacking him. Pakistan was ready to take advantage of the situation and invade. The Americans were also trying to take a Cold War advantage. The Russians would not help for fear of causing a split in the Communist bloc. Some of the non-aligned nations were beginning to doubt Nehru's non-alignment—they thought that he really was looking to the West for help.

He was obliged to drop V. K. Krishna Menon, his Minister of War, who had come under the most severe attack for the Chinese defeat of the Indian forces. That Menon was made the scapegoat for the defeat was a sad blow for Nehru because he had never trusted the Indian military people. He found them much too British in their outlook, isolated from Indian thinking. He would say "they are more British than the British." And Menon, as War Minister, was his counterweight to their rigid attitudes. Yet when all the people who would have liked to attack Nehru attacked Menon instead, Nehru was put in an untenable position and he was forced to fire Menon. Nehru was deeply distressed.

Nasser's quiet diplomacy on Nehru's behalf culminated in the Colombo Conference in January 1963. The proposals adopted there eventually contained the Indo-Chinese problem and led to the end of the fighting. Nasser, despite the malicious campaign waged against him, was justified and, to the extent that the Chinese attack did not lead to the downfall of non-alignment in India, he won a victory for the non-aligned nations.

But there was no victory for Nehru. He was a shattered, demoralized man. Seeing him afterward, one felt that he had been broken on the Himalayas. He had believed that he had his world arranged when, suddenly, the Chinese soldiers started to pour over those high mountain passes. That world was broken into fragments and could never be put together again.

Everything was wrong. His China policy had collapsed. Menon was gone. The military had gained more power. Planning was disturbed. Nehru thought there had been a deliberate effort to make what he used to call the "third road" fail. His third road was neither capitalism nor Communism, it was socialism without Communism.

He certainly felt that he had failed, and I believe that this helped to kill him because Nehru was always obsessed with the judgment of history: "What will history say about us?"

Once he told Nasser that when Gandhi was asked why he had chosen Nehru as his successor, despite the fact that he had been educated outside India and there were other, more obvious candidates, Gandhi had replied: "Because Nehru is the only man who can link India with the twentieth century." And Nehru, typically, had self-doubts: "I don't know if I can live up to the expectations of Gandhi."

Now he was a diminished figure, and Nasser used to suffer agonies when they met because the man whom Nasser had admired so much, the father-figure and the star of Bandung, had lost hope.

On May 24, 1964, Nehru died a disillusioned man.

X

Chou En-lai: East and West

Gamal Abdel Nasser, like most of us, used to move in a series of different circles, some of them just touching, others making complete contact at certain points, and others almost overlapping. But whereas with most of us the circles are those of business and sport and hobbies, his were statesmanship, national struggle, and revolution.

He moved in Afro-Asian circles where he had his great friendship with Chou En-lai of China and Sukarno of Indonesia. He moved in the non-aligned circle where his friends were Nehru and Tito. There was the Arab circle with Ben Bella of Algeria and Arif. And the African circle of Nkrumah of Ghana and Sekou Touré of Guinea. Each circle was different, each had its similarities, and each had its friends.

Nasser's friendship with Chou En-lai was particularly intimate.

They used to enjoy each other's company and they would sit for hours talking of many things. They were relaxed with one another and Nasser especially admired Chou's determination and completely organized way of approaching anything he wanted to do. I calculate that they spent some seventy-four hours sitting together and talking. During one visit when Chou was in Cairo for twelve days, they met sixteen times for discussions.

Chou told Nasser that the first contact he had with Egypt was when he passed through the Suez Canal on his way from Paris to start his revolutionary work in China. The second time was in 1954 when he was on his way back to China from the Geneva Conference on Indochina. He was going home by way of India and as the Indian government had put one of their aircraft at his disposal, the Indian Ambassador was at Cairo Airport to meet him. But, apart from the airport authorities, there was only one protocol officer from the Egyptian Ministry of Foreign Affairs[1] to welcome him—a strange beginning in the light of his subsequent friendship with Nasser.

Chou, whose interest in Egypt had been quickened by his voyage through the Suez, sent a message from the plane saying that if any food was going to be put on the aircraft, would they please make sure that it was Egyptian food. The Indian Ambassador got the message and he hurried round the airport to find kebab and tahina for the Chinese Premier.

Nasser and Chou met for the first time at Rangoon on their way to the Bandung Conference of non-aligned nations in 1955. The Chinese were very keen to make contact. Egypt was beginning to emerge as the leader of the Arab world, and the Chinese were watching Egypt's behavior closely for Egypt's attitude toward China meant a whole area's attitude, not just her own.

The Chinese Ambassador in Delhi asked to see Nasser when

[1] Egypt had no diplomatic relations with Communist China at this time.

he stopped there to pick up Nehru and asked if he would like to see Chou. Nasser accepted with pleasure, thinking that they would meet in Bandung. But when Nasser and Nehru touched down at Rangoon, Chou was waiting for them at the airport.

Nehru performed the introductions by saying: "Do I need to introduce you to each other?"

It was very hot. They stood together for some time, drinking fresh coconut milk and being sprinkled with perfumed water by people celebrating the Shai Gan, the Burmese water festival. One got the impression that Chou was looking at Nasser with some admiration. And that evening the two men held the fateful discussion that ultimately led to Egypt's first arms deal with the Soviet bloc, the deal that itself was to have so many consequences for Egypt, the Middle East, and the world.

In Bandung itself they had two meetings at which they talked of many things—Afro-Asian solidarity, the need for contacts, common endeavor against imperialism—but one felt that Chou was more interested in listening than in talking. They dined together and Chou talked about his Egyptian meal at Cairo Airport and the bird's nest soup they were then eating. Salah Salem, Egypt's Minister of National Guidance, who was at the dinner, asked what was in the soup. "Birds' nests" said Chou. "Just as they are?" asked Salah Salem. "Yes," said Chou, and the interpreter explained about the dish to Salah Salem. He began to feel ill, shouted a protest, and rushed from the room to be sick. Nasser signaled the interpreter not to translate what Salah Salem had said. Chou viewed the scene with astonishment.

Chou visited Cairo for a week in December 1963 and, in a strange hark-back to his previous arrival at Cairo Airport, Nasser was not there to meet him. This was thought in some quarters to be a slight to Chou. The fact was that Nasser had been obliged to go to Tunisia for twenty-four hours to attend the celebrations marking the French evacuation of Bizerte. Nasser was trying to patch up his differences with Tunisia's leader, Habib Bourguiba, and judged that it was more important for him to establish friendly relations with Tunisia than to go through the formalities of meeting Chou.

Some people took this as an affront, but Nasser had left Chou a message explaining the situation and Chou understood perfectly.

Chou insisted that the week of talks be informal. He went to the Egyptian Museum and was greatly impressed by what he saw, and it seemed to spark the theme for him for his second meeting with Nasser. He talked about the ancient civilizations of the East and their struggle for the future. He was bitter about the contempt the West showed for the countries of the East: "With all our centuries of civilization, with all our contributions to the human race, all we get from the West is humiliation."

His themes throughout the day were:

1. We must have independence.

2. The meaning of independence, and this is the only meaning, is that we will be our own masters.

3. If we are our own masters, we can equal the West.

4. If we can equal, we can surpass.

When we can do that, he argued, when we surpass the West, we will shift the world's center of gravity back to the East.

He talked for an hour on these themes and he used the Suez Canal as an example. "What is the lesson to be learned from your nationalization of the Canal? It is that we of the East can run things as well as the West." He kept underscoring this point: the East is as good as the West. "They have always tried to fill us with complexes and convince us that we are not as good as they are, that we are poor, low-grade material. Your management of the Suez Canal is not important financially—it is important only in proving that what they can do, we can do."

Equality in all things with the West was his watchword. Egypt had just signed the nuclear non-proliferation treaty, but Chou told

Nasser that China would not sign it because: "There has to be either complete nuclear disarmament and destruction of all the weapons, or China will have to make its own nuclear weapons, for it cannot leave the big powers with a nuclear monopoly."

After that visit Chou returned to Cairo for one long day of talks in April 1965, and he passed through on several other occasions. Each time the friendship grew between himself and Nasser. Then in June of that year he arrived in Egypt to spend twelve days with the President. It was a most important visit. So many events were on the boil. Khrushchev had fallen. China had exploded its first atom bomb. Chou had been to Moscow in a last attempt to patch up China's differences with Russia.

Nasser was worried by this Sino-Soviet quarrel because he thought that it was hindering all the national liberation movements and was harming the people of Asia and Africa. Nasser had, in fact, sent a message to Chou when the Chinese Premier was in Moscow in 1964. The message was conveyed by Marshal Amer who was also in Moscow and it started by congratulating Chou on China's achievement on building its own atomic weapons. (Nasser was enthusiastic about China's atomic success. He looked on it as a triumph for the East.) He then went on to plead with Chou to reconcile his differences with the Soviet Union because of the harm the quarrel was doing to the liberation movements.

Chou saw Amer and sent a message in return, thanking Nasser for his message of congratulations. He said that China would not be like others and try to keep a monopoly on its scientific achievements but would throw its knowledge open to everyone. He replied to Nasser's plea for a reconciliation with the Russians by saying that he was trying, that that was why he had gone to Moscow. Khrushchev had forced the quarrel and now that Khrushchev had gone, he was attempting to work out an agreement with the new leaders. But, he said, he did not think he would succeed because the "Russians are Europeans and the Europeans, the whites, are alike and they look on us as inferiors."

He was correct in his pessimism. There was no reconciliation, and when he came to Cairo for his visit in June 1965, China's dispute with Russia was one of the two main topics of his conversations with Nasser.

The other major topic was Vietnam. American involvement in Vietnam was growing under President Johnson and the whole world was concerned with the dangers of the situation. The nonaligned nations played a large part in expressing the world's concern. Nasser, Nehru, and Tito all called attention to Johnson's folly and spoke long and often about the danger into which he was putting the world. Nasser wanted the Americans to withdraw and allow the people of Vietnam to settle their own fate.

But when he and Chou dined together in Alexandria on June 23, Chou said that he did not want Johnson to withdraw any American soldiers—on the contrary, he wanted the United States to send more and more of its young men to Vietnam.

"We are afraid that some American militarists may press for a nuclear attack on China and we think that the American involvement in Indochina is an insurance policy against such an attack because we will have a lot of their flesh close to our nails.

"So the more troops they send to Vietnam, the happier we will be, for we feel that we will have them in our power, we can have their blood. So if you want to help the Vietnamese, you should encourage the Americans to throw more and more soldiers into Vietnam.

"We want them there. They will be close to China. And they will be in our grasp. They will be so close to us, they will be our hostages."

One of the remarkable things he said that night when talking about the demoralization of the American soldiers was that "some of them are trying opium. And we are helping them. We are planting the best kinds of opium especially for the American soldiers in Vietnam."

President Nasser looked at him in some disquiet, but Chou went on: "Do you remember when the West imposed opium on us? They fought us with opium. And we are going to fight them with their own weapons. We are going to use their own methods against them. We want them to have a big army in Vietnam which will be hostage to us and we want to demoralize them. The effect this demoralization is going to have on the United States will be far greater than anyone realizes."

Nasser felt that possibly Chou was exaggerating a little. But Chou had his plan absolutely clear in his mind. There was no doubt that he intended to do exactly as he said.

When Johnson called his bombers off North Vietnam at the end of 1965, he sent a number of emissaries round the world telling the leaders of other countries what he hoped to gain by the pause. Ambassador Averell Harriman came to Egypt on this mission and saw Nasser on January 4, 1966.

The bombing pause had been accompanied by a propaganda campaign from the Americans, and so when Harriman arrived, Nasser expected to hear something important from him. Harriman started by asking the President what he thought about Vietnam and Nasser answered that it was a problem that he wanted to see an end to because it was in nobody's interest. Harriman asked him for his suggestions. But it was all minor-key talk. The meeting lasted for two hours with nothing positive coming of it. Harriman had come with nothing new. He had no suggestions. And there were silences during the talks that lasted for several minutes at a time.

Eventually Nasser said to Harriman; "Do you really think you are going to defeat them? If you increase your troops in Vietnam, you are only going to play into your enemy's hands. Strangely enough, I've heard something from Chou En-lai and you are carrying out the Chinese plan precisely." And he told Harriman what Chou had said about wanting more and more American soldiers to be sent to Vietnam. But he did not tell Harriman about Chou's plan to fight the American army with opium.

That was the only time during the whole of that two-hour meeting that Harriman showed any real interest in the proceedings. Afterward, Nasser said he got the impression that Harriman's mission was just show, that he had been sent so that Johnson could say that he had tried all round the world to find a way to peace in Vietnam.

Later, Nasser felt that possibly he ought not to have told Harriman about Chou's plans, so he sent messages to Chou and to Ho Chi Minh about the meeting. As a matter of fact, Chou had cabled Nasser asking him not to meet Harriman because his mission was only a maneuver, but the cable had arrived too late and Nasser could not have refused to see the American in any case.

Nasser told Chou about the meeting and explained that there was nothing new in it "but I must confess to you that I did something which I hope you will not consider a mistake. I told him what I heard from you about the American troops in Vietnam and that they were falling into your trap."

Chou replied that he knew Harriman's visit was only propaganda and he did not mind Nasser telling the Americans of his plans because, he said, "They are not going to learn anything. They are set on a certain course and nothing is going to change their minds."

During the Nasser-Chou talks in June 1965, both President Mohammed Ayub Khan of Pakistan and President Sukarno of Indonesia passed through Cairo. The four of them met one night to discuss international affairs. Ayub Khan left first, then Sukarno said: "Enough of politics, I'm going to leave," and he looked at Nasser, saying: "Brother Nasser, I know you have good intelligence men and they will follow me to find out what I am going to do. I am going to see a belly dancer. So they need not follow me and write reports about it tomorrow." He then asked Chou if he would like to go with him to see the dancer, but Chou replied: "No, the intelligence reports tomorrow will say that I either stayed with President Nasser or I spent the night working."

There was not much light-heartedness in Chou on that visit. He was bitter to the core about the Russians. Nasser told him that the Soviet Union was helping Egypt, but Chou insisted: "They are not going to help you. They are only interested in helping themselves."

He told story after story about the way the Russians withdrew their technicians and their aid from China, about the unfinished factories and industrial projects abandoned by the Russians, and how they tried to cripple China's atomic progress by calling their scientists home. "Yet," said Chou, "we did it ourselves." His bitterness was complete.

It was this bitterness that led to the first lasting dispute between Nasser and Chou.

At the end of 1965 preparations were being made for the second Afro-Asian Conference and the Soviet Union asked to take part as an Asian country. The Chinese were vehemently opposed to Soviet participation, believing that the Russians would try to take over leadership of the Afro-Asian movement, a position that Chou felt belonged to China. So Nasser wrote to Chou pointing out that the Soviet Union included vast areas of Asia and that the Afro-Asian nations would benefit from the Russians' presence at the conference.

But Chou had an entirely different point of view. He argued first of all that all Russia's Asian territories were grabbed from China. Secondly, he said, the Russians would bring one bloc of the Cold War into the conference.

In a letter to President Nasser, Chou left no doubt about

China's position: "If the conference should be forcibly convened as scheduled in violation of the principle of consensus through consultation in spite of the opposition of China, the kingdom of Cambodia, and other countries, the Chinese government will be compelled to absent itself from such a conference, which will lead to a split."

The Chinese were so opposed to Russian participation that they wrecked the conference. It was first postponed, then canceled three days before it was due to open in Algiers, where a beautiful new auditorium had been built for the occasion. It has never been reconvened. And the Afro-Asian movement was killed.

There had been a previous split between Chou and Nasser in 1959 when Khaled Bagdesh, the Communist who had fled from Syria after the formation of the United Arab Republic, was invited to attend the tenth anniversary celebration of the Communist victory in China and was allowed to attack the United Arab Republic at a rally in Peking. Chou actually introduced him to the meeting. The next day Nasser withdrew his chargé d'affaires from Peking and closed the Chinese consulate in Damascus. The Chinese retorted by laying siege to the Egyptian Embassy in Peking.

Chou wrote to Nasser asking him what could be done to heal the breach. Nasser replied that he was affronted because China had allowed Bagdesh to stand up and attack the United Arab Republic, with Chou himself introducing him.

Chou's reaction was unprecedented: China apologized to the United Arab Republic. Later, Chou told Nasser that this was the only time that China had ever allowed itself to apologize to anybody. That dispute was settled well. But the Sino-Soviet quarrel left its scars on everybody involved in it.

President Nasser once made a speech in which he talked about the Cultural Revolution in China and said: "One day we must have a Cultural Revolution to knock the rust off our political organization and political thinking." Later, when he was visiting Moscow, one of the Russian leaders referred to this speech, saying: "I have noticed that you are friendly with Chou En-lai. Why do you have such admiration for them?" And the President replied that: "For a movement to change a country like China and to build its own atomic weapons is a very great achievement. To rid China of famine, to get China moving, to make China one of the superpowers, to move into the atomic era, that is a great achievement for an Asian country and I think that the men who have done this, especially Mao, must be great."

The Russian sprang to the attack: "No! He is only an opportunist. He profited from the circumstances and the events but he never created them. In the war against the Japanese he left all the fighting to Chiang Kai-shek and he did not fight himself. He left Chiang to do the fighting and he fled to Yenan.

"And then when the Japanese withdrew, we ordered Malinovsky to enter China with an army that encircled half a million Japanese soldiers and opened the road to Peking. So Mao Tse-tung sent to Stalin and asked for permission to march on Peking. And Stalin gave him permission. It was then and only then that he came out of hiding."

"Do you know," said the Russian, "that his two sons were living in the Soviet Union? One of them even had a Russian name, Yuri. But he did not care for them. We gave them a good education. But Mao was so ungrateful that when the boys returned to China after Mao had entered Peking, he had them brought to his office and asked them what they had learned. They told him. And he said that it was all nonsense and they had learned nothing. And he sent them to a commune.

"That was an insult to the Soviet Union, because we had done our best for his sons."

Nasser replied that even if that was the case, if the capture of Peking had been made easy for him, even so, he had gone on and ruled China and achieved great things. The Russian argued that he had the backing of a very powerful party and of course things were easy for him. Nasser countered by saying that Mao had even fought the party during the Cultural Revolution. And the Russian said: "Yes, but he used the Army against the Party."

There was no easy way out of the argument. From the Chinese, one would hear only the worst things about the Soviet Union, and from the Russians, only the worst things about the Chinese. It was an impossible situation for someone who was a friend of both sides.

In 1967 the Chinese took a strong attitude against Egypt's acceptance of the cease-fire with Israel. Both Mao Tse-tung and Chou En-lai wrote to President Nasser urging him not to accept but to fight on.

Nasser replied, explaining that Egypt had lost its Army. Not to accept the cease-fire would only be giving the Israelis the opportunity to destroy Egypt piecemeal without Egypt being able to do anything about it.

Mao then sent Nasser a military plan of action. The basis of it was the breaking up of the Egyptian Army into independent brigades which should lose themselves in the population in guerrilla fashion. They would depend on the people and strike out at the Israelis when and where they could.

Nasser had to send him back a complete description of Sinai. "It is a desert and we cannot conduct a people's liberation war in Sinai because there are no people there." There were no more than thirty thousand people in the whole of Sinai, he told the Chinese, the whole area was arid and you could see for thirty and forty miles. The independent brigades would stand no chance. But still the Chinese were not convinced.

At this time the Israelis were threatening to develop atomic weapons—and use them, if the Arab countries did not do as they wished. One day the President wrote to Chou, reminding him of his promise to share China's nuclear knowledge, and he sent a delegation from Egypt's nuclear authority to China to ask for help in making a break-through in nuclear techniques. Chou received the men kindly. His advice to them was simple and, he said, he wanted it conveyed to President Nasser. Self-reliance was his message. Nobody was going to give anybody anything as a gift. If the Egyptians wanted to step into the atomic field, they would have to do it themselves. This was the way China had done it and it was the best way.

So the delegation came home empty-handed, and while there were no hard feelings against the Chinese, there was disappointment that they had not helped Egypt with their nuclear knowledge.

The differences between China's leaders and Nasser over the cease-fire and the sharing of nuclear knowledge were differences between friends and there remained a basic understanding of each other's position. But soon afterward there was a crisis between Egypt and China in which Chou and Nasser completely failed to understand each other.

At an Afro-Asian solidarity meeting in Peking in February 1967, a young Chinese called Kwan Yu-shin had been a member of the reception committee for the arriving delegation.

Upon leaving, one member of the Japanese delegation handed his passport to Kwan Yu-shin and asked him to complete a few formalities for him before takeoff. The passport was already stamped with an exit visa and the delegate's airline tickets were tucked inside. Kwan Yu-shin peeled off the passport photograph of the Japanese, stuck in his own, and caught the only plane out of Peking Airport that day. By ill luck it was coming to Cairo. So Kwan Yu-shin arrived in Egypt and asked for political asylum.

There was an immediate uproar. Everybody jumped in. Chou sent a personal letter to the President, asking for the young man to be put on the next plane to Peking. The Americans claimed he had contacted a Western embassy and asked for asylum in the United States; they wanted him. The Russians claimed that he had contacted the Soviet Embassy and asked to be flown to Moscow; they wanted him too. Quite innocently, Egypt was in the middle of an international quarrel.

There were further complications because the tradition of asylum is very strong in Egypt. This tradition dates from the time after Napoleon's invasion of Egypt when the country was virtually independent of the Ottoman Empire and many political refugees came to Egypt from the Arab East. They were mainly intellectuals who had been forced to flee their own countries by the Ottoman authorities. The Khedive, showing his independence, granted them asylum. These people, these intellectuals, were those who, with their counterparts in Egypt, spread the idea of Arab unity and molded the intellectual renaissance in the Arab world at the turn of the century. When the Sultan demanded their return, he was opposed by both the intellectuals and the religious authorities of Egypt.

The whole concept of political asylum thus became so entrenched as a part of the Egyptian way of life that all of Egypt's constitutions since that day have included an article that expressly forbids the giving up of political refugees.

So when Chou demanded the return of Kwan Yu-shin, it put Nasser in an appalling dilemma. He had no wish to offend Chou, but he could not break a tradition as sacrosanct as that of political asylum.

The Chinese claimed that Kwan Yu-shin was not a proper political refugee but had left the country with state secrets and was therefore not worthy of being granted asylum. He was a spy and a criminal.

But on those grounds Nasser could not break the tradition. Even his own sworn enemies were given asylum in Egypt. It was an explosive situation. Nasser wrote to Chou and tried to explain his point of view. But there was no understanding from the Chinese.

Kwan Yu-shin was by now asking to leave Egypt. The Russians wanted him. The Americans wanted him. And the Chinese were furious. So the compromise that Nasser worked out was that he would put Kwan Yu-shin in prison indefinitely. The Chinese were still unhappy about it. They wanted him back. But Kwan Yu-shin was put into Cairo prison where he stayed for a year and a half before being let out. The last definite news of him was that he had left Cairo on an SAS plane for Brussels.

This disagreement left relations strained between Chou and Nasser, and they were not improved by a problem Egypt had concerning the Palestinian Resistance. The Resistance, like the Vietnamese, had an admiration for Chinese ideas on guerrilla warfare. But Nasser had his reservations about the possibilities of a people's war in the Middle East. He had already pointed out to Mao and Chou that such a war was impossible in Sinai. However, the Chinese were hammering their theories of a people's war into the guerrillas, who made their way from Palestine to China where they had a special camp for training in guerrilla warfare. They came back to the Middle East full of Chinese theories, believing that they could apply them to the Middle East.

So Nasser was obliged, when he was talking to the guerrillas, to criticize the Chinese methods. He told them they were wrong because of several factors. In the first place, nowhere in the Middle East was the population dense enough for the guerrillas to move among the people. In Algeria there had been ten million Algerians while the occupying force had amounted to only half a million. In Vietnam there were forty million Vietnamese while the foreign army amounted to only half a million. Nowhere in the Palestinian guerrillas' fighting area was there anything like those ratios between the population and the occupying forces.

In the second place, Nasser told them, they had no real sanc-tuaries. In both Algeria and Vietnam there were areas beyond the reach of the enemy, where the guerrillas could retire to lick their wounds, rest and train, and plan before coming out to fight at their own time and on ground of their own choosing. There were no such sanctuaries in Israel. Everywhere was within the enemy's reach.

All this was in direct contradiction to what the Chinese were teaching the guerrillas. He further annoyed the Chinese by taking Yasir Arafat, the guerrilla leader, to Moscow where he introduced him to Kosygin, Brezhnev, and Podgorny, who had had reserva-tions about the guerrilla movement but who now started to have some contacts with them. This irritated the Chinese because they wanted to have a monopoly on helping the liberation movements.

Nasser heard that the Chinese were telling the guerrillas that he was selling them to the Soviet Union. It was his turn to be annoyed. So when Yasir Arafat called on him before the Pales-tinian went on a visit to China, he told Arafat to tell Chou that he was not selling anyone to the Soviet Union but that he was doing what he saw as best for the general Arab movement.

Arafat brought back a message from Chou saying that he was very sorry for the misunderstanding with President Nasser. Chou En-lai looked to President Nasser as the leader of the national liberation movement in the Arab world, but he was afraid for him because the Soviet Union was not going to help him and he said that the Russians were trading the Arab problem as part of their over-all deal with the United States.

Chou said that despite the misunderstanding, he liked and re-spected the President, and the proof of that respect was that during the Cultural Revolution he had let only one Ambassador outside China and that was the Ambassador to Cairo.

Nasser took advantage of the friendly tone of this note to write back, in an attempt to rebuild their bridges. But it was too late. He died before it could be done.

As I wrote in the first chapter, Chou remained true to form: he blamed the Russians for Nasser's death.

XI

Ludwig Erhard: Conflict Imposed

Gamal Abdel Nasser, President of Egypt, and Ludwig Erhard, Chancellor of the Federal Republic of Germany, were pushed into a conflict that neither planned and neither wanted. Both of them were surprised by what happened. But Nasser went into the conflict decisively. He was angry because he felt he had been deceived. Erhard, however, went into the conflict hesitantly, because the conflict was not of his making. As one of his ministers told Gamal Mansour, the Egyptian Ambassador in Bonn: "The walls round Erhard fell down suddenly, and there he was, in full view, in the bathroom."

What made the whole business even more sad was that there was no need for any quarrel between the two countries. Traditionally, there had always been good relations between them. They were never intimate but they were close enough to create the feeling of a comfortable friendship. In fact, the Arab world admired Germany. This admiration stemmed from many things. It was a German scientist who first isolated the parasite Bilharzia, the disease that was the scourge of Egypt. A German-Swiss explorer was the first to bring the temples of Abu Simbel to the world's notice. There was the legend of the reliability of German machinery. And, in particular, the Arabs admired Germany for its discipline, power, and the way in which it built its unity from a collection of states that had a common language and a common heritage but had no power until they were welded together. When Arabs studied how they could achieve their own unity, they sometimes looked to the example set by Germany.

It also happened that at the time of two upheavals in Egypt— the events leading to the revolution of 1919 and the ferment that started in 1939—Germany was fighting the same enemy as the Egyptians. They were fighting the British.

Egypt has been accused of being pro-Hitler. This is not true. What is true was that Egypt and Germany found themselves fighting the same enemy and this created a certain bond. But even those army officers like Anwar el Sadat who had contact with the Germans, were not pro-Nazis. They were simply anti-British. Not all the officers who were working to free their country wanted to help the Germans. Men like Colonel Nasser believed they would merely exchange the British for the Germans as an occupying power. So while Sadat was being arrested for his contacts with the Germans, Nasser was guarding the British rear against the Germans at El Alamein.

Sadat was not the only one to open channels to the Germans. King Farouk sent one of his relatives as a special emissary to Hitler. This man, an army officer, made his way to Switzerland where he met the Germans and was taken to see Hitler in Germany. Farouk had a second contact through his father-in-law, Youssef

Zulfikar Pasha, in Teheran who went to see German Ambassador Ettel.

The purpose of these contacts was for Farouk to obtain a promise from Hitler that if the Germans were victorious, they would grant Egypt independence.

There were a series of incidents early in 1942 which turned the Egyptians even farther from the British and toward the Germans. The British felt that the Germans were working through the Vichy French consulate in Cairo and ordered the Egyptian government to close it. Farouk was on a fishing trip on the Red Sea and did not hear about this until he returned to Cairo. Farouk was furious and ordered his Foreign Minister to resign. Whereupon the Prime Minister resigned and there were demonstrations in the streets during which the students of Al Azhar University shouted "Forward Rommel!"

It was this plus British suspicions of the Italians holding responsible posts in the Palace that led Lord Killearn to encircle the Abdin Palace with tanks on that notorious day, February 4, and force Farouk to accept Nahas Pasha as Prime Minister.

But even after Nahas came to power there were situations in which the Egyptians favored the Germans. As part of the plans for "the defense of Egypt," the British were prepared to make the Nile Delta impassable to tanks by opening the Nile Barrage and flooding the farmland. It might have stopped Rommel's tanks but it would certainly have ruined Egypt's agriculture. Instead, the Cabinet gave an official letter to the governor of Alexandria ordering him to go and give the keys of Alexandria to Rommel if ever he advanced on the city so that there would be no fighting and no flooding.

But Germany was defeated. Egypt was shocked at the devastation wrought on the nation that had been the source of so much admiration. Egyptians who went to Berlin after the war were appalled at the way one could buy anything for a cigarette. The old admiration therefore became even greater as Egypt watched the miracle of the German economic recovery.

It was against this background of traditional good relations, of fighting against the same enemy, and of renewed admiration that Nasser found himself facing his first major political problem after the revolution.

In December 1952 the West Germans signed the reparations settlement with Israel. Under this settlement they agreed to pay the Israelis three billion dollars over a twelve- to fourteen-year period. The argument was that this was to be compensation for Nazi crimes against the Jews. But the Arab world was shocked. Its effect would be the military and economic strengthening of Israel—which had not been touched by the Nazis, which did not even exist when the Nazis ruled Germany.

As Nasser explained later to Erhard, "What makes it necessary for Israel to inherit from the Jewish victims of the Nazis? We can understand private reparations to individual Jews and individual families, but why give the money to Israel? There is no proof that the survivors of Nazi Germany went to Israel. Most of them emigrated to America and Western Europe."

The President saw the reparations as an enormous injection of power into Israel but there was little he could do about it. He was preoccupied with other things, and, moreover, at that time West Germany was taking every possible opportunity to build friendship with Egypt. So although the Arab League was bitter about the reparations to Israel, Egypt took no action.

However, Nasser was astonished when he raised the matter with the West German Ambassador and the Ambassador said: "You must understand that this is not Germany's will. Germany behaved according to the dictates of the Allies, especially America, and you must remember that Germany is occupied." He could not understand why Germany should bow down to Israel.

Erhard came to Cairo in January 1960 when he was still Vice-

Chancellor and the man responsible for the "German economic miracle." Nasser was fascinated to hear from Erhard how this miracle had been brought about. After they had discussed it, Nasser came to the conclusion that it could not be repeated because it was due to the skill of a certain people, that it was the human element, the determination of the people to succeed, rather than a magic formula that had made West Germany prosperous again.

Erhard also talked about the German wish to foster good relations with the Arab world. Nasser told the German that he too was interested: "We do not have good relations with the British. We do not have good relations with the French. We have very bad relations with the Americans. Nevertheless, we are trying to keep two bridges open to the West and those bridges are Italy and Germany, and we feel that Germany can help us maintain our relations with the West because there is a reservoir of good will between us."

Nasser touched on the question of West German arms for Israel and the reports he was receiving that the Germans were supplying the Israelis with weapons. He did not believe the reports, Nasser said, but there were some strange goings on.

He told Erhard that at the end of 1957 he had received one report from Israel that Ben Gurion had talked about the possibility of getting arms from West Germany. Two Israeli cabinet ministers had resigned at that time and it was said they had been forced to resign because they had leaked Cabinet secrets. But the information Nasser received was that they had resigned on moral grounds, arguing that Israel should not accept arms which had been previously used for killing Jews. Ben Gurion had replied to their arguments by saying that the matter of obtaining arms was not a question of morality.

Nasser had spoken to Hammarskjöld about this during one of their meetings, and in January 1958 Hammarskjöld told several ambassadors, among them the Soviet Ambassador and the Egyptian Ambassador at the UN, that he was worried by hints that Israel was getting arms from West Germany because this would further complicate an already complicated question.

The West German government thereupon issued a declaration that said: "The Federal German Government does not intend now or in the future to sell arms to Israel." This would be, it said, an act which was completely contrary to the policy of the Bonn government. This policy was not to send arms to any part of the world where there was tension. "The Federal German Government looked with astonishment at the statements attributed to Premier Ben Gurion and others that Israel wants to obtain submarines and other arms from Germany. This Government is convinced that legally, constitutionally, and politically it cannot export arms to the Middle East." The statement pointed out that the reparation agreement specifically excludes any reference to arms from the items with which Germany paid reparations.

It was such a categoric denial that everybody believed it. So when President Nasser brought the subject up with Erhard, he did not go into details and did not press the matter. The German denial had been explicit. Erhard brushed the whole matter aside and it was dropped.

Two months after Nasser's meeting with Erhard, Chancellor Conrad Adenauer met Ben Gurion in New York. The extreme Zionists demonstrated wildly against Adenauer and even Ben Gurion had to slip out of the back door in order to meet the West German leader.

Egypt did not learn what had happened at that meeting until a long time afterward when the Germans explained their conduct to President Nasser. Ben Gurion, said the Germans, told Adenauer that France, which had been supplying Israel with arms, was changing its policy under De Gaulle, Britain was playing the hypocrite's role, the United States was still hesitating about supplying Israel with arms, and so, said Ben Gurion, "if Germany really wanted to compensate for the concentration camps, it must give the Jews, whom the Germans had tried to wipe out, the means to defend themselves against another attempt at national genocide."

Adenauer did not commit himself immediately but said he would think about it and discuss it with his colleagues. He put it before the German Cabinet but they were not very happy with the proposal. When Ben Gurion saw Eisenhower and asked for his backing in getting arms from Germany, the American President told him that it was a matter that needed to be carefully weighed because of its implications.

The Israelis continued to press the Germans but Adenauer still held back until he met President Kennedy in November 1961. Adenauer was planning to bring up the question of arms for Israel because the Israelis were putting such great pressure on him, but before he could broach the subject, Kennedy himself said that he knew the Israelis had asked Adenauer for arms. The United States would like to give them what they wanted, he said, but they could not for the time being because of Kennedy's friendship with Nasser and America's ties with the other Arab nations. And he said that he would appreciate it if the Germans would make the deal with the Israelis so that the United States would not be involved.

Adenauer started to offer weak objections, saying that he understood the Israelis' problem but that the Germans also had ties in the Arab world. Nasser knew all this because he was told later by Eugen Gerstenmaier who, when he was head of the German Bundesrat, was sent as an emissary to the President by Erhard. Gerstenmaier told Nasser that Adenauer was practically ordered by Kennedy to give arms to Israel.

So the deal was arranged. Israel was to get a credit of $60,000,-000 from the West Germans with which they could shop anywhere. Among the weapons they bought with this grant were two British submarines, 200 American Patton tanks, 200 armored carriers, 72 105-mm. self-propelled guns, 36 155-mm. howitzers, 6 torpedo boats, American F-84 jet fighters, and Italian G-91 jet fighters, along with French Noratlas transport aircraft and 15 helicopters. They also bought 200 40-mm. rapid-firing guns equipped with radar. They even tried to buy the Leopard, a brand new tank being developed by the West Germans.

It was enough to equip a small army, air force, and navy.

However, despite Kennedy's assurances, the story started to leak. There were signs of a special sort of relationship developing between West Germany and Israel. The Germans contracted to buy Uzzi sub-machine guns and uniforms from the Israelis for the German army.

The Uzzi weapons created a scandal at a meeting of the Organization of African Unity where some were displayed by the head of the Angolan liberation movement. These guns had been sold to the Germans who had passed them on to Portugal and they were then used against the liberation movement in Angola. In another Uzzi incident, the Sudanese government contracted to buy machine guns from the Germans, and when the guns arrived in Khartoum it was discovered that they were Uzzis. So it was obvious that something was going on between the Germans and the Israelis.

By the beginning of 1964 Egypt's Military Attaché in Bonn was sending back reports about the extent of the co-operation between Germany and Israel. The Attaché was Mohammed Sadek, who is now a lieutenant general and the Minister of War, and he had discovered most of the details of the secret deal.

President Nasser read the reports but for some reason he tended to not believe the deal was as large as was reported. In fact, it was even bigger because the arms were all bought at enormous discounts. The Americans, for instance, sold the Patton tanks very cheaply so the Germans' $60,000,000 credit was worth two or three times that much in arms for Israel.

Other Arab embassies in Bonn began to hear about the deal and to report to their governments, the Arab League's office in Bonn picked up the story and the Arab League held meetings to discuss this intelligence. Yet the President was still reluctant to take these reports too seriously. It was almost as if he did not want to believe them. And it was because of this initial reluctance that he reacted so violently when the time came for him to see what had really happened. He became furious with himself for being late in reacting and he compensated by overreacting.

By the end of 1964 the situation was getting out of hand: arms were pouring into Israel because of the deal with West Germany and Arab protests were mounting. So Erhard, who was Chancellor by now, sent Gerstenmaier to explain the situation to Nasser.

The President was preoccupied with other things when Gerstenmaier arrived in November 1964. Khrushchev had fallen and Nasser was re-examining the whole of Egypt's foreign policy. So when Gerstenmaier came in for his appointment, Nasser had not read the full dossier on the arms deal, he was not aware of the real extent of the deal, and he did not push Gerstenmaier too hard. He talked about the dangers of giving the Israelis arms and about the rumors he was hearing and the reports he was receiving, but still he held back.

Two considerations affected his attitude. He did not want a crisis with West Germany at a time when he was re-evaluating Egypt's foreign policy, and he had the feeling that some of the information he was getting about the arms was being deliberately fed to him by the Israelis to turn him against West Germany.

Gerstenmaier admitted to the President that there had been an arms deal and said that it was a mistake, that it had been forced on Germany, and that there was opposition in Germany to the deal.

Nasser almost sympathized with him: "Why should you be blackmailed by the Israelis?"

I had seen Gerstenmaier before he went to meet the President and I warned him that he was in for a difficult time, so he was prepared for the President's being very angry with West Germany. But when, after the meeting, he had lunch with the West German Ambassador, Anwar el Sadat, who was then head of the Egyptian Parliament, and me, he gave the impression that he had got off much lighter than he expected and he went back to Bonn feeling that the whole business could be contained.

He was rapidly disillusioned. President Nasser, who had actually asked to see the full dossier on the arms deal but had no time to read it before Gerstenmaier arrived, finally found time to study it two or three days after Gerstenmaier had returned to Bonn.

Then the balloon went up. He recalled the Egyptian Ambassador and the Military Attaché from Bonn and listened with growing fury to their account of the military strength being pumped into Israel by West Germany.

It was at this precise moment, January 1965, that a completely new element came into the story, like a joker being thrown on to the card table. Walter Ulbricht, the East German leader, wrote to President Nasser and in a cordial letter said that he was ill and his doctors had advised him to go to a warm country to recover. Some of the doctors had mentioned Aswan as having the most suitable climate. Could he, asked Ulbricht, please come to Egypt and spend a few days at Aswan?

At the time Egypt had consular relations with East Germany but had not recognized East Germany as a separate nation. Nasser's position was that he wanted Germany to be united again and it would not help if he recognized the East as well as the West and so confirmed the existence of two Germanys. However, how could he refuse a sick man's request for a few days' holiday in Egypt's sunshine? So he wrote to Ulbricht agreeing to his visit.

It has always been said in West Germany that Nasser's invitation to Ulbricht to visit Egypt was a deliberate snub, a calculated reply to Bonn's arms deal with Israel. But it did not happen that way at all. The initiative was entirely Ulbricht's and the purpose was medical, not political. However, a major crisis was to stem from that innocent beginning.

Ulbricht wrote back to Nasser and said that if it was agreeable with the President, he would like to come to Egypt in February 1965. The visit was arranged.

Then a small news item published in East Germany gave the news that Ulbricht was going to holiday in Egypt, and the West Germans started a tremendous uproar. They accused Nasser of inviting Ulbricht because of his displeasure over the arms deal. And Nasser, as always, reacted with pride and anger. He hit back at the West Germans by changing the status of Ulbricht's visit from an informal convalescence to a formal state visit.

The sequence of events after that had a certain inevitability. Ulbricht wrote to Nasser on January 27 thanking him for his invitation, which by now had been published officially.

The following day Erhard called a special meeting of his Cabinet and issued a statement deploring the visit. Political meetings throughout West Germany discussed the visit—it was to be Ulbricht's first outside the Eastern Bloc and it was to the Middle East, where so much was happening. The implications were therefore thought to be very dangerous. The newspapers were full of the story.

However, Erhard started to send verbal messages to Nasser telling him that he was being forced to make the fuss. In one message he informed the President that after Gerstenmaier had returned from Cairo, he told President Johnson that he wanted to stop the Israeli arms deal, but that Johnson had forced him to continue, arguing that it would be critical for Israel if West Germany stopped half way. The German Ambassador had been recalled to Bonn for consultations with his government—he even sat in on the Cabinet meeting and his report was distributed to the leaders of all the coalition parties. He added: "Mr. President, we are not like you, an independent nation. Germany is not independent."

The President became very angry when he heard this: "With all your economic potential, you come and tell us, an underdeveloped country, that you are not independent? We are trying to borrow money from you, technical skill from you, and then you come and tell me that you are not independent? This is an argument which I will not accept!"

This fierceness was part of his overreaction at not having responded sooner to the reports about Germany helping Israel. He felt he had been deceived. He said that logically there was absolutely no reason for the West Germans to help the Israelis and that his failure to react was a classic example of the mistake of depending on logic in politics.

The West Germans by now were anxiously looking for a way out of the crisis into which their relations with the Arab world had slumped. It was a two-headed crisis: arms and Ulbricht. The Egyptians did not want West German arms in Israel and the West Germans did not want Ulbricht in Egypt.

If a German may ever be described as scurrying, then West German diplomats scurried round the world looking for a way out of the impasse with Egypt. Erhard wanted a mediator, and he hit on General Francisco Franco of Spain because Franco had never recognized Israel. Franco agreed and he sent a messenger to President Nasser with a plan for a settlement of the quarrel. Under this settlement the Germans said that they were ready to declare publicly that the deal was over. However, there was a sum of money still outstanding on the arms credits and they proposed to hand this money over to the Israelis and allow them to do as they wished with it.

On February 10 Nasser ordered the terms of this settlement to be announced in Parliament. It was now the Israelis' turn to be furious. They accused Erhard of crawling on his knees in front of Nasser.

Erhard, wanting to dramatize to the Arab world the fact that he was stopping the arms, called the head of the Israeli procurement mission before him in Bonn and gave him the news personally. The Israeli Cabinet met and announced that they considered Israel had entered a binding contract with the West Germans that Bonn should implement and execute completely.

But then, the day after the settlement was announced, the Spanish emissary returned to Nasser and said that Erhard wanted Ulbricht's visit canceled. Nasser replied: "How can I? They want me to cancel Ulbricht's visit because it displeases them, but at the same time they are giving arms to the Israelis that are going to kill us. I want to annoy them. But there is no comparison between what they have done to us and what we have done to them in reply. It is unfair. I am only annoying them and they are killing us."

However, Erhard continued to press Nasser to cancel Ulbricht's visit and in the process he made a great mistake. He invited Nasser to go to Bonn. The German Ambassador, when passing on the invitation, told Nasser that Bonn was expecting Queen Elizabeth II in the spring and Germany would be more than happy to put the red carpet out for President Nasser to walk on before Queen Elizabeth.

This was distasteful to Nasser. "I have no interest in walking on the red carpet before Queen Elizabeth," he replied. "I am not in competition with her."

He refused to go to Bonn, he said it was wrong for West Germany to give the Israelis the unexpended portion of the arms money, and he refused to cancel the Ulbricht visit.

Ulbricht by now was taking political advantage of the situation. He stood up in the East German Parliament and said that this invitation to Cairo was a great honor to him, the greatest honor he had ever received in his life. And he appealed to Erhard to retain the dignity of the German people and to stop the deal with Israel.

Erhard was frightened that Ulbricht's visit would lead to Egypt's recognizing East Germany and that the rest of the Arab world would follow. So he was trying to do two things—first, get the visit canceled and, second, to isolate Egypt from the rest of the Arab world.

Erhard sent a message to Ben Bella saying that he hoped Ben Bella would not follow Cairo if Nasser decided to recognize East Germany. West Germany was giving aid to Cairo and in the event of Egypt's recognizing East Germany, he would order that aid to be switched to Algeria.

Ben Bella told the German Ambassador that this was a bribe he would not accept, and he sent a telegram to Nasser telling him of Erhard's proposition. Nasser was in Aswan when he received it and he stood up and read out the telegram publicly, saying: "This is a cheap bribe."

Poor Erhard; wherever he moved, things blew up in his face. It was as if he was walking through a minefield. He angered everybody—the Egyptians, the Algerians and the Israelis.

Ulbricht continued to take advantage of the explosions. He sailed for Alexandria on a ship called *Friendship Between Nations*, and one day I received a telegram from the ship asking if *Al Ahram* was interested in an interview with him. I telegraphed back, saying that we would be ready for him when he arrived. But the same afternoon we received from the ship something like twenty long takes of questions asked by Ulbricht of himself and answered by himself. Some of the answers were an all-out onslaught on Bonn.

I was dubious about it because we had not asked the questions. I contacted President Nasser and told him that I had received a gift I hadn't asked for, although it was a perfectly acceptable gift. The President said: "Go ahead, publish it."

Erhard was beginning to get frantic. He asked President Johnson to calm the Israelis and Johnson sent Averell Harriman on this mission. Erhard sent envoys to Jordan, to Baghdad, to Algiers. The situation was getting completely out of hand. On the very day that the *Friendship Between Nations* arrived in Alexandria, Erhard was still appealing to Nasser to cancel Ulbricht's visit. The burden of that last message was that the moment Ulbricht set foot on Egyptian soil, the West German government would break off diplomatic relations with Egypt. Even that threat did not deter Nasser. He replied that he was due to meet Ulbricht at the Cairo railroad station the following morning: "How can I cancel the visit?"

The two men met on February 24, 1965. Ulbricht kissed Nasser and told him: "I come to your country as a comrade in arms." That night, at an official dinner in Cairo, Ulbricht stood up. He said that he spoke for "all the traditional friendship between the Arab world and the German people."

Nasser, however, was still anxious to salvage something from the debacle with Erhard. He tried to be careful and in his speech he said: "Our policy is that we would not do anything that would deepen the division of Germany and endanger the possibilities of German reunity." It was a clear reaffirming of our position on Germany.

The East Germans were full of honey and sweet words. They promised all kinds of assistance. It was a question of "ask and it shall be given"—a medical unit here, a factory there, contracts for everybody. They were very generous.

Meanwhile, the Bonn Cabinet met twice to decide if they were going to break off relations. There was a split between Chancellor Erhard and Foreign Minister Gerhard Schröder. The first day they could not reach a decision. Erhard was hesitant. He was caught with his pants down. Then, after the second meeting, Erhard announced that West Germany was not going to break off relations with Egypt but would normalize relations with Israel.

And so another crisis unfolded. These crises seem to be self-generating. One grew out of another and each one was worse than the previous one. It would have been easy for the whole business to have been stopped. Ulbricht had arrived in Egypt. Nasser had reaffirmed his policy of supporting the re-unification of Germany which was so dear to West German hearts and Erhard had decided not to break off relations with Egypt. It could have stopped there.

But Erhard was so anxious to save face that he decided to punish Egypt by recognizing Israel—and he trod on another mine.

The Arab League was convened to answer this move by Erhard. The representatives of the kings and presidents recommended three moves:

1. They would withdraw all Arab ambassadors from Bonn.

2. They would break off diplomatic relations with West Germany.

3. They would stand by Egypt economically if Erhard broke off the aid agreements.

President Nasser added that if Bonn went ahead with its plan to recognize Israel, not only would Egypt follow the Arab League's recommendations but it would also recognize East Germany and sequestrate all West German schools and capital in Egypt.

The Israelis, fearing that Erhard would back down again in face of this Arab determination, hit back on the very same day, announcing that they would not accept the normalization of relations with West Germany unless:

1. Germany would do all in its power to have all German scientists who were working in Egypt withdrawn.

2. That the German Ambassador would establish his Embassy in Jerusalem and not in Tel Aviv.[1]

[1] Despite the UN declaration of 1947, Israel still claimed Jerusalem.

3. That the time limit for bringing Nazi war criminals to trial—which was running out—would be extended.

The German scientists working in Egypt were not as important as the Israelis had made them out to be. They had already begun to leave under threat of murder by the Israeli parcel-bombers. The fuss created about Nazis working for Egypt was nonsense. There was only one former SS man working in Egypt and he was Wolfgang Lotz, an Israeli spy who posed as a horse dealer. He was caught and imprisoned and when Egypt and Israel exchanged prisoners after 1967, he was at the top of the Israeli list for exchange.

There was much movement between Bonn and Israel after the Israelis had made their demands, and the process of negotiation has never been made absolutely clear. But on March 14 the Israelis announced that they were accepting Erhard's offer to normalize relations "after receiving the necessary clarifications."

This announcement was taken in Cairo and the other Arab countries to be a West German surrender to Israel. So that same day the foreign ministers of the states accepted the recommendations of the representatives of the kings and presidents. Seven Arab states accepted completely; three—Tunisia, Libya, and Morocco—made the reservation that they would not sever diplomatic relations with Germany.

On March 20 Gamal Mansour, the Egyptian Ambassador in Bonn, prepared a report for President Nasser on all that had happened. He said that it was known beyond doubt the previous October that there was an arms deal between West Germany and Israel. When he raised the matter in Bonn he was told that it was a deal made by Adenauer and Ben Gurion in New York in 1960 without the knowledge of the Bundestag and that the West German government had held up the deal until Kennedy confirmed it in 1961. Mansour's report continued:

I was told by Foreign Minister Schröder that when they took office he tried to convince the Cabinet that they ought to stop it. But unfortunately he failed to convince the Government, principally because Washington was insisting that the deal should be carried out. Gerstenmaier told me soon afterwards that the general opinion in the Bundestag was against the export of arms to areas of tension and that he was completely against such exports. After Gerstenmaier had visited Nasser, he returned to Bonn thinking that the crisis could be contained and, full of enthusiasm, he saw Schröder and tried to get a law passed banning the export of arms to areas of tension. He failed.

The Cabinet's point of view was that they would complete this deal because of the pressure from Washington but would not enter into another one. . . .

But then, Mansour reported, there came the invitation to Ulbricht and there was a division in the West German government.

I would say that there were three tendencies. The first is represented by Schröder and [Kai-Uwe] Von Hassel, and their position is that Germany must not rush into any economic or diplomatic measures against Egypt, must try to stop the military assistance to Israel, and must try to reach an understanding with the Arab countries. They argue that any strong measures against Egypt will only result in East Germany replacing West Germany in the Arab countries.

The second tendency includes the group belonging to [Franz-Josef] Strauss and those who are loyal to Adenauer and their position is that all economic aid for the United Arab Republic must be stopped the moment Ulbricht sets foot on Egyptian soil.

They argue that this would serve not only as an ultimatum

to the Arab countries but also to the African and Asian countries which might try to establish relations with East Germany.

They would also break off diplomatic relations with United Arab Republic on the grounds that Ulbricht's visit is a violation of the Hallstein Doctrine.[2]

The third tendency, which comes from outside the Cabinet, is supported by Strauss and Adenauer who are themselves involved in the arms deal and they say that Germany should go ahead and establish diplomatic relations with Israel and give the Israelis unlimited military and economic aid. . . .

When Erhard gave his ultimatum to the United Arab Republic over the Ulbricht visit, Adenauer telephoned Erhard and criticized his behavior throughout the crisis and told him that he ought not to threaten to break off relations, "instead the moment he does set foot in Egypt you must recognize Israel and announce that you are going to give the Israelis arms and economic help."

According to the Cabinet Minister who told Mansour about Adenauer's telephone call, Erhard was annoyed with Adenauer because he thought he was caught in a web woven by Adenauer. "You know," the Minister said to Mansour, "we have a problem here. The relations between Adenauer and Erhard are a Churchill-Eden relationship with all its complexes."

On May 9 Erhard wrote a letter to Nasser that made it obvious that a break between West Germany and the Arab world had become inevitable.

I deeply regret [wrote Erhard] that the traditionally

[2] A policy formulated in 1955 by West German State Secretary Dr. Walter Hallstein, by which West Germany refused to have diplomatic relations with any country that recognized East Germany.

friendly relations between our two countries have deteriorated recently. I do not want to go into the cause of this deterioration now. I am writing this letter with a view to the future and with the sincere intention to prevent—despite everything that has happened—an irreparable breach.

Within a few weeks ambassadors will be exchanged between the Federal Republic of Germany and Israel. This is based on a decision which the German Government has taken after thorough consideration. Eighty-seven States of the Western, Eastern, and non-aligned world maintain diplomatic relations with Israel; among these there are many who have always enjoyed friendly relations with the Arab States. Public opinion in my own country and in many other countries has again and again wondered why the Federal Republic of Germany does not also establish diplomatic relations with Israel. This question was asked all the more persistently because, as you know, Germans have inflicted upon the Jews very serious suffering in the past.

The establishment of diplomatic relations with Israel enables us to normalize our policy in the Middle East. It is in no way directed against any Arab state. It is our firm conviction that the conditions agreed upon in this connection do not in any way constitute a violation of Arab interests.

Previous commitments on the supply of arms to Israel will no longer be executed. These commitments will be commuted. In the new agreements to be concluded with Israel there will be no provision for any supply of arms.

I regret that a number of Arab States have decided to take measures against Germany because of the establishment of diplomatic relations between the Federal Republic of Germany and Israel. I cannot accept that this decision is justified, for by exchanging ambassadors between Bonn and Tel Aviv, Germany takes a step which many other states have taken before without the Arab States undertaking anything against them.

Whatever you may ultimately decide to do about the relations between our two countries, I must draw your attention to the following point: If the United Arab Republic establishes diplomatic relations with the so-called German Democratic Republic, I fail to see a possibility by which you or I could prevent the ties of friendship between the German people and the people of the United Arab Republic, for which both of us bear a historic responsibility, being severed for an unforeseeable length of time.

I should like you to accept these declarations of mine as the words of a man who has been deeply hurt by what has taken place, and of a man who will nevertheless not cease, for as long as it is possible, to work for German-Arab friendship.

Please accept, Mr. President, the expression of my highest esteem.

He wanted it both ways. He wanted to recognize Israel but he did not want East Germany recognized.

The President replied to this letter of May 13. He referred to the traditional friendship between Germany and the Arabs and said that he believed that the German people were the victims of the Nazi agony and not its creator. He went on:

If the German people feel a responsibility for what happened to the Jews under the Nazis, it is my belief that the German people should also feel crisis of conscience toward the Arab nations, because racial Zionism had exploited the suffering of the Jews under Hitlerite Germany in order to carry out a conspiracy against the Arab nation by taking part of its territory to build a homeland for the Jews.

It seems to me that we are therefore paying Germany's blood money for her to salve her conscience. . . .

The reparations paid by the German people to Israel were a great help to the Zionists in their aggression and I do not need to recall for you what they did with the power they acquired from those reparations. . . .

The Arab nation received a terrible shock when it learned of the secret arms deal between Germany and Israel. The fact that Germany had decided to compensate Israel with aggressive arms was a deep and agonizing shock to us. I cannot find the words to explain to you what I and everybody else felt when we realized the dimensions of this operation. . . .

We were even more upset when we heard that this deal was part of a special relation between Bonn and Tel Aviv.

Egypt had tried to make Bonn understand, the President wrote,

but we were greeted with news that we did not understand. When we tried to soften the crisis we were motivated by the wish to keep our traditional friendship with the German people . . . the deterioration in the situation could have been halted if the West German Government had simply said it was ready to stop its arms gifts for the Israelis. But what happened after that was, in my opinion, a collapse in decision-making which we did not understand.

It is a pity that the Federal Republic of Germany decided at that time, in that tense atmosphere, to create diplomatic relations with Israel. It meant that this decision became part of a big operation to challenge the Arab nations. . . .

Finally, concerning our relations with East Germany, let

me tell you that the United Arab Republic puts its principles
first and it cannot accept any pressure. . . .

This exchange of letters left no more room to maneuver. On
the day that Nasser replied to Erhard, the Arab states, one after
the other, began to recall their ambassadors from Bonn and break
off diplomatic relations with West Germany. And once again the
Middle East saw the exodus of the representatives of a Western
nation from the Arab countries. Ten ambassadors and their staffs
went home to Bonn, their missions at an end, their embassies
closed.

When the Arab League had first discussed what measures to
take against West Germany, Nasser had suggested that they should
not end relations with Bonn but retaliate by recognizing East
Germany, and thus force the West Germans to stand by the
Hallstein Doctrine and break off relations with all Arab states.
He argued that with so many countries involved, it would be a
serious challenge to Erhard and to the Hallstein Doctrine.

However, the Saudi Arabians said that on religious grounds they
would not be able to recognize a Communist government. For
them, it was taboo to establish relations with the Communists.

Other countries then argued for breaking relations with West
Germany and this course was adopted, but only because the
Saudis had blocked Nasser's proposal. After that, the President
delayed recognition of East Germany because he wanted to maintain the position of ten states acting in unity. He did not want to
spoil that unity by acting independently, and so he postponed the
decision to recognize East Germany for a long time for the sake of
Arab unity. Eventually, on July 10, 1969, full diplomatic relations were established between the U.A.R. and East Germany.

I believe that it was the hesitancy with which Erhard behaved
in this crisis, the way in which he darted to and fro, and his inability to cope with the situation that really finished him as

Chancellor. He was faced with a major challenge and he demonstrated that he was not capable of coping with that challenge.

This crisis, this confrontation, which neither West Germany nor Egypt wanted, but which had its origins in Kennedy's commitment to arm Israel, had another far-reaching effect. With West Germany closed off as a source of weapons, Israel was forced to turn to the United States, and America, under Johnson, became the acknowledged source of Israel's military strength.

The United States was forced to show its true colors.

XII

Guevara and Revolution

When Fidel Castro and his victorious men marched into Havana in January 1959, slung round with guns and bandoliers and sporting their bushy beards, President Nasser tended to dismiss them as a bunch of Errol Flynns, theatrical brigands but not true revolutionaries. He did not pay much attention to Castro's movement because there was a great deal of American support for Castro at that time, and although Nasser thought Latin America was ripe for revolution, he did not think any change could succeed there without American approval. He was too conscious of the way the CIA had overthrown President Arbenz of Guatemala five years before to have any illusions about United States power in the area.

So this suspicion of American support combined with his suspicion of Castro's theatricality and his own preoccupation with events in the Middle East made Nasser shy away from involvement with Castro and his bearded, booted followers.

There was no real contact between the Egyptian and Cuban revolutionary movements until June 1959 when Che Guevara, Castro's second in command, arrived in Cairo on a fifteen-day visit to study Egypt's methods of land reform.

At their first meeting Guevara told Nasser that in 1956, when things were going badly for Castro, fighting his guerrilla war up in the Cuban hills, he used to be encouraged by the way Egypt had overcome the attack by Britain, France, and Israel. Nasser was a source of moral strength for them.

However, when they turned to the subject of land reform the differences between the two men became immediately apparent. Guevara's first question was: "How many Egyptian refugees were obliged to leave the country?" And when the President told him that there were not many—and they were mainly "white Egyptians," men of other nationalities who had become Egyptianized—Guevara was unhappy. "That means," he said, "that nothing much happened in your revolution." Guevara added: "I measure the depth of the social transformation by the number of people who are affected by it and feel that they have no place in the new society."

Nasser explained to him that what he was doing was "liquidating the privileges of a class but not individuals of that class." He would destroy the power of the landowners but would not deny them a chance to become useful members of the new society.

Guevara insisted on his point of view and so nothing much arose from his visit. President Nasser still gave little attention to the Cubans and their policies.

The following year Nasser had another Cuban visitor—Raúl Castro, Fidel's brother, who headed a delegation to the celebrations marking the eighth anniversary of the Egyptian revolution. The brother was to speak in Alexandria on the anniversary of King

Farouk's departure. He had prepared a blisteringly anti-American speech, for relations had soured between the United States and the new Cuba and they were on the eve of the Bay of Pigs.

One of our protocol people asked Castro what he was going to say in his speech, and when Castro showed him the text, he was horrified. The violence of its anti-Americanism frightened him and he asked Castro if he would tone it down.

So Castro went away into the stadium and tried to take out some of the more powerful parts of his speech. He was very upset and became even more upset when the chief of protocol told him that the revised version was still too harsh. In the end he took out something like two thirds of his speech and felt like not talking at all, but as he had given his word to speak and all the arrangements had been made, he felt compelled to go on with it. But he was sadly disappointed. He thought his speech had fallen flat, that no guts were left in it.

He was followed on the podium by Nasser, whereupon the President made a bitter attack on the United States, far harsher than Castro's first version. The Cuban, naturally enough, was both puzzled and very angry.

They drove away from the stadium together to have dinner, Castro silent the whole way despite the enthusiastic cheering of the crowds. When they arrived at the President's house, Castro said, "I am sorry, perhaps I should not bring the subject up, but I don't understand . . . here is my speech." It was in Spanish, but the President saw that more than half of it was crossed out.

"What puzzles me," said Castro, "is that you spoke ten times more harshly about the Americans than I intended to do."

The President was astonished and asked Castro who had censored his speech. He started an investigation over the telephone and soon found the man who had censored the speech. That unhappy fellow said that he felt he had to ask Castro to tone down his speech because the American Ambassador was going to be present at the celebrations.

Nasser turned to Castro and said: "And that is how revolutionaries suffer from bureaucrats."

Castro told him that if the President had not spoken out against the Americans, prompting him to ask why his speech had been censored, he would have gone back to his brother and reported that the Egyptians were not revolutionaries.

Nasser met Fidel Castro for the first time in New York three months later when they took part in "Khrushchev's session" at the United Nations in September 1960. Castro repeated what Guevara had said about the encouragement given to them in 1956 by the way Egypt had stood up to the British, French, and Israelis over Suez and had come out on top. He asked Nasser for an exposition of the Egyptian experience at the time of Suez and throughout he showed genuine admiration for Nasser.

The Egyptian President came to his support in New York where some Americans had mounted a campaign against Castro, designed to force him to leave the country. He and his delegation had booked into the Shelburne Hotel where he was insulted by being asked for a guarantee. Then scandalous stories were printed about his delegations' rooms being filled with feathers from the chickens the Cubans were supposedly killing and eating. Castro moved up to Harlem and Nasser went to visit him there in the New York black ghetto. He wanted to propose that if the Americans made it impossible for Castro to attend the United Nations, then the United Nations would have to be moved to some other country. Castro brought Nasser a present, a wooden box lined with crocodile leather. When Nasser opened it, he said: "I thought it was cigars." And Castro apologized, saying, "I didn't know you smoked cigars but I will make sure you are sent some. Perhaps I made a mistake in giving you crocodile leather because you have plenty of crocodiles in Egypt."

"Yes," said Nasser, "we have got exactly"—and he looked at the ceiling—"exactly four."

Castro looked at him startled. "How do you count them?"

"Because," said the President, "they are all in the zoo."

Castro asked Nasser if he was going to listen to the major speech which the Cuban planned to make at the United Nations the following afternoon. But Nasser replied that as much as he wanted to he could not because his appointment with President Eisenhower had been fixed for precisely the time that Castro would be talking. Castro was very unhappy. He thought the Americans had fixed the timing deliberately in order to hinder the rapprochement between Castro and Nasser. If that was the intention, they did not succeed. There was a mutual and growing admiration between the two men.

Nasser urged two things on Castro during their meetings in New York. The first was that he should not attach too much importance to the American base on Cuban soil at Guantanamo and not be drawn into a military conflict because of the base.

The second was the importance of a basis for revolution, a basis like Egypt's Arab unity. The President explained to Castro how the idea of Arab unity gave great depth to the Egyptian struggle, supplying strategic moral and political depth to the revolution. And he asked Castro if there was any basis for unity in Latin America.

Castro said that there were some bases: religion, language (except for Brazil), and an oppression of the peasants that was common to all Latin-American countries. But so far there had been no unifying factor as strong as the idea of Arab unity.

Guevara made a second visit to Cairo on February 11, 1965, and stayed in the area until the end of March. By this time Nasser had completely rejected his initial suspicion of the Cubans and he admired them for their struggle over the Bay of Pigs. He thought that their fight against the United States during the Bay of Pigs and the missile crisis was the fight of the sardine against the whale. His admiration was all for the sardine. Nasser met Guevara on the second day of his visit and he felt immediately that Guevara was saddened by some deep personal distress. Nasser pressed him to talk. How were things in Cuba? Was everything all right between him and Castro? But Guevara would not be drawn. He remained uncommunicative.

The Cuban said that he was going to Tanzania where a committee for helping African liberation movements had been set up in Dar es Salaam. Still, Nasser felt that his heart was not in it.

Guevara returned after ten days during which time he had been into the Congo. He told the President that he was distressed by what he had seen there. He had been visiting the force of two battalions of black Cubans that had been raised and sent from Cuba to fight for Antoine Gizenga, the man who had tried to inherit Premier Lumumba's mantle, and Guevara said to Nasser that he was thinking of going to join the struggle and take over command of the black Cubans. Nasser was astonished.

Guevara was accompanied by the Cuban Ambassador to Tanzania, Señor Rivalta, who had been a leader of the cigar workers union. Guevara added: "I spent all night pacing my hotel room in Shepheard's, trying to decide if I ought to come and tell you of my decision. My friend Rivalta here," he added, "spent the time making two cigars for you."

(Rivalta always carried tobacco leaves with him and whenever he had time he rolled cigars; indeed he had made two long cigars for the President while Guevara tried to decide whether or not to tell the President he was planning to fight in the Congo.)

Guevara then started to talk, to explain himself to the President: "I feel that we must do more for the revolution in the world and I thought I would come and do something in Africa. I have experience in revolutionary activities and organization and I think the situation is ripe in Africa.

"And I think I shall go to the Congo because it is the hottest spot in the world now. With the help of the Africans, through the committee in Tanzania, and with the two battalions of Cubans, I think we can hurt the imperialists at the core of their interests in Katanga."

Nasser told him: "You astonish me. What happened to all that you were doing in Cuba? Have you quarreled with Castro? I don't want to interfere, but if you want to become another Tarzan, a white man coming among black men, leading them and protecting them . . . it can't be done."

Guevara laughed about the idea of being a Tarzan and they broke off the meeting, but it was the start of a series of talks, of a dialogue between Nasser and Guevara, a dialogue between two revolutionaries whose thinking on the way that revolution ought to be achieved was often fundamentally different.

Nasser was fascinated by Che Guevara; he felt a certain affection for him. As they talked, the reasons for Guevara's distress emerged. He said that he respected Fidel Castro very much and considered him a brother and a teacher. But that there were several things that had not been right between them. The first was that Che had introduced Raúl Castro to Communism while they were both in Mexico. He made Raúl a party member and they decided to hide the fact from Fidel. When Fidel found out, he was furious with both of them, furious because it had happened and because it had been kept secret from him.

A second thing was that although he had no doubts about the revolutionary sincerity of Fidel, he had sometimes had reservations about his leader's social convictions while they were struggling in the mountains.

However, both Castro's anger and his own doubts had now passed. Castro had given him his chance to fight, had given him, an Argentinian, Cuban nationality and had made him Minister of Industries. But the difficulties of that post were tremendous, and now so many people were attacking him because of his lack of success that he felt he was opening a path for an attack on Fidel himself.

He felt himself to be in a crisis. He had so many questions to which he could not find the answers. Cuba was faced with tremendous problems and there were no quick solutions. "We made blunders," he admitted, "and possibly I am responsible. We nationalized ninety-nine per cent of everything we found, even the barbershops. And then we found that we had to leave some people outside the scheme of nationalization.

"I used to talk a lot about social transformation. Then I was given the task of supervising that transformation. The first problem that greeted me was finding the people to run the nationalized concerns. We found them and we thought they would be representatives of the revolution. But we found they did not belong to the revolutionary party; they belonged to the managerial party. They forgot their revolutionary fervor in the arms of beautiful secretaries, in their lavish cars, with their privileges and their air-conditioning. They started to close the doors of their offices to keep the cool air in instead of opening them to the working people.

"I felt that we were giving a chance to opportunism; we found one man with seventeen television sets in his office!

"And I felt that we did not have a party . . . I am a Communist and I have read so much Communist literature and I am tormented between the Revolution and the State . . ."

He talked at full spate. His disillusion and distress were now apparent. He was full of questions and no answers.

"Who is a Communist? What's the role of the party? Is a Communist only an atheist? Is he a man who should be working more than others? I said one day that the Communist should be the last to eat, the last to sleep, and the first to rise, but that may describe a man who is a very good worker but not a very good Communist.

"Who makes the laws? . . . What is the relation between the

party and the state? . . . Between revolution and the people? Until today these relationships were conducted by telepathy, but telepathy is not good enough. We are so unhappy with many of the things we see around us. We are not happy with Stalinism but we do not accept the reaction against Stalinism . . .

"And then there is a paradox in Communism. Sometimes when I was negotiating with the Soviet Union, I found that the Russians wanted to buy our raw material at the market price fixed by imperialists. I cannot accept this from a socialist country. I discussed this with them and they said they were obliged to sell in a competitive market. I then asked what was the difference between them and the imperialist who fixed the prices, and they told me that they understood my point of view very well, that they knew the raw material was gathered by the agony of the people of backward countries, but, they argued, they had no alternative. 'We are obliged to sell in a competitive market.'

"I asked them about the finished goods they were selling us. I told them: you have automation, you don't pay very high wages, and you can produce these goods cheaply; yet you sell them to us again at the same market level. So we are crushed. There is no hope for us this way."

Guevara went on to discuss Cuba's role in Latin America, arguing that the only movement that deserved attention before the Cuban revolution was Perón's in Argentina. He said that Perón did some important things in the field of industrialization but that he had completely failed to understand the role of the proletariat, and his movement failed because it lacked the element of popular struggle. It failed also, said Guevara, because Perón was a coward; he could not gather enough courage to face death, and when the time came to show courage he ran away.

"The turning point in each man's life," said Guevara, "is the moment when he decides to face death. If he faces death, then he is a hero whether he becomes a success or not. He can be a good or a bad politician, but if he cannot face death, he will never be anything more than a politician."

And that was the creed he lived and died by.

The talks went on for several nights at the President's house. One of the things that Guevara told Nasser was that they had decided to start the revolution in Cuba even though the conditions were not right, because they felt the very decision to start it was a revolutionary factor to be reckoned with.

Nasser picked up his arguments. He understood that the decision to start a revolution can itself be a factor even if the subjective conditions were not yet right. But, he said, there are basic requirements that cannot be ignored, and if they are ignored, then the act of revolution would be desperate.

"First of all," he told Guevara, "you must forget all about this idea of going to the Congo. It won't succeed. You will be easily detected, being a white man, and if we get other white men to go with you, you will be giving the imperialists the chance to say that there is no difference between you and most mercenaries.

"I believe the revolution is a world-wide phenomenon which makes no distinction between different colors and races, but there are certain things that must be taken into consideration. What we should do is to help the Africans, try to give each people the right to do what it feels is correct.

"But if you go into the Congo with two Cuban battalions and if I send an Egyptian battalion with you, it will be called foreign interference and it will do more harm than good."

Nasser went on to argue about the necessary bases for a successful revolution. "Perhaps," he said, "I disagree with the dogmatic Marxist view that a revolution can only start where there is a developed proletariat—both Lenin and Mao have proved that thesis incorrect—but there must be at least a nucleus of *petite bourgeoisie* and workers.

"You must also have an infrastructure of communications. Ideas need communications just as the economy does. If the economy needs roads and airports, then ideas also need the means to travel. You cannot have a mass revolution unless there is a basic infrastructure.

"I experienced this in Yemen when the revolution started there. I jumped to its help, and although I received reports that the situation was not right for revolution, I said, like you, that the mere fact that it had started was an important subjective element in itself and it should be helped.

"But then I discovered, first, that it could not be helped from outside; second, that it would take a long time and much agony; and while we can accelerate the historical process of the revolution, we cannot jump over the natural and chemical process that creates the forces of revolution."

At the time of their talks, Nasser was offering himself for reelection as president, and he was traveling around the country making speeches. So after one of their long sessions he told Guevara they would not be able to meet the next day. He would be out of Cairo opening a factory.

That turned the talk again to industry and Guevara said that to build and to manage a factory was a very difficult business. He thought that the most gratifying aspect of a revolution was political activity among the masses and that running factories was a dull, depressing business. Nasser said that mobilizing the masses came in the romance stage of revolution. The day of the revolution was the consummation of the romance—the wedding night. But after that you had to make the marriage succeed. You had to earn money, build a house, and produce children. And that was what a revolution meant: it meant going through the dull, difficult business of building factories and reclaiming land.

Guevara said, with a grin: "I've already broken two marriages."

The President hammered away at him on the theme of making the revolution work. "If we had only the romance of the revolution without the necessary developments, it would be a catastrophe. If you don't do all those difficult and dull tasks, then there will be no revolution.

"You were a doctor," he said to Guevara. "Well, you will be like the surgeon who put his patient up on the operating table, anaesthetized him, opened him up, and then refused to go on with the operation. You cannot do that."

Guevara replied, all his frustration showing: "But after a revolution it is no longer the revolutionaries who do the job; it is the technocrats and the bureaucrats, and they are anti-revolution.

"You know, I think that there must be one basic law in socialism and nobody has yet discovered it. I have read Marx and Lenin, followed all their experiences, and I am convinced that nobody has yet found that basic law. There was a time when I thought it was planning, because through planning man was able to remold his future for the first time. But then I discovered that when we come to planning, we are faced with the technocrats and the bureaucrats and they work against the revolution."

The President asked him if he would like to go to the opening of the new factory where they could see some practical results of the Egyptian revolution. Guevara said he would, and so they set out together the following day.

Nasser received a tremendous reception. Whole villages came rushing to greet the car; they tried to stop the car by throwing themselves in front of it. At the factory there were thousands and thousands of people cheering for Nasser. Guevara became very excited. "This is what I want," he said. "This is the revolutionary ferment."

"Yes, all right," said Nasser, "but you can't have this"—and he pointed to the crowd—"without that"—and he pointed to the factory. "This is the substance of the problem; unless you make that factory, you cannot succeed."

Guevara was overwhelmed by it all. He stood up at a meeting and said: "I wish I could vote for you."

The Cuban also visited the Aswan High Dam, and he, like everyone else who goes there, was immensely impressed. The President took the High Dam as an example to follow up his arguments about the need to build the revolution. "We fought a battle over the High Dam," he said. "There was all the romance of the revolution, all the romance of a big battle against three powers. The Suez invasion took place because of the High Dam. But after the fighting was over we had to get down to the real task. Dulles used to tell us that we would curse the day we thought of building the Dam because of the sacrifices it would impose on the Egyptian people. But this is the revolution. Those sacrifices *are* the revolution. Working day after day to put rock beds in place, build tunnels, install machinery. That is what changes society. The peak of revolutionary activity is to mobilize the people to accept the sacrifices and to give you support all the time."

The next time they met, Guevara said to Nasser: "Perhaps we can find a way. Perhaps we can politicize the bureaucrats and the technocrats. If we can do that, then perhaps the revolution will be safe."

He kept returning throughout their talks to his theme of having questions but no answers, and Nasser kept trying to get him to talk out his problems in the hope that some answers would emerge. "What is the matter?" Nasser asked one day. Guevara shook his head and replied: "Honestly, I feel I am not fit to do what I am doing and I am looking for somewhere else to go. I thought of going to the Congo but having seen what is happening there, I am inclined to accept your point of view that it would be harmful if I went there.

"I thought of going to Vietnam. I am more impressed by what is happening there than I am by anything else. To think that those people were able to fight the Japanese, the French, and the Americans in continuous war is an extraordinary achievement.

"What they have done to the Americans is simple and brilliant. They have obliged the Americans to fight in places and conditions contrary to their style of life."

He wanted to go to Vietnam very badly but did not because he thought his presence there would cause too much trouble for Cuba. But, he said, "Maybe we can create other Vietnams. We want as many Vietnams as possible." He was to return often to this theme of creating Vietnams.

"I want to do anything that will shake the world order because I do not consider that what we have now is peace. It is not peace and we should not defend it. What we have is peace at any price, arranged by compromise among the big powers, and if we accept peace at any price, we will, in effect, be accepting continuous war, but hidden war."

He asked the President about the phenomenon of military coups d'état in Africa and whether such coups would abort the revolutionary process. Nasser said that in his analysis the revolutionary process in Africa was being aborted by neocolonialism, with the imperialists changing immediately from old-style colonialism to new colonialism, faking revolution, staging coups, stealing the slogans of the revolution, and deceiving the people.

At their last meeting Guevara told Nasser that he did not think he would stay in Cuba. He had not yet decided where to go, he said, but the only thing he was searching for was "where to go, where to find a place to fight for the world revolution and to accept the challenge of death."

Nasser said to him: "Why do you always talk about death? You are a young man. If necessary we should die for the revolution, but it would be much better if we could live for the revolution."

But Guevara knew his own destiny. He was so disillusioned with his life, with what he saw as the failure of the application of the revolution, that he had developed a death wish. He did not want to run factories and cope with technocrats and bureaucrats. He wanted to fight. He wanted to look death in the face.

Nasser was tremendously moved by the letter Guevara wrote to Castro when he set out on his fatal adventure in Bolivia. It contained so much of what Guevara had talked about in their long dialogue:

". . . man either wins or dies, so many of our friends died on the road to victory . . . now everything is less dramatic . . . I feel that I have done that part of my work that tied me to the Cuban revolution . . . other countries in the world need my efforts . . . I can do what you cannot because of your responsibilities in leading Cuba . . . now it is time to part. I want you to know that I am leaving with a mixture of pleasure and pain . . . if my hour comes under other skies, you and the Cuban people will be in my thoughts before I take my last breath . . . to victory, revolution, or death . . ."

So he went off to carry the revolution to Bolivia. But there he found what Nasser had warned him about: there was no base for revolution. He had arrived with the spark, but there was no explosive mixture ready. He failed. He was betrayed. And he was killed.

EPILOGUE FOR AN ERA

This book, as noted at the outset, is not a biography of Nasser but a book about men of power and their relationships. Whether or not the portraits and sketches are favorable, nearly all these men represent an era. These were men of a certain character, of what came to be called, too glibly, "charisma."

Churchill, Adenauer, Eisenhower, Nehru, De Gaulle, Khrushchev, Nasser . . . the names that once paraded before our consciousness are gone, for better or for worse. Even our new revolutionaries do not seem to be towering or romantic figures. Guevara is replaced by nameless Tupamaros. The Irish rebels go into battle hidden under stocking masks.

The men in this book came out of traditional or revolutionary politics . . . and the time for that seems to be changing, too.

Such giants came out of war, the underground, revolutionary or orthodox party machinery. Now, it appears, nations are to be run by technocrats. One major state is led by three engineers. The similarity of their background is no accident. Technology invades ideology. The problems presented to a head of state are, less and less, the ones that once confronted him. The challenges of space, rocketry, and missiles, of city and regional planning and development, of military and social machines, these give technocrats a political role that was not theirs before. Everywhere you look, there are dozens of newcomers without faces. In Britain there are no Churchills in evidence; instead, in Brussels and in Bonn, we see a shift: questions and decisions of great magnitude being planned and made by nearly anonymous men in committees. In the United States the last three Presidents have had vastly important technocrats in the White House. These men in "the Basement"—McGeorge Bundy, Walt Rostow, Henry Kissinger—have competed with, reduced, and sometimes eliminated functions of the State Department, the Defense Department, the Congress itself. Such men rule not by election but by influence, under Executive privilege—and protection.

Even Lyndon Johnson, in his vulgarity, had a certain earthy energy that was recognizable, even reassuring—not dissimilar in some ways, perhaps, from the childish displays and tantrums of a Khrushchev. Once, in certain societies, a man needed a political party to win a position of power. The technology of the media— and its "personalities"—have changed that fact. Now the party is most important to the leader who does not *want* to become exposed. Today's rising men are managers by-passing the open political challenges.

This epilogue is an observation, not a lament. What we have seen here is a group of men who saw and knew each other, talked or corresponded, men who affected the course of nations and who will not be easily, if ever, replaced. One of them, Gamal Abdel Nasser, is at the heart of the book. What he accomplished is best summed up, beyond all details or arguments, in the statement André Malraux made to me some months after Nasser's death:

"Regardless of everything, regardless of success or failure, victory or defeat, Nasser will go down in history as the embodiment of Egypt, just as Napoleon became the embodiment of France."